THE METROPOLITAN DAILY NEWS

The
METROPOLITAN

DAILY NEWS

Understanding American Newspapers

Joan Corliss Bartel

Prentice Hall Regents
Englewood Cliffs, New Jersey 07632

Library of Congress Cataloging-in-Publication Data

Bartel, Joan Corliss, (date)
   The metropolitan daily news: understanding American newspapers /
Joan Corliss Bartel.
       p.   cm.
   Includes bibliographical references (p.) and index.
   ISBN 0-13-043258-X : $15.00 (est.)
   1. English language--Textbooks for foreign speakers.   2. American
newspapers--Problems, exercises, etc.   3. Current events--Problems,
exercises, etc.   4. English language--United States.   5. Newspapers
in education.   6.Readers--Current events.   7. Americanisms.
I. Title.
PE1128.B354   1994
428.2'4--dc20
                                                         93-25881
                                                         CIP

CREDITS

p. ii: Boston Chamber of Commerce. p. 7: Reprinted by permission of AP/Wide World Photos, Inc. p. 17: Boston Globe Photo. p. 19: Boston Chamber of Commerce. p. 21: *The New York Times.* p. 22: *USA Today.* p. 23: *The Christian Science Monitor.* p. 24: *Boston Herald;* AP/Wide World Photos. p. 31: Ken Karp. p. 40: (left) Dennis Stein. (right) Houston Tourist and Convention Center. p. 41: Map of Canada courtesy Prentice Hall Canada, Inc. p. 47: Weekly World News, Inc. p. 51: UN Photo 172543 by Y. Nagata. p. 55: Arlington Advocate. Photo by Peter Severance. p. 61: Charles Gatewood, Box 745, Woodstock, NY 12493. p. 73: Irene Springer. p. 82: *Boston Herald.* p. 94: Marc Anderson. p. 102: *International Herald Tribune.* p. 112: © 1988 by Herblock in the Washington Post. p. 113: Architect of the Capital. p. 124: Architect of the Capitol. p. 132: Neil Goldstein. p. 136: Marc Anderson. p. 144: Ken Karp. p. 156: Joan Bartel. p. 159: Norbert Bartel. p. 168: Irene Springer. p. 170: Vermont Development Commission.

Editorial/Production Supervision and
   Interior Design: *Ros Herion Freese*
Acquisitions Editor: *Nancy Leonhardt*
Cover Design: *Mike Fender*
Prepress Buyer and Scheduler: *Ray Keating*
Manufacturing Buyer: *Lori Bulwin*

 © 1994 by Prentice Hall Regents, Prentice-Hall, Inc.
   A Simon & Schuster Company
   Englewood Cliffs, New Jersey 07632

Printed in the United States of America

10

ISBN-0-13-043258-X

Prentice-Hall International (UK) Limited, *London*
Prentice-Hall of Australia Pty. Limited, *Sydney*
Prentice-Hall Canada, Inc., *Toronto*
Prentice-Hall Hispanoamericana, S.A., *Mexico*
Prentice-Hall of India Private Limited, *New Delhi*
Prentice-Hall of Japan, Inc., *Tokyo*
Simon & Schuster Asia Pte. Ltd., *Singapore*
Editora Prentice-Hall do Brasil, Ltda., *Rio de Janeiro*

BHB

Contents

Preface

The ability to pick up a newspaper and make some sense of the news reported in it is a fundamental skill that all adults should have. The news reflects what is important in our lives; understanding it broadens our perspectives.

Being able to read and discuss current issues empowers non-native–English speakers in the United States to interact responsibly within their environment and socially with their American peers. For citizens in other nations of the world, understanding an English-language newspaper means being able to take a first-hand look at the issues and viewpoints of another country. The skills learned from this book can be used for a lifetime.

The main goals of this book, then, are to help adults and young adults feel comfortable with and understand news articles in current English-language newspapers. Mastery of these ends requires time and practice, and no one book can hope to cover everything, in part because *current* news topics and even vocabulary are continually evolving. But *The Metropolitan Daily News* provides a solid base on which intermediate and advanced readers can build: Besides learning to understand headlines and sentences in the newspaper, students will read background information on topics such as government censorship, elections, and the role of advertising in the news business. These topics reveal the greater context of American journalism in society.

This book is intended for either individual or classroom use. Individuals can work through it independently, checking their comprehension of the news articles in Part Two with the Answer Key. For both mono- and multicultural classes, several types of discussion questions are provided throughout the book. The text and news topics will be of interest to students in general ESL/EFL classes as well as in reading and American culture courses; they will also be useful to people in the fields of journalism, international business, and political science who wish to improve their English and to read English-language newspapers more. Because major American newspapers can be found in cities around the globe, this book can be read effectively both in the United States and in other countries.

It is my hope that, with the help of *The Metropolitan Daily News*, readers will go on to peruse newspapers regularly and enjoy discussing current issues in English with confidence.

I would like to express my appreciation and thanks to many people for their help with this work, especially: to members of my family for their encouragement during the three years of writing and rewriting; to Paula Gassman and Margaret Thomas for their constructive comments on the first version of Part One; to the people at Prentice Hall, who have given the book a chance; to their anonymous reviewers, several of whom provided thoughtful suggestions that improved the later drafts; and last, but not least, to my students at Harvard University—Pnina, Tony, Ingrid, Mihyeh, and all the others—whose good questions and comments motivated me to write the book in the first place and then to continue on to publication.

J.C.B.

THE METROPOLITAN DAILY NEWS

PART ONE

Prereading Conversations

CC **Conversation with a Classmate**

Pair work (two people working together) gives you intense practice in speaking and listening for a short time. Use the vocabulary and structures that you already know for this conversation. (In later chapters you will be asked to practice the language presented in the chapter.) You shouldn't worry if your English is not exactly correct. Do not use a dictionary during the conversation, just as you would not use one out of class. Your teacher will listen in.

1. Introduce yourself to a classmate. Exchange information on where you come from and why you are taking this course.

2. Look at the map of the United States. Tell your partner which cities or states you have been in, or which ones you'd like to visit.

THE UNITED STATES OF AMERICA

Before you begin discussing the topics in this book and in the news, note the following "unwritten rules" or techniques for discussions that are common in North America. Are they the same in your native culture?

In North America all individuals involved in a discussion are expected to say something. A discussion or conversation is most interesting if everyone expresses his or her opinion and/or comments on someone else's statements. If you do not contribute to a group conversation, Americans might think you are bored, or you don't understand English, or you are not an interesting person.

It is not acceptable to remain silent when someone speaks directly to you. Americans usually feel uncomfortable in a silence during a conversation. They think that their partner either has not understood the question (so they repeat it) or does not want to make the effort to answer, which is impolite. So if you need to think for a minute before responding, begin your remarks while you are thinking with something like "Well, . . ." or "Hmm, let me think . . . ."

A good conversation or discussion depends on give-and-take behavior. It is just as important to ask others questions as it is to answer theirs. Both questions and answers tend to be quite direct in the United States (compared to Japan, for example). But it is also OK *not* to answer a question directly. If a topic is too personal or unpleasant, or if you don't know an answer, you can avoid giving a direct response (see the Helpful Expressions box on p. 5).

If members of the group have differing opinions, they can disagree politely and in a friendly way without becoming defensive or aggressive. If a discussion becomes *too* one-sided or angry, the discussion leader or host may try to get the conversation back to a safer, more pleasant tone by changing the subject or by saying something light or humorous.

Certain nonverbal behavior is also important. Eye contact (looking at people) is considered polite; when speaking, Americans look at the other group members. And they, reciprocally, show their interest through facial expressions or gestures, such as smiling (showing encouragement, pleasure, or sometimes, amusement), raising their eyebrows (showing surprise or doubt), or nodding their heads (showing agreement). Such nonverbal behavior gives the speaker feedback about the group's reactions.

Practice the verbal expressions in the box as well as nonverbal feedback during the group discussion that follows. Your teacher will tell you the topic to be discussed and the number of students in each group (about four to six). The instructor may also ask you to count the number of times you:

- *volunteer* to speak,
- ask a question, and
- respond to a question or comment.

Your group discussion can be considered a success if everyone has participated in all three ways at least once.

Remember to practice these expressions and discussion techniques every time you participate in group conversations—in class and outside of class.

Helpful Expressions

The following expressions are commonly used in discussions. Expand this list with further expressions that you know.

to ask for a clarification: I didn't quite follow what you said about. . . .
Could you say that again, please?
I'm sorry, I don't understand what you mean.

_____

to ask someone's opinion: What do you think, Tony?
Don't you think so? [You expect the answer
    "Yes, I do (think so)."]
Is it the same in your country too, Ya Ming?

_____

to say your opinion: I think/feel that . . . .
As I see it, ...
In my opinion, ...

_____

to avoid a direct response: It's hard to say.
I'm afraid I don't know (can't answer) that one.
Well, in my country we don't usually discuss that.

_____

to agree with someone: I agree (completely).
I think so too.
I don't think so either. [= Me neither].

_____

to disagree politely: But if you consider . . . , ...
I'm not sure that I agree. As I see it, ...
Well, in my country, many people think . . . .

_____

to change the subject: I think we should also hear from Alex.
That's all very interesting, but . . . .
I hate to interrupt, but shouldn't we go on?
By the way, [introduce a new topic] . . . .

_____

CHAPTER 1

Newspapers in America: An Introduction

PREREADING QUESTIONS
---

1. a. How often do you read a newspaper in your own language?

   b. Do you read any English-language newspapers? Name some that you know.

2. a. Are the owners of a U.S. newspaper allowed to publish whatever they want to?

   b. How is it in your native country?

3. Do you think that the government influences news reporting in the United States?

Reporters and camera crews at work, observing a struggle between a demonstrator and a police officer (New Haven, Connecticut). (AP Photo)

1.1 Introduction

There are thousands of different newspapers printed in the United States. They range from thick *daily* newspapers (called *dailies*), which are read by millions of people across America and the world, to small, local, weekly newspapers, which offer news of interest to a specific area. This book is about dailies; there are more than 1,700 of them,[1] and six have been chosen as examples in this book.*

About nine out of ten adult Americans read some part(s) of a newspaper every day. Sweden is the country in which the most people read one every day; Japan, Germany, and Finland also have a very high percentage of newspaper readers.[2]

Before you begin to read an American newspaper, you probably want to know something about the kinds of dailies that exist in the United States and about the role of the *press* (newspapers and reporters in general) in American society. This chapter will give you that background information.

1.2 Newspapers for the Nation

In your country there may be one or a few national newspapers, and the press may be a national institution. Out of all the newspapers (also called *papers* or *journals*) in the United States, only three are considered national.

The *Wall Street Journal* was the country's first national daily and is one of the largest. Because it specializes in economic and financial issues, however, it will not be described further in this book.[3]

The *New York Times* is a journal with a relatively long and respected history. Its national edition is read by about one million people in the United States. It is air-mailed to capital cities around the world for international readers who are interested in events in the United States. About two-thirds of its readers live in the New York City area; their full, New York edition includes local news in an extra "Metropolitan" section and more cultural and sports articles than the national edition.[4]

The third national newspaper is *USA Today*, started only recently, in 1982. This new paper had no precedent: It was not an expanded version of any traditional journal but instead was the first newspaper to start out as a truly national one. It calls itself "The Nation's Newspaper" and claims over five and a half million readers altogether.[5] Its main office is in Washington, D.C., but it is printed in several places in the country. In 1988 it could be found daily in 53 countries outside the United States.[6]

The *New York Times* and *USA Today* offer readers two very different styles of journalism and focus on different kinds of issues. We will compare them in detail in Chapters 2 and 5.

Two other newspapers that also represent American journalism in the areas of national and international news will enter into the comparisons as well. They are the *Christian Science Monitor* and the *International Herald Tribune*.

---

*Superscript numbers refer to Appendix 1, "Notes and References," at the back of this book.

The *Christian Science Monitor* has its headquarters in Boston, Massachusetts, next to the main Church of Christ, Scientist. Mary Baker Eddy founded both the religious denomination and the newspaper, the latter in 1908. It is smaller in size and readership than the other papers mentioned here. About 200,000 copies are printed in the United States every weekday, and most of them are mailed to regular subscribers. It includes a daily religious article but specializes in national and international news, calling itself "an international newspaper." A weekly edition is printed in a few other countries. It is generally respected for its high-quality journalism.

The *International Herald Tribune* is partly owned by the New York Times Company and the Washington Post Company. About 40% of its articles come directly from those two American papers. Its main office is in Paris. Printed simultaneously in ten major cities in the world, it calls itself "The Global Newspaper." It offers political and financial news about many countries, especially the United States, Western Europe, and the Far East.

1.3 The Importance of Metropolitan Newspapers

Three national newspapers in a country with a population of more than 230 million may seem like a small number. There are several reasons why there are not more. In the past, the main reason was the size of the country.

Distance still separates readers from one another today. What is news in Maine may not be interesting to readers in Arizona, for example. There are differences in climate, in economic basis, and to some extent in lifestyles and origins of the population across the country. These differences are regional.

There are loosely defined regional areas within the U.S.A. An American citizen is likely to identify with and feel at home in one region more than the others. He or she may tell you, for example: "I'm a New Englander/ Midwesterner/Texan, etc." or "I'm from the South/the West Coast, etc." People like to read about happenings, places, and persons that they are familiar with. So newspapers represent the particular interests of readers in their community or region. They carry advertisements for businesses there and announce upcoming events in that region.

Until recently, it was technically difficult and expensive to transport tons of newsprint great distances. In the 1980s, some journals began to use satellites to transmit information. Using a satellite, the *New York Times*, for example, prints its national edition in nine cities. Even the *Boston Globe* uses a satellite to reach its branch printers, in a northwestern suburb of Boston, rather than using much slower truck transportation. *USA Today* could not exist without satellite transmission.

A GLANCE BACK IN HISTORY

Early America

From the very beginning, in Colonial America, settlers were proud of their town or state. As the population moved from the east coast westwards, communities in the western territories grew up. They were quite self-reliant and gradually produced their own newspapers. These journals often emphasized the positive aspects of their hometowns, trying to attract new citizens and stimulate economic growth. Far from the influence of the nation's capital, they watched the federal government critically. They began to speak for their readers in asking for more rights and better laws for the territories. A few of them grew into modern newspapers of today. Local newspapers have a long tradition in this country.

Today most of the biggest newspapers come from the biggest cities in the country. They serve the readers in that city and the area around it. Some of the metropolitan dailies with the largest number of readers are the *New York Daily News*, the *Los Angeles Times*, the *Washington Post*, the *Chicago Tribune*, the *Detroit News* and the *Detroit Free Press*, the *San Francisco Chronicle*, and the *Boston Globe*.[7] (See the map on p. 3.) Sample articles from some of these can be found in Part Two of this book.

1.4 Newspapers and Government

In some countries the government influences or even controls news reporting. There is no official *censorship* in the United States in peace times. Newspaper owners do not even need a license to publish.

In times of war, the President can classify some kinds of military information as "secret" and not available to the public. *Censorship* can occur during times of war: During the U.S. military action in Grenada in 1983 and the war in Iraq in 1991, the Defense Department restricted reporting and censored news reports. Journalists and the public criticized that. Many were frustrated because they could not get as much objective information as they wanted.

Indeed, the role of newspapers in American society is based on their independence from governmental control. At the national and state levels, the government in America is made up of three parts: the legislative, the executive, and the judicial branches. Each of these three branches is supposed to check and balance the power of the other two. The press is not part of the government. Instead, its role is to report the news freely, including news about government actions and officials. So newspapers are supposed to check or watch over all three branches. (The press is sometimes called the *fourth estate*, but that just means a fourth power, not the fourth branch of government.)

In order to be a good critic, or "watchdog," of the government, the press has to be free from government interference. The Watergate affair (see box) is a major example of how the press succeeded in uncovering a scandal in spite of the government, in this case the executive branch. This kind of journalism is called *investigative reporting*. However, it is not typical of the ordinary, day-to-day work of a reporter. In fact, it is usually done by special teams of journalists for the big dailies.

A GLANCE BACK IN HISTORY

The Watergate Affair

Two *Washington Post* journalists were effective "watchdogs" when they helped to uncover the Watergate scandal. This scandal is named after the Watergate Hotel in Washington, D.C., where the Democratic National office was located. In 1972 five men from the Committee for the Re-election of the President (Richard Nixon, of the Republican Party) were caught inside their rivals' office. They had wiretapped the telephones there and were looking for information. During the Watergate Affair, 1972–1974, President Nixon's White House staff participated in the obstruction of the official investigation of the wiretapping and in other illegal activities. The two journalists were able to get information about these illegal actions from someone inside the government, confirm his statements, and report on them. They later received the Pulitzer Prize for excellence in reporting for their work.

The Watergate affair has had a lasting effect on American society. Nixon, in the end, resigned from the presidency. Members of his administration were brought to trial and found guilty of wrongdoings. The Watergate scandal is still used as a kind of measuring stick for such crimes in government. For example, about 15 years later, when a scandal was discovered in President Ronald Reagan's administration involving the sale of weapons to Iran, some reporters called the affair "Irangate"; and a play about a similar, fictitious situation was named "Mastergate."

Sometimes, however, the press does not act as a separate power. In their search for the latest news and "inside" information, reporters who cover government affairs often form close contacts with a few of the policy makers. These people can, knowingly or unknowingly, feed reporters certain information that they want to see published. Good journalists report where they got their information and how reliable it is.

1.5 Objectivity in Reporting

Most Americans today—both newspaper people and readers—agree that it is the role of the press to be fair, or *objective*, in reporting the news. One of the first things that a young journalist must learn is to separate fact from opinion. Readers should form their own opinions or judgments about the news after reading the reported facts.

But this point of view was not always popular. The first journals in the country represented their editors' points of view. Readers bought them in order to read an opinionated account of events. Today such opinions are openly expressed only on *editorial* pages, where they are clearly presented as the publishers' views. They are accompanied by the opinions of other writers and experts and by letters from readers.

Carlin Romano, a noted journalist and editor, suggests that the ideal and development of objective writing is good for the United States:

> It may be that our mixed society maintains relative internal peace only because so many differences are masked behind a journalism that discourages the vocabulary of class, race, and ideology. If every newspaper here took an openly partisan position, closer to the model of Italian and French journalism, we might face a far more conflict [-filled] society.[8]

Do you think it is possible to produce news articles, or *stories*, completely objectively?

If you look at the front page of a few different newspapers, you will immediately see that they do not look the same. (See Chapter 2 for examples.) Their front-page editors have chosen various news stories to print there; and no two papers will feature exactly the same ones. The limited space on the front page has forced this choice. Here we see the first element of subjectivity (that is, something coming from someone's personal ideas): Which news stories are important enough to appear on the front page? Which ones must the reader turn one or more pages to find? And which reports never get written up at all in a particular news-paper? (In Chapter 2, we will examine the front page in more detail.)

Look also at the *headlines* above the articles. They condense the important information of a report into a very few words. The reporter who writes the story usually does not write the headline to it; an editor writes it. He or she may interpret the story differently from the reporter or may want to emphasize a certain part of it. This point of view represents a second element of subjectivity.

Now look closely at the article itself. Is the author's name given? An author's name is given in the *byline* (the article is *by* that person).

Reporters like to be acknowledged for their work. A byline also makes them responsible for it. Readers may be able to judge the objectivity of a signed report on the basis of other pieces by the same journalist or on the basis of facts they know about him or her.

Of course the journalist may have written a *biased* story (that means a report that expresses a point of view). That opinion may be openly expressed through the use of certain words. Descriptive adjectives and adverbs, for example, are often added to sentences to "color" them or "bring them to life." Although they are important in fiction, adjectives and adverbs are not used much by serious journalists in factual news reports because "colors" are experienced subjectively.

A more subtle form of bias can be found in the choice of what news is included in an article on each topic. Most reporters cannot personally gather all the facts they want, so they rely on experts' or witnesses' stories. People who give information to a journalist are called *sources*. Just whom a reporter chooses as a source can seriously affect the kind of information that is included in or left out of the final article. Bias can be expressed through the omission (leaving out) as well as the inclusion of facts or statements. [Ex.VV.2]*

On the other hand, sometimes there is no byline. Instead, the Associated Press (AP), the United Press International (UPI), Reuters, the Knight-Ridder Service, or Agence France Presse (AFP) may be given as the source of the facts of the story. These are news services, called *wire services*. They sell factual news reports to many newspapers in the world. Their news is telegraphed (*wired*) to subscribing papers in compact form. The papers' journalists then rewrite it into understandable sentences.

In order to get a lot of subscribers, the wire services have had to be sure that their news is not biased, or partisan, toward any one point of view. The result is fairly objective news. The many articles written on the basis of wire service facts are very similar, regardless of what newspaper they appear in.

A GLANCE BACK IN HISTORY

Agnew vs. the Press

In 1969 (three years before the Watergate scandal got into the papers) Vice-President Spiro Agnew suddenly and dramatically attacked the press in a speech. In his opinion the news media, especially television news programs, were biased against President Nixon. He tried to discredit the newspeople, saying that they purposely produced stories that hurt the president politically and in the eyes of the public. He maintained that the television stations were run by a small group of liberals who alone determined what millions of Americans saw on their news programs each night. He also spoke against the liberal press, but then some writers showed that newspapers are often owned by conservatives.

All of the news media carried stories about Agnew's message. The press was very angry but many citizens agreed with the Vice-President.

---

*Exercise VV.2, in the Exercises section at the end of this chapter, is related to the paragraphs you have just read.

1.6 Criticism of the Press

The objectivity of news stories was not discussed much for the first 200 years or so of the history of American newspapers. Even after Vice-President Agnew attacked the news media for their bias (see box on p. 12), there were no big changes in journalistic policies. The government cannot force changes on the press.

Most publishers say they try to present news fairly; they need a good reputation so that many people will buy their papers. But Agnew and Nixon succeeded in influencing the public to be wary of the news media.[9]

Only a few years later, the Watergate affair in Nixon's government was discovered. The public then learned to be wary of the powers of the presidency as well. The relationship between the press and the presidents has often been uneasy.

Presidents and other public figures in America must accept the fact that journalists will follow their lives closely. Reporters say that the public wants to know about the lives of elected officials as well as about famous entertainers and sports heroes. They even say that the public has a "right to know."

Recently there has been a lot of discussion about *how much* the public should know about people's private lives. This issue often arises during election years (see box below for an example). Other issues with which the press is still struggling are the privacy of individuals in a trial and of crime victims in general.

A GLANCE BACK IN HISTORY

The Privacy of a Presidential Candidate

In 1987 several men were campaigning to become the Democratic party's candidate for president. Of course, journalists reported about them—about their speeches and political goals and also about their private lives to a certain extent. Reporters said they were informing their readers about the whole person so that they could choose whom to vote for. But when the *Miami Herald* printed a story and a photo of one married man, Gary Hart, with a good-looking young woman sitting on his lap, some people said the newspaper went too far into his private life. At a meeting with the press soon after that, one reporter even asked Hart: "Have you ever committed adultery?" (*Adultery* means being unfaithful to your marriage partner.) Hart replied that he did not have to answer that question. Almost no one disagreed with Hart's answer. But many readers and journalists asked themselves and the press whether the public has the "right to know" about a political candidate's extramarital affairs. Gary Hart's reputation was so damaged that he ended his campaign. The debate about the public's right to know continues.

Exercises

RR **A Review of the Reading**

1. Answer the following comprehension questions:

   1. Is the *Boston Globe* a national newspaper? The *New York Times?*

   2. In what way are the *New York Times* and *USA Today* similar? How are they different?

   3. Why are metropolitan newspapers so popular in America?

   4. Does the United States government ever censor the news?

   5. What happened in the Watergate scandal? What was the role of the press?

   6. Why don't serious journalists use many adjectives and adverbs in their news articles?

   7. Do U.S. reporters write about the private lives of politicians?

2. Check your understanding of this chapter. Make the following statements exact by adding *may*, *should*, or *have to* OR their negative forms in the blanks.

   1. Many newspapers _____ use satellites to reach branch printers.

   2. State governments _____ close a newspaper business because it does not have a license.

   3. Readers _____ never know what really happens during wars.

   4. Young journalists _____ learn to separate fact from opinion.

   5. Readers _____ form their own opinions.

   6. U.S. presidents _____ accept the fact that journalists will follow their lives closely.

   7. Politicians _____ answer questions about adultery.

3. *Extra-credit, Writing Exercise:* Write a paragraph giving a young reporter some advice about his or her work.

4. This chapter has six sections: Introduction, Newspapers for the Nation, The Importance of Metropolitan Newspapers, Newspapers and Government, Objectivity in Reporting, and Criticism of the Press. Review in your mind the contents of each section. If you have trouble summarizing one, go back and read it again. Then write some notes—important words or phrases—about each section.

Valuable Vocabulary

1. In this chapter you were introduced to some newspaper vocabulary. Match each word on the left with the correct definition on the right. Write the corresponding letter in the blank to the left of each number. One word is not defined; explain it in your own words.

_____ 1. **dailies**

_____ 2. **journalist**

_____ 3. **censorship**

_____ 4. **byline**

_____ 5. **editorial**

_____ 6. **bias**

_____ 7. **source**

_____ 8. **wire service**

a. author's name below a headline

b. prejudice, or a personal point of view

c. reporter

d. company that gathers news and sells it to journals

e. newspapers that are published every day

f. · someone who gives a reporter information

g. · official examination of newspapers, books, films, etc., with the purpose of removing anything that is considered to be offensive or harmful to the public good

2. Do *objective* and *biased* mean the same thing? Is an objective report also a biased one?

For Discussion and Debate

Talk about the following topics; remember to use the discussion techniques described on pp. 4 and 5.

1. Comment on the objectivity of the following two headlines. Both concern a 15% raise ("hike") of state income taxes that members of the Massachusetts government (House of Representatives) agreed on. Headline *a* is from the *Boston Herald*; *b* is from the *Boston Globe*.

a.

b.

SATURDAY, JULY 8, 1989

Fury!

Taxpayers in uproar over 15% tax increase rushed through House

JULY 7, 1989

House votes to hike state income tax

Initial OK calls for temporary 15% rise

2. Do you think journalists should be allowed to write about the private life of an elected politician or a candidate for election? Does the public have a right to know about it?

   If during the discussion two points of view develop, debate the issue: The class should divide into two groups with opposing views. (Undecided students may act as a third group, of judges, if desired.) Each group writes down as many supporting arguments as it can and then selects one or two group speakers. The speakers then debate the issue; first each team gives arguments for the group position, then each can rebut (answer) the other's arguments. Finally, the judges, if any, summarize the most convincing arguments.

3. Look at the photograph below. In small groups, discuss why the press might be interested in the young woman; use your imagination. Then tell the class your group's story. *Option*: Write the story.

GLOBE STAFF PHOTOS/JOHN TLUMACKI

4. Are you interested in working for a newspaper? Tell the class about your interest and/or experience in the field of journalism.

5. One of the Prereading Questions was: "Do you think that the government influences news reporting in the United States?" Has your opinion changed since reading this chapter? Do you think the author's presentation of information has been objective? (If you are not ready to answer this question yet, wait until you can gather more experience with American newspapers.)

Intercultural Issues

1. Do many people in your country read a newspaper daily?

2. Tell your classmates about the kinds of newspapers in your country. Does the government (local or national) influence news reporting in your country? Should it?

3. Do newspapers (or radio or television) in your country report on the private lives of politicians?
   Do you remember whether they reported the Gart Hart affair?
   Would similar reports about a politician in your country force him or her out of office or out of a campaign?

CHAPTER 2

Looking at the Front Page

PREREADING QUESTIONS

1. a. How important are photographs in a newspaper?

   b. Are color photos more important than black-and-white ones?

   c. Can photos be biased? For example, look at the pictures in Chapter 1.

2. Can you locate the most important news story on the front page of an English-language newspaper? Try it, using a current paper or the front-page copies in this chapter.

3. a. Is your native country in the news "spotlight" right now?

   b. If you read an American or other English-language newspaper *today*, what, if anything, might it report about your country of origin?

2.1 Examples of Front Pages

Let us look at the front pages of the dailies available in a major city. In this book, Boston, Massachusetts, is used as an example. Boston hosts two local dailies—the *Boston Globe* and the *Boston Herald*—and the internationally oriented *Christian Science Monitor*. The national newspapers *New York Times* and *USA Today* can be found anywhere that newspapers are sold. And the New York edition of the *International Herald Tribune* can be bought at many newsstands. Throughout the remainder of this book, the newspapers will be referred to by their commonly used short names (except for *USA Today*): the *Globe*, the *Herald*, the *Monitor*, the *Times*, and the *Tribune*. As you work through this chapter, you may want to have some newspapers from your own area ready to look at and compare with Boston's.

Look at the following front pages of four of these newspapers. All of them are dated Thursday, January 17, 1991. As you can see, they look quite different. Even the size of the paper is not uniform.

The *Monitor* and the *Herald* use a smaller format, called the *tabloid size*. It is cheaper to produce and easier to open and read, especially while sitting in a bus or subway. Since many journals with these smaller pages print lots of photographs and little serious news, the noun "tabloid" has come to mean a newspaper for sensational stories. An example is the *Weekly World News*, pictured on p. 47. The *Monitor* is certainly not a tabloid in this sense, and most people would agree that the *Herald* is not either.

The larger-sized newspaper holds more information on each page, of course. In fact, you can read more words on just the front page of a full-sized newspaper than you hear in a half-hour television news program![1]

2.2 Placement of Articles on the Front Page

In the first chapter it was mentioned that the publishers (who are usually also the owners) and editors choose which articles to print on the front page. Large papers even have a "front-page editor" who does this as a full-time job.

Among the several stories, there is one that is the most important news of the day. It is called the *lead* (for <u>lead</u>ing, or main) story or article. It is easy to see which that is in the *Herald*. The *Herald* chooses only one or a few stories (plus two or three extra headlines) for its front page every day. One headline is printed in huge letters, often across the middle of the page.

Although most of the papers shown here followed this pattern because of the seriousness of the news that day, the lead article is not always distinguished by oversized type. It is the policy of most newspapers, such as the *Globe*, to print the most important news article of the day on the right-hand side of the page directly under the newspaper's name. The second-most important article is on the left-hand side.[2] The *Times* emphasizes the stories in these same positions with headlines in capital letters. *USA Today* emphasizes its lead story with boldface (thick letters) headlines; its second-most important story, however, is placed under the lead.[3] *USA Today* also labels one article "Cover Story" and centers it on the front page; there is usually a color photo to this story.

The New York Times

New York: Today, partly cloudy, windy. High 49. Tonight, clear, cold winds. Low 32. Tomorrow, variable clouds. High 40. Yesterday, high 55, low 38. Details are on page D22.

VOL.CXL... No. 48,483   Copyright © 1991 The New York Times   NEW YORK, THURSDAY, JANUARY 17, 1991   50 cents beyond 75 miles from New York City, except on Long Island.   40 CENTS

U.S. AND ALLIES OPEN AIR WAR ON IRAQ, BOMB BAGHDAD AND KUWAITI TARGETS; 'NO CHOICE' BUT FORCE, BUSH DECLARES

RELIEF AND ANGER

News of Attack Sweeps the Country, Stirring Profound Feelings

By JAMES BARRON

In one long moment yesterday evening, word that the United States had attacked Baghdad swept the country. In split-level suburban homes on the East Coast where dinner was in the oven, in big-city restaurants where bars were jammed with the happy-hour crowd and in skyscraper offices on the West Coast where people were still at work, there was an odd mixture of apprehension, sadness and relief.

In malls, shoppers emptied out of stores and cried. Some rushed to call relatives and share the news that after five months of waiting and wondering, America was at war. Some stood silently in front of television sets, stunned that the Bush Administration had decided to act so soon after the United Nations deadline for Iraq to withdraw from Kuwait. Some worried how close to home the conflict might come.

"You don't know what to expect and then you think, 'Am I really going to be affected by this?' " said Carla Houston, 26 years old, of Cupertino, Calif. "Physically, I probably won't be. Mentally, I know I will be. I mean, I was only 6 years old during Vietnam."

Something Had Happened

On college campuses, on sidewalks and in city parks, people who had not heard the news realized that something had happened just by the way friends said hello on the telephone. "I called home and my boyfriend was in tears," said Robin Cheevers, a 27-year-old legal secretary in San Francisco.

In bars and restaurants, managers made somber announcements. At Joe's Stone Crab, a restaurant on Miami Beach, George Silas punched the button on the public-address system.

"Ladies and gentlemen," he said, "I've just received word that the United States has started to bomb Iraq. The war is on." There were about 50 people in the restaurant. He said the waiting had been the hardest part. There was no cheering and no clapping.

At the Mirage Hotel in Las Vegas, ex-

Continued on Page A18, Column 1

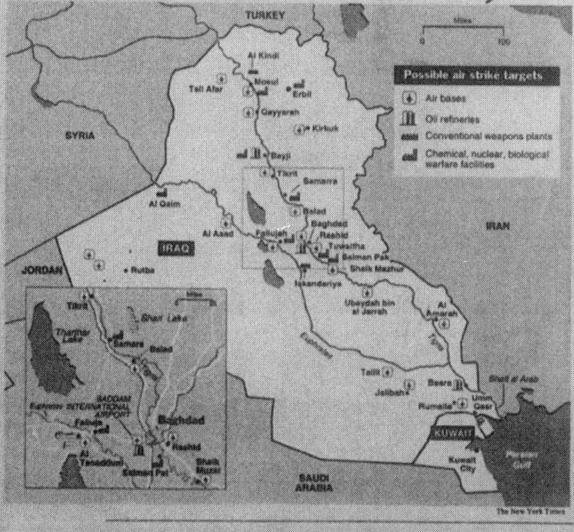

OTHER NEWS

Gorbachev Is Moving To Muzzle the Press

Faced with mounting condemnation of the assault by Soviet forces on demonstrators in Lithuania, President Mikhail S. Gorbachev moved to undermine a law guaranteeing freedom of the press — a hallmark of the era of openness that he himself ushered in. Page A8.

In a show of defiance in the Lithuanian capital, hundreds of thousands of mourners streamed through the streets to bury the dead. Page A8.

Dinkins Offers Budget With Layoffs and Cuts

Mayor David N. Dinkins presented a preliminary New York City budget of $29.3 billion for the next fiscal year.

The announcement was met with a mix of pain and uncertainty. Some questioned whether he had gone far enough in making cuts; others complained that he had gone too far. The plan includes thousands of layoffs and service cuts. Page B1.

Daily News Threatens To Close or Sell

The management of The Daily News threatened to close or sell the paper unless it stems heavy losses.

Both sides in the 12-week-old strike agreed the move was an ultimatum to the unions to make major concessions or lose their jobs for good. The News said a shutdown could occur as early as March 20. Page B1.

Trenton Gun-Law Challenge

Both houses of New Jersey's Legislature have moved to weaken the state's assault weapon law, the nation's most restrictive, and may set off a national battle. Page B1.

Raids, on a Huge Scale, Seek to Destroy Scud Missiles

By MICHAEL R. GORDON
Special to The New York Times

WASHINGTON, Jan. 16 — The military campaign to evict Iraq from Kuwait began, as expected, with air strikes on a huge scale at targets deep in Iraq and Kuwait.

American officials said the onslaught included Tomahawk sea-launched cruise missiles, F-117 Stealth fighter-bombers, F-15E fighter-bombers and a wide variety of other Air Force and Navy planes.

The aim of the attack was to damage Iraqi command and control centers, knock out Iraqi air defenses, and destroy Scud surface-to-surface missiles and airfields throughout Iraq.

Reassurance for Israel

In mounting the air attack, the United States is also trying to make good on its assurances to the Israelis that the Washington would blast the Scud missiles that threaten Israel to make it unnecessary for Israel to enter the war, the officials said.

Asked what aircraft would be used in the attack, an official replied, "Pretty much everything."

Air Force officials in Saudi Arabia said that a squadron of F-15E's took off from an air base in central Saudi Arabia at 4:50 P.M., Eastern standard time.

The dispatch of the squadron was only a fraction of the air power that can be unleashed against President Saddam Hussein's forces. The number of

aircraft involved and the intensity of the assault in the opening hours and days of an air campaign is expected to be among the biggest such attacks in history.

The expectation that the United States would unleash air strikes on Iraq built in recent days as the Pentagon maneuvered two aircraft carriers inside the Persian Gulf, the first time that two carriers have ever been in those waters simultaneously.

Ever since the American military buildup began in the Persian Gulf, there has been considerable debate about the efficacy of air power, particularly whether American and allied air power can defeat Iraqi ground troops. But the Pentagon is confident that the allied air force is vastly superior to its Iraqi counterpart. Some members of Congress who were briefed by the United States Central Command last year were told that American military experts to achieve air superiority within 48 hours.

Iraq, however, has been trying to develop ways to counter an allied air assault by dispersing its planes and preparing camouflaged sites for its surface-to-surface Scud missiles, which could be fired at airfields.

Shielding Iraqi Weapons

Some Administration officials say Iraq might try to preserve some of its aircraft by hiding them in concrete shelters and using camouflage and decoys to deceive the Americans. The planes, and any surface-to-surface missiles that Iraq managed to hide, could then be used to launch surprise attacks later in a war, this line of speculation goes.

United States military officials say American casualties are inevitable in an air campaign, with some crew members killed and others captured at the Dhahran International Hotel were held as prisoners. Many former military officials anticipated that to reduce casualties, an air attack would begin at night. This enabled the American military to take advantage of its edge in

Continued on Page A15, Column 1

News Summary	A2
Editorials/Op-Ed	A22-23
Obituaries	B10
Sports	B11-14
Weather	D22

No Ground Fighting Yet, President Tells the Nation

By ANDREW ROSENTHAL
Special to The New York Times

WASHINGTON, Jan. 16 — The United States and allied forces attacked Iraq today, striking Baghdad and other targets in Iraq and Kuwait with waves of air attacks at the start of the long-threatened war to force President Saddam Hussein's army from Kuwait.

"The liberation of Kuwait has begun," President Bush said in confirming the start of the attack with a three-sentence statement that was read by his spokesman, Marlin Fitzwater, shortly after the raids began.

Later, in a televised address to the nation, Mr. Bush said, "We have no choice but to force Saddam from Kuwait by force. We will not fail."

Chemical Weapons Targeted

But he also said, "We are determined to knock out Saddam Hussein's nuclear bomb potential. We will also destroy his chemical weapons facilities."

Assuring Americans that ground forces were not yet engaged in the battle, the President added: "Five months ago, Saddam Hussein started this cruel war against Kuwait. Tonight, the battle has been joined."

He said initial reports indicated that "our operations are proceeding according to plan.

"Our objectives are clear," he said. "Saddam Hussein's forces will leave Kuwait, the legitimate Government of Kuwait will be restored to its rightful place and Kuwait will once again be free."

In the written statement issued earlier, Mr. Fitzwater said: "In conjunction with the forces of our coalition partners, the United States has moved under the code name Operation Desert Storm to enforce the mandates of the United Nations Security Council. As of 7 o'clock P.M., Operation Desert Storm forces were engaging targets in Iraq and Kuwait."

The nighttime attack, which began at about 6:30 P.M. Washington time, (2:30 A.M. Iraqi time Thursday) was first revealed in television reports by American correspondents in Baghdad that the skies over the Iraqi capital were alight with anti-aircraft and tracer fire. Initial reports were that multiple waves of warplanes bombed central Baghdad, hitting oil refineries and the airport.

British and Saudis Attack

White House officials said an undisclosed number of British warplanes and 150 Saudi planes were taking part in the initial attacks.

Mr. Bush notified Congressional leaders of the planned attack between 6 and 7 P.M., telephoning House Speaker Thomas S. Foley and Robert W. Byrd, the President pro tem of the Senate. He also sent notification, as required under the war resolution passed by the House and Senate last week, that all efforts at diplomacy had failed.

"We must now pray for a conflict that ends quickly, decisively and with a minimum loss of life," Mr. Foley said. "We must now stand united in support of our armed forces in the gulf who have embraced the duty and burden of conducting the war."

In New York, the United Nations Secretary General, Javier Pérez de Cuéllar, said, "I think it is for me to express deep sorrow."

Code Word to King Fahd

The United States put into motion the actual order for battle at 8 A.M. today, when Saudi officials said Secretary of State James A. Baker 3d called in the Saudi Ambassador, Prince Bandar bin Sultan, and told him that American forces would attack Iraq tonight.

The Ambassador immediately telephoned King Fahd of Saudi Arabia, using a code word that Mr. Baker and the King had arranged during the Secretary's trip to Saudi Arabia last week, the informants said. The King then repeated back a code word that constituted his formal authorization for the American warplanes take off.

Mr. Bush directed the offensive from the Oval Office, where he watched the evening news and waited for the first

Continued on Page A14, Column 1

MORE ON THE GULF

Bush Evokes Glory of Past, not Vietnam

To tell Americans that war with Iraq has started, President Bush harked back to one of the great days in American military history — D-Day, June 6, 1944. On that day, Gen. Dwight D. Eisenhower said that "the liberation of Europe was under way." Last night, the White House spokesman said, "The liberation of Kuwait has begun." News analysis, page A16.

Oil Prices Jump $3 on News of War

Oil prices shot up $3 a barrel in cash trading off the exchange floors late night on word of the attack on Iraq. Crude oil prices almost instantly hit $35 in cash trading in New Orleans and Houston Business Day, page D1.

A Nation Reacts

Across the United States, there was an odd mixture of apprehension, sadness and relief as people stopped to absorb the realization that their country was again at war.

Israel on Alert

Israel declared a state of emergency minutes after word of the attack. There was no immediate indication an Iraqi attack on Israel. Page A16.

Rumble in the Sky Ends a 5-Month Wait

By PHILIP SHENON
Special to The New York Times

IN SAUDI ARABIA, Thursday, Jan. 17 — "It's absolutely awesome, I mean the ground shook and you felt it," said Col. Ray Davies, describing the takeoff of the first planes departing to attack Iraq from a big Saudi air base where he is chief maintenance officer.

The 44-year-old colonel said the first group of jets took off at 12:50 A.M. about an hour before the first word of attack was broadcast by television reporters in Baghdad.

"We've been waiting here for five months; now we finally got to do what

we were sent here to do," Colonel Davies told a group of American reporters who were brought to the base. "This is history in the making."

Thundering Off in Pairs

The F-15 fighter bombers, heavily loaded with bombs and supplemental underwing fuel tanks, thundered off in pairs into what had been a still desert night. The aircraft, which quickly became faint red dots, were armed with cannon and air-to-air missiles to be used for their own defense.

The activity at the airfield, whose exact location cannot be identified under military reporting rules, was the

first indication here that the assault was under way. All commercial traffic at the airport had been suspended a short time earlier.

Just before 4 A.M. Saudi time, hundreds of journalists and other guests at the Dhahran International Hotel were herded into the hotel bomb shelter in the basement and instructed to put on gas masks. Sirens started to wail throughout the city.

Waiting for the Signal

As the guests, primarily journalists, waited for the signal "gas clear," a hotel employee serving as warden directed guests to spread out in the area, which serves as a kitchen. The air conditioning had been turned off as a precaution to prevent the spread of chemical agents in case the hotel in the eastern Saudi oil city was hit by Iraqi missiles. The room was quiet except for the sound of a radio, on which a news announcer somewhere was reporting that operation Desert Storm had begun.

A British defense consultant who is working for the hotel, Philip Congdon, allowed reporters to leave after he

Continued on Page A16, Column 1

The War Begins

"The liberation of Kuwait has begun. In conjunction with the forces of our coalition partners, the United States has moved under the code name Operation Desert Storm to enforce the mandates of the United Nations Security Council.

"As of 7 o'clock P.M. Operation Desert Storm forces were engaging targets in Iraq and Kuwait."

STATEMENT, PRESIDENT BUSH, 7:06 P.M.

President Bush as he announced in a televised address last night that an air attack had been launched against Iraq.

HOW THE ATTACK UNFOLDED 3A

VIA SATELLITE

THE NATION'S NEWSPAPER

USA TODAY

NO. 1 IN THE USA . . . NEARLY 6 MILLION READERS A DAY

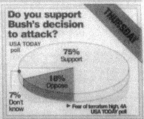

THURSDAY

Do you support Bush's decision to attack?
USA TODAY poll

75% Support

18% Oppose

7% Don't know

► Fear of terrorism high 4A
USA TODAY poll

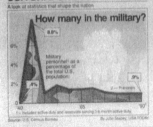

THURSDAY, JANUARY 17, 1991

NEWSLINE

THE GULF WAR AT A GLANCE

THE ATTACK: With a historic, lethal air strike, troops of Operation Desert Storm rain bombs on Iraq. 3A. President Bush: "Just the way it was scheduled." 4A.

MARKETS REACT: Japan's Nikkei shoots up 1004.11 points to close at 23,446.81. "What happens in Tokyo follows in London and then the U.S." 1B.

PAYING THE PRICE: U.S. officials deny it, but Iraqi leader Saddam Hussein, left, also may have been a target. 2A. Connoisseur of violence. 8A.

NO RESISTANCE: U.S. and allied forces met "no air resistance" from Iraq, USA says. 4A.

EARLY TARGETS: Iraq's air force and chemical, nuclear plants took a pounding. 3A.

SADDAM: Said to instill fear in enemies.

UNITY URGED: Democratic leaders of Congress who voted against war urge support from all in United States. 4A.

MEDICAL AID: No clear view exists on number of military casualties. 4A. Hospitals ready. 9A.

THE DISPUTE: A look at the issues and answers surrounding the gulf crisis. 8A. Peace marches. 3A.

DESERT FIGHTERS: Twenty-eight nations have sent ships, aircraft or personnel to gulf. Airplanes total more than 1,800; ships, 167. Ground forces total 745,000. 3A.

THE WEAPONS: How leading U.S. weapons and weapons systems compare to Iraq's. 9A.

PEOPLE IN CHARGE: The leaders in charge of Operation Desert Storm under Gen. H. Norman Schwarzkopf, commander of U.S. forces. The taskmaster. 3A.

TODAY'S DEBATE: War in the gulf. In USA TODAY's opinion, "The villain is not a U.S. president thirsty for blood. . . . It is a tyrant named Saddam Hussein who thumbed his nose at the world and dared an attack." 10A.
► "This war is unnecessary. The crisis in the gulf didn't need to end this way," says George Thompson. 10A.

SPECIAL EDITION: In addition to its weekend edition published Friday, USA TODAY will publish a Saturday edition this week to cover the gulf war. The edition will be available at newsstands, vending machines, airports and other sites.

ABROAD: Soviet President Mikhail Gorbachev urges lawmakers to suspend press-freedom laws. 4A.

MONEY: Labor Dept. says consumer prices rose 6.1% in '90 from '89; largest annual hike since '81. 1B.

SPORTS: Ticket brokers are salivating at the thought of an all-New York Super Bowl in Tampa. 1,4C.

LIFE: Long-term use of banned painkiller — phenacetin — linked to an increased risk for hypertension. 1D.
► CBS wants Delta Burke to continue Designing. 1D.

Compiled by Mary-Christine Philip

Inside USA TODAY

News		Sports	
Editorial/Opinion	10-11A	Basketball	1,3,8C
Nation at large	6A	Football	1,4C
Washington/World	4A	Hockey	10C
Weather	12A	Lotteries	11C

Money		Life	
Amex/OTC	8B	Classified	6-7D
Insiders	2B	Crossword	6D
Market Scoreboard	3B	Jeanne Williams	2D
New York exchange	5B	Television	3D

© COPYRIGHT 1991 USA TODAY, a division of Gannett Co., Inc.

USA SNAPSHOTS®

A look at statistics that shape the nation

How many in the military?

Military personnel as a percentage of the total U.S. population

8.8%

.9%

'40   '65   '90

1 — Includes active duty and reserves serving 2-6 months active duty.

Source: U.S. Census Bureau

By Julie Stacey, USA TODAY

U.S. BOMBS BAGHDAD

Iraqi air force 'decimated'

President Bush:
"Tonight the battle has been joined."

"When the troops we've sent in finish their work, I'm determined to bring them home as soon as possible."

Targets

Iran

Iraq/Kuwait
At least half of Saddam's 150,000 elite troops were reported wiped out by allied bombing.

Syria   Iraq

Rutba   Baghdad

Israel   Jordan   Kuwait City

Iraq
Scud missile batteries were targeted, with "high priority" given to a pair near Rutba, Iraq, the closest batteries to Israel. Numerous blasts were reported on the west bank of the Tigris River in Baghdad, the location of a number of government buildings, Iraqi television and radio.

Saudi Arabia   Kuwait

Saudi Arabia
Air Force AWACS flew above Saudi Arabia to direct the attack.

Key ■ Air base ▲ Missile site

Source: CNN; USA TODAY research

Photo by Tim Dillon, USA TODAY. Graphic by John Sherlock and Julie Stacey, USA TODAY.

By Bill Nichols
USA TODAY

U.S. bombers continued attacking Baghdad throughout the morning today after a pre-dawn raid reportedly decimated the Iraqi air force and destroyed nuclear and chemical weapons facilities.

"The battle has been joined," President Bush said Wednesday night in a TV address. "The world could wait no longer. . . . We will not fail."

Iraqi President Saddam Hussein, looking resolute, was seen for the first time since the bombing began by a CNN staffer about 1 a.m. EST.

Saddam earlier said that Iraq would crush "the satanic intentions of the White House."

Super Design, a Kuwaiti spokesman in Saudi Arabia, said Iraqi troops in Kuwait are defecting to escape fighting, "taking any cars they can get."

He was reporting at 3 a.m. EST bombs were still falling.

Said a communique read on Baghdad radio at 6 a.m.: "The cursed offensive continued from 2:30 . . . until the moments of preparing this statement."

Defense Secretary Dick Cheney told reporters early action had gone "very, very well."

Six waves of F-15E bombers left Saudi Arabia at 12:56 a.m. (4:50 p.m. EST) for strategic targets in Baghdad; the first bombs hit about 6:35 p.m. EST.

CNN, in unconfirmed reports, said all U.S. and allied planes returned safely and that as many as 100,000 of Iraq's elite Republican Guard in Kuwait and Iraq were killed.

Reports of the destruction of nuclear and chemical facilities also could not be confirmed.

Civilian casualties in Iraq were unknown.

The attack, which some estimate dropped 18,000 tons of ordnance in and around Baghdad, did not involve ground forces, Cheney also said.

► There was no Iraqi air response. Pentagon and Saudi officials both knocked down reports Iraqi Scud missiles were fired at targets in Saudi Arabia.

► The focus of the raid was the "destruction of Saddam Hussein's offensive capabilities," Saddam was not a target.

Israeli officials reported no retaliation and missiles that posed a threat had been hit.

Turkey was seeking permission from parliament for the use of bases there, potentially opening a second front.

Gen. H. Norman Schwarzkopf, commander of U.S. forces, told troops before the attack: "I have seen in your eyes a fire of determination. . . . You must be the thunder and lightning of Desert Storm" — the operation's new name.

Bush Wednesday authorized distribution of oil from the Strategic Petroleum Reserve.

COVER STORY

19 hrs. after deadline, the war began

As planes took off in pairs, 'the ground shook, and you felt it'

By Johanna Neuman
USA TODAY

When the lights went out in Baghdad, it was 3 a.m. Thursday in Iraq, 7 p.m. Wednesday at the White House.

"I've never been there, but it feels like we're in the center of hell," said CNN's Bernard Shaw. In Baghdad filled with red and white flashes. Buildings shook.

By all preliminary accounts, it was a massive display of superior power. Reports said Iraq's vaunted air defenses were virtually silent. That the allied forces suffered no casualties. That Iraq's elite air force was said to be wiped out, its sophisticated Republican Guard troops destroyed, its 100 air bases scrambled, its Scud missiles eliminated. And that all the allied jets had returned safely to base.

As a second wave began, experts cautioned early combat reports might unduly favor the allied forces. But for now, it seemed that President Bush had done what he said when he told congressional leaders Dec. 20: "If we get into an armed situation, (Saddam Hussein) is going to get his ass kicked."

They called it Operation Desert Storm. It was precise, thunderous. It was consecutive, with wave after wave awaiting the streets, the telecommunications centers, the strategic command post, the missile sites. And it was perhaps the most complex air bombing mission of the century.

More than five months after Iraq's Saddam invaded Kuwait, 48 days after the United Nations laid out an ultimatum, one week after Secretary of State James Baker faced Iraqi Foreign Minister Tariq Aziz in Geneva, 19 hours after the U.N. deadline passed, the war had begun.

"This is history in the making," said Col. Ray Davies, chief maintenance officer at the largest U.S. air base in central Saudi Arabia, who watched the first F-15E fighter.

Please see COVER STORY next page ►

On the scene: Baghdad 'eerie'

Foreign correspondent Don Kirk was on the phone with USA TODAY when the bombing of Baghdad began. With an abrupt "bye," he left the U.S. Embassy to get a view of the destruction, but returned later in search of a telephone.

He found his way to the 14th floor of the Al Rashid Hotel where CNN reporters Bernard Shaw, John Holliman and Peter Arnett had been reporting live through the air raid. They immediately put Kirk on the air.

He was among the first journalists to be in the streets of the Iraqi capital.

His observations:

"I just drove back. . . . The streets were dark and calm and somewhat eerie and there were no sign of bomb damage to the center of the street where we drove. I was at the American embassy calling USA TODAY. . . .

"I came back here — the driver made me pay full fare — and the first thing that happened was they put me in a bomb shelter with a lot of other journalists.

"There were no people on the streets. My driver wanted to drive with lights out, but I persuaded him to put his dim lights on from time to time. We passed some others with dim lights on.

"I did see some taxis dashing throughout the night, but that was about it.

"From the embassy I could see anti-aircraft, with tracer bullets going on all over the place. I passed the presidential palace, and for all I knew it might not have been there, because it was pitch black.

"There are no local telephones at this point, and there's no communications overseas. This is the only phone that's working, which is why I'm here."

By Tim Dillon, USA TODAY

FITZWATER: 1st official word

"The liberation of Kuwait has begun. In conjunction with the forces of our coalition partners, the United States has moved under the code name Operation Desert Storm to enforce the mandates of the United Nations Security Council. As of 7 o'clock p.m. Operation Desert Storm forces were engaging targets in Iraq and Kuwait."

Call 1-800-USA-0001 . . . for your USA TODAY subscriptions and customer service

---

22   PART ONE

AN INTERNATIONAL DAILY NEWSPAPER THURSDAY, JANUARY 17, 1991 50¢ ($1.00 CANADIAN)

THE CHRISTIAN SCIENCE MONITOR

Massive, Mobile UN Force vs. Dug-In Iraqis

GRAPHIC BY SHIRLEY HORN – STAFF. RESEARCH BY KURT SHILLINGER – STAFF

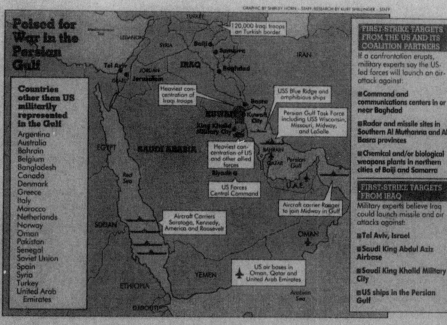

Poised for War in the Persian Gulf

Countries other than US militarily represented in the Gulf
Argentina
Australia
Bahrain
Belgium
Bangladesh
Canada
Denmark
Greece
Italy
Morocco
Netherlands
Norway
Oman
Pakistan
Senegal
Soviet Union
Spain
Syria
Turkey
United Arab Emirates

FIRST-STRIKE TARGETS FROM THE US AND ITS COALITION PARTNERS

If a confrontation erupts, military experts say the US-led forces will launch an air-attack against:

■ Command and communications centers in or near Baghdad

■ Radar and missile sites in Southern Al Muthannia and Al Basra provinces

■ Chemical and/or biological weapons plants in northern cities of Baiji and Samarra

FIRST-STRIKE TARGETS FROM IRAQ

Military experts believe Iraq could launch missile and air attacks against:

■ Tel Aviv, Israel

■ Saudi King Abdul Aziz Airbase

■ Saudi King Khalid Military City

■ US ships in the Persian Gulf

Strategy of US-led armored units is to lure adversaries into open, then strike them

By Peter Grier
Staff writer of The Christian Science Monitor

WASHINGTON

THE months of diplomacy and debate, troop deployments, and United Nations maneuvering, have come down to this: the silence of waiting for war to begin.

As of this writing the United States-led multinational coalition had not yet begun military action to drive Iraq out of Kuwait. But it was clear that with the passing of the Jan. 15 deadline such an attack could come at any moment.

Grim White House officials were indi-

GULF ■■■■ CRISIS

cating that no politically meaningful time would elapse before bombs began to fall. The Pentagon said that the 415,000 US troops in the Kuwaiti theater of operations were just waiting for the word.

"The Department of Defense is ready to execute any order we might receive from the president," said spokesman Pete Williams on the 15th.

Iraq gave every indication of stepping up to meet the battle. Its fortification line within Kuwait was being adjusted to make it more defensible, while being extended westward into Iraq proper by a constant influx of more troops and heavy guns.

"We don't see any evidence that they are in any way pulling out of Kuwait," said Mr. Williams.

Thus, the fate of the Gulf was passing from the hands of politicians into those of generals. At the US command level this seemed little occasion for rejoicing. Discussions in recent months with a wide range of US officers, both in Washington and the field in Saudi Arabia, found only an isolated few sounding gung-ho about ousting Saddam Hussein from his "19th province"

See STRATEGY next page

Soviets Try to Mollify West as Grip Tightens at Home

By Daniel Sneider
Staff writer of The Christian Science Monitor

MOSCOW

WHILE the Lithuanian parliament waited nervously behind home-made barricades for the tanks to come, a smiling Mikhail Gorbachev appeared before his parliament on Tuesday to present his new foreign minister.

Alexander Bessmertnykh, hastily flown in from his post as the Soviet ambassador to Washington, wasted no time in assuring a worried world. The Soviet government would pursue a "political solution" to the crisis in the Baltics. And as the world seemed headed for war in the Gulf, Soviet foreign policy, including support for the anti-Iraq coalition, holds firm.

"The policy of new thinking will be preserved, will continue and develop," he told the Supreme Soviet.

Hours later, Mr. Gorbachev appeared again before the parliament. He angrily denounced a string of enemies who have defied him, from Russian President Boris Yeltsin and the democratic press to the leaders of Latvia and Lithuania.

As the Baltic and Gulf crises unfold in parallel, Gorbachev's government increas-

ingly shows two faces – one to the outside world and one at home. The move to the right in domestic affairs, spearheaded by the crackdown on the nationalist governments in the republics, has not yet been mirrored by any retreat from the post-cold war outlook labeled "new thinking."

Some Soviet analysts argue that there is a clear logic to that apparent contradiction. At a time when the Kremlin is struggling to keep control at home, it seeks to avoid any conflict abroad, especially with the West.

"Foreign policy is the area that Gorbachev will try to keep as stable as possible

See SOVIETS next page

Other Gulf Coverage

Military analysts in Egypt say Saddam seriously underestimates the strength of the allied forces or ayed against him. **3**	To balance a post-crisis Middle East, many experts say that Iraq should retain some military power. **4**	Saddam's bravado is not reflected in empty streets and gloomy mood in Baghdad. **5**	Exiled Kuwaiti opposition leaders call for end to sheikhdom and more democratic institutions. **5**	Terrorism experts don't expect attacks to occur within the US. Still, defense firms, airports, and others are beefing up security. **7**

Back to Nature at Yosemite
A Monitor columnist supports a master plan to cherish the park's native attractions.
13

Cold-Weather Warmers
Après ski, après school, après sledding – winter calls for cozying up with soups, hot chocolate, and other 'comfort' foods.
15

24   PART ONE

Less important articles are farther down on front pages. Sometimes a headline without an article appears. In order to read the accompanying story, the reader has to turn to another page.

Now turn to pp. 21–24 and find the lead stories.

2.3 Photographs

Most newspapers also have photographs on the front page. Often a photo accompanies a main article. This is typical for *USA Today*. If so, it is generally positioned directly next to that article: above, below, or to one side of it. Some editors enclose a story with a photo in a rectangle (*box*) of black lines.

At other times a picture refers to a story on another page. If so, then the sentences or words under it (called the *caption* or cutline) direct the reader to the accompanying article. The caption may end with instructions such as: "Please see SPORTS, p. 25" or "Turn to page 25" or "Continued on page A25". Or it may end simply with a page number or with the name of a section of the paper plus a page number (for example, "SPORTS, p. 25"). The *Globe* and the *Times* typically put photographs on the front page that refer to a story on an inside page.

Almost all photographs are black-and-white. By 1991, only *USA Today* and the *Monitor* offered full-color pictures on the front page. The use of color set these newspapers apart from their competitors. Now, more papers are acquiring the technology and resources to print color photos on their pages. *USA Today* also includes a colorful graph or drawing in a box in the lower left-hand corner every day. Its policy is to include a combination of women and men from different ethnic and racial groups in pictures on its front page.[4]   [Ex. PP]

2.4 Foreign, National, Local News

Now that you can identify the lead story, you will want to look at its contents. The subjects of the news articles on the page in general, and of the lead article in particular, are examples of the kinds of news that the journal emphasizes.

Newspapers differ in the amount of international news they carry. The following chart shows the percentages of foreign, national, and local (state or metropolitan) news on the front pages of the five U.S.-based papers for one week in June, 1988, for example.[5] (It also shows typical data for the *Tribune*.[6]) Clearly, the events that happened in America and the world that week were the same for all the journalists. But the publishers emphasized the kinds of news that interest their readers.   [Ex. RR.1]

These statistics support, for example, the claim of the *Monitor* to be an "international newspaper"; it is surpassed only by the *Tribune*. They also support the roles of the *Times* and *USA Today* as national newspapers—with distinct differences. And they contrast the interests of the readers of the two Boston dailies, which must attract different circles of readers in order to stay alive financially.

Front-Page News Stories of Six Papers

	Foreign	National	Local	(= state, city)
Herald	6%	35%	59%	(18, 41)
Globe	21	32	47	(12, 35)
USA Today	7	93	0	
Times	41	41	18	(3, 15)
Monitor	50	50	0	
Tribune	74	26	0	

2.5 Index to the Sections Inside

On their front pages, most newspapers refer to some of the articles on the inside pages. The *Monitor* and the *Times* and many other papers have a box at the bottom of the page that contains short headlines and descriptions of a few stories with their page numbers. The *Herald* has such headlines at the very top or bottom of the front page; they often concern sports. *USA Today* prints such headlines in the upper left and right corners of the front page. Because these headlines help sell the newspaper by attracting readers with varied interests, they are chosen very carefully.

USA Today has its entire, short index on the front page. The paper is organized by sections; each is highlighted by a different color. The four removable sections are: "News" (usually 8 pages, including two editorial pages and a full page of weather), "Money" (8 pages), "Sports" (10 pages), and "Life" (10 pages, including about 2½ pages of Classified Ads). All of the sections can include one or more full-page advertisements.

In contrast, the *Times* and many other newspapers print their full indices on the second page. Each index takes up one to two columns of print on that page. They feature such titles as "National," "International," "Regional" or "Metro/Region," "The Home Section" or "Living/Arts," "Business," "Sports," and "Editorial/Op-Ed/Letters." *Op-Ed* means opposite the editorial page; here opinions, letters from readers, and political cartoons are presented. The *Globe* and the *Times*, which contain many advertisements, each have about 112 pages in four separate sections (A–D).

The full-sized *Tribune* basically contains only two parts: a political and a financial section. There is no index, since the paper generally has only about 24 pages. There are a few advertisements.

The *Monitor* has 20 pages. In January 1989 it was given a new design. Now it is the only journal to print its editorials on the back page, where they can be found easily. It carries almost no advertisements.

The tabloid-sized *Herald* has about 112 pages, as many larger papers do, but all the pages are in one section like a magazine. It does not have an index for its news articles. Its index, on page 2, lists mostly smaller items of particular interest to certain readers, such as "Comics," "Crossword Puzzle," "Horoscope," "Obituaries" (notices about the deaths of well-known people), "Television Schedule," and "Weather." Besides the Classified Ads, it carries many other advertisements as well.

These newspapers contain much more than news about current events.

EXERCISES

PP | **Purposeful Practice: Adjectives and Prepositions of Location**

As you use this textbook, you will want to talk about articles you find in newspapers. You may want to refer to the front pages on pp. 21–24 for examples. Or you may want to talk about articles from your own local paper. In the box are some adjectives and prepositions you can use to describe the positions of articles, photographs, and headlines on a page.

Adjectives:	upper	or	top	**Prepositions**:	*at* the top	*across* the page
	left	or	left-hand		*at* the bottom	*across* two columns
	lower	or	bottom		*at/on* the side	*in* a column
	right	or	right-hand		*on* the page	*in* the middle/center
	middle	or	central		*on* the right/left	*in* the corner

Adjectives are added to make the position more exact, for example: the *central* column, the *lower right-hand* corner.	*Prepositional phrases* can be combined with "of" phrases to make, for example: *in* the middle *of* the column, *at* the top *of* the page.

More useful prepositions you know are: *next to, above, below/under*.

1. **Look at the newspaper page below (right) and answer these questions:**

    1. What is written across this front page?
    2. Is the paper's name at the top of the page?
    3. What is at the bottom of the middle column?
    4. Is there a photograph in the lower right-hand corner?
    5. What is in the left column?
    6. How can you describe the location of the biggest photo more exactly?
    7. What is in the top left corner?
    8. What is another way to describe the flag's location?

2. **Now look at the newspaper front pages on pp. 21–24. Describe the location of the following (your teacher will tell you whether to say or write the descriptions for one or all four newspapers):**

    1. the name of the newspaper
    2. the date
    3. the lead article
    4. the biggest picture(s)
    5. the index (if there is one)

VV Valuable Vocabulary

In this chapter you learned some more newspaper vocabulary. Match each word on the left with the correct definition on the right. Write the corresponding letter in the blank to the left of each number.

_____ 1. **tabloid**

_____ 2. **tabloid-sized**

_____ 3. **lead article**

_____ 4. **caption**

_____ 5. **column**

_____ 6. **Op-Ed**

a. section opposite the editorials, for opinions, etc.

b. newspaper of sensational stories and photographs

c. most important story

d. words under a photograph

e. about half of full-sized

f. a narrow rectangular space on a page, which lines of print span (go across)

RR A Review of the Reading

1. Check your understanding of the table on p. 26.

    1. Which newspapers emphasize local news?

    2. Which newspaper emphasizes national news?

    3. Which journal has the greatest percentage of international news?

    4. Which papers carry about an equal number of international and national news stories on the front page?

2. Answer these questions about the reading:

    1. Why does the *Times* use capital letters in some headlines?

    2. What are some examples of sections inside a newspaper?

CC Conversations with a Classmate

1. With a partner, look at the photographs in a current newspaper. Are any so interesting that they make you want to read the accompanying article? If so, find the article.

2. a. Interview your partner about the newspaper she or he reads. Which sections or parts are her/his favorites?

    b. Present the information to the whole class. Someone should write a list of the favorite sections on the blackboard. If many students favor one or a few sections, your class may want to choose local newspaper articles from these sections to read together.

DD For Discussion and Debate

1. If you want to read about events in your country, which American newspaper can you read? Why?

2. The newspapers described in this chapter emphasize different kinds of news. Which paper would you prefer to read? Why? (You will see this question again in a later chapter.)

3. The front pages of most newspapers were filled with news of the war with Iraq on January 17, 1991. What was your reaction to that news?

4. In which of the newspaper sections *a–f* below might you find the following stories? Give reasons for your answers.

_____ 1. results of a national golf tournament	a. International News
_____ 2. a new fruit that was created from two common fruits	b. National News
	c. Editorials
_____ 3. a new corn plant that is very healthy and productive	d. Business
	e. Living
_____ 4. opinions for and against scientific creation of new plants and animals	f. Sports
_____ 5. plans of several countries to mine coal in Antarctica	
_____ 6. a demonstration in Washington, D.C., against mining in Antarctica	

5. *Optional Pairwork* (or individual writing exercise): Your teacher will give you a newspaper photograph without a caption. Discuss what is happening in the picture; use your imagination! Then write an appropriate caption.

6. *Extra-credit Project*: Choose an English-language newspaper and look at the number of international, national, and local news articles. Compare it to the papers described in the table on p. 26. Discuss your findings.

II Intercultural Issues

1. Look at the number of international, national, and local news articles on the front page of a newspaper from your country. Compare it to the American papers described in this chapter. Discuss your findings.

2. Did your native country play a role in the war in Iraq? Or in later developments in that geographical area?

CHAPTER 3

Understanding Headlines

—————————— PREREADING QUESTIONS ——————————

1. a. When you pick up a newspaper, do you scan the headlines before choosing an article to read?

   b. What kinds of articles do you look at first?

2. Who are some of the world's leaders in the headlines today, and what countries are they from?

3. Who are some people from your community that are in the news, and why are they in the news?

4. Do you think individuals can "make a difference" in today's world?

3.1 Introduction

The purpose of a headline is to summarize the news content of an article in very few words. The headline should report the topic, and perhaps a main fact, accurately. It should also present the information in an interesting way, so that the reader is encouraged to read the article itself. The kinds of news that appeal to the readers of one newspaper may differ widely from those of a competitor. But all headlines include one or more of the following elements that attract a reader's interest: newness or unusualness, personal relevance or consequences, and emotions.

Sometimes one headline is not enough to summarize the important information, so a second headline, in smaller letters, is added below the first. It is called a *subheadline*.

Note that when you are reading a newspaper, you will find that many words in the headlines are repeated in the article. Thus you see them in a larger context in the article and can understand their meanings more easily than in the brief headline. Because this chapter is only about headlines, the news stories are not given here; however, you can look up those referred to by page number. You probably will not know every word in the sample headlines, and you don't have to. It is important only to understand them as examples. (You may use a dictionary to look up main words if you want to.)

In the rest of this chapter, the structure of newspaper headlines and some special headline vocabulary are explained.

3.2 Syntax

Newspaper editors differ somewhat as to the types of headlines they prefer. In the *Times* the average headline (eight to nine words) is longer than in most papers, and it strongly favors the syntax (structure) of a typical English sentence: subject–verb–(completion). The other five newspapers also use this syntax more than 60 percent of the time.[1] Examples:

U.S. BOMBS BAGHDAD [p. 22]

Inner-City Teen Talks About Drugs [p. 134]

The second form for headlines is a noun phrase without a verb.[2] Such headlines can be as simple as a noun with a qualifier, as in this one about a very big hurricane (wind storm):

Killer 'cane! [p. 82]

Or, more often, they are or include a prepositional phrase:

Sting on the jungle [p. 108]
[Ex. VV.1]

No matter what form a headline takes, it is often *elliptical*; that means that some words have been omitted from (left out of) the sentence or phrase in order to make it shorter. The articles (or determiners) *the* and *a(n)* are frequently omitted, for example:

[*The*] Prime ministers of [*the*] two Koreas agree to meet   [p. 98]

And the verb *to be* in all its simple forms (especially *is/are*), is often left out, too, as in these headlines:

Otsuki [*is*] found guilty of murder

West Bank, Gaza [*are*] quiet on uprising anniversary   [p. 90]

In the last example above, the word "and" has been replaced by a comma, which also saves space. (See Punctuation box.)

Punctuation Marks in Headlines

The **comma**
1. takes the place of *and*: **Income, spending up sharply**   [p. 130]
   OR
2. is used with its normal function of separating words in a list (in the following case, adjectives):   **Massive, Mobile UN Force. . .**   [p. 23]
   OR separating phrases: **19 hrs. after deadline, the war began**   [p. 22]

The **colon**
1. is used after a word or phrase to explain it:

   Washington prediction: slow growth, no recession   [p. 126]

   OR
2. following a name, tells what a person said *without* quoting his or her exact words: **Junkie: I'll take test**   [p. 136]

Single quotation marks
1. tell what a person said, using his or her exact words. The whole headline (or subheadline) can be a quotation or just a few words. The speaker can be named in the headline or not:

   'The liberation of Kuwait has begun'—President Bush   [p. 24]

   Iraqi air force 'decimated'   [p. 22]
   OR
2. are used instead of the name of a person who is not well-known or instead of a thing that has a difficult or technical name:

   Just 2 years [jail term] for 'beauty queen' thief

   'Suicide machine' takes first life   [p. 146]

Serious journalism requires that the source of quotations be named at the beginning of the article.

3.3 Verbs

Verbs are usually in a *present tense*, which emphasizes the immediacy of the report. The "news" is only new(s) when it is fresh, immediate, current. There are some exceptions, of course. Occasionally some past events are reported in the past tense, as in this headline:

19 hrs. after deadline, the war began   [p. 22]

The future tense—as in this headline:

4 large corporations will reduce emissions that harm ozone layer   [p. 152]

—is not usually used for future events. Notice, instead, the present tense form "*is to* + verb" (or "*are to* + verb") with future meaning in the following example:

Liz Taylor, 8th husband [*are*] *to* be wed this week

(The verb *are* could be omitted; here it has been added to the headline in order to make it easier to understand.)

Headlines in the Passive Voice

The passive voice is formed by the verb *to be* and the past participle of a main verb. Example:

Passive headline: **Westchester mayor is stabbed by angry voter**

agent

Active sentence: **Angry voter stabs Westchester mayor.**

agent

When the agent is unknown or unimportant, it is omitted:

Westchester mayor is stabbed

Note: Do not confuse the present tense passive voice in an elliptical headline with the past tense active voice (which is rare in headlines). Example:

Passive: **Mayor stabbed at midnight = Mayor <u>is</u> stabbed at midnight**

not

Active: **Mayor stabbed <u>someone</u> at midnight**

Present tense headlines are sometimes written in the passive voice (see Headlines box, p. 34). In fact, the *Times* and some metropolitan dailies like the *Globe* use the passive in one out of four headlines. In other papers the passive voice seldom appears.

There are several special verb phrases in headlines that show that the information is a report of what someone else, a *source*, told a journalist, rather than information that the reporter gathered alone. The source might or might not be named in the news article. American laws protect the identity of a secret source; a journalist cannot be forced to tell his or her name. The three most common expressions that indicate such indirect reporting are: *is said to, is reported to,* and *reportedly* (see Indirect Reporting box).

There are several reasons for editors to be careful and accurate in their choice of words. Maybe the journalist was not sure that the source was completely reliable. It is likely that he or she had no opportunity to check the facts personally. Or the topic in the headline may be a rather sensitive political matter, and the publisher wants to remain objective by reporting only facts and statements made. Especially in stories about crimes or trials, journalists must be careful not to prejudge the case or make false accusations.

Indirect Reporting in Headlines

1. [is] said to

Westchester mayor <u>said to</u> be near death

A source, probably from the mayor's or hospital staff, said that the mayor is near death.

---

2. [is] reported to

Westchester mayor <u>is reported to</u> have Mafia connections

A believable source said that the mayor has connections to the Mafia.

(No newspaper would print this statement as a fact unless it had been proven in court.)

---

3. reportedly

Mayor's birthday party <u>reportedly</u> cost city $25G

A believable source, probably with evidence of some kind, said that the party cost $25,000 of the city's money.

(See Section 3.5 about numbers.)

3.4 Names

How can you quickly discover what kind of news is in an article? What clues do the headlines give you? Answer: names, names, names—of persons, countries, sports teams, and places in the United States. The *Times*, for example, has more than one name in every headline, on the average! And, except for *USA Today*, which uses few names in its headlines, the other newspapers analyzed had names in about 75% of their headlines.[3]

The personal names in headlines refer usually to people in government but also to famous and formerly famous figures in all areas of American and world culture. You cannot quickly understand the main news stories of the day unless you know the names of the "movers and shakers" (and the places in which events are happening). In fact, James W. Carey, professor of journalism and communications, suggests that

> American journalism always begins from the question of "who" ....
> The primary subject of journalism is people—what they say and do.
> Moreover, the subject is usually an individual—what someone says and
> does. Groups, in turn, are usually personified by leaders or
> representatives who speak or act for them, even when we know this
> is pretty much a fiction.... If journalists cannot find a representative
> individual, they more or less invent one.... This is the sense in which
> American culture is "individualistic": We assume that individuals are
> authors of their own acts.... The world is the way it is because
> individuals want it that way.[4]

The leaders of nations are truly representatives of their countries; they speak and act for their citizens. In the United States, the President, presidential candidates in an election year, leaders in Congress, and so on are individuals whose names are often in the headlines. Leaders of other countries, their foreign ministers, and so on are named only if they are in the news often enough to be well known to the American public.

Some newspapers with a somewhat informal style, such as the *Herald*, like to shorten public figures' names. For example, the *Herald* used former Massachusetts Governor Michael Dukakis' nickname "Duke" continually in the headlines. And it often calls Boston by one of its nicknames: the Hub. (A *hub* is the center of a wheel, such as a wagon or bicycle wheel; everything originates from it. The nickname comes from the story that the early Bostonians, very proud of their culturally active city, called it the "hub of the world".) [Ex. VV.2]

You may not yet know all the names, and nicknames, of the American people and places in the headlines. All personal names, American or not, are explained in the first sentence or two of the article. So, if you do not recognize names in a headline, continue reading! The individuals will be described in more detail in the news story. They will become more familiar with time. The more you read, the easier it will become.

3.5 Numbers

Numbers are also called *numerals, digits,* or *figures,* and the abbreviation *no.* is used in some contexts. Numbers usually function like adjectives and are written together with a noun or symbols that explain them (as in "$51" or "20 years"). But there are a few space-saving conventions that use numbers alone, especially in headlines. Often, when numerals appear alone, they refer to a number of *people,* as in this headline:

Anti-smoking efforts will save 3 million [p. 65]

It is three million people's lives that are meant here.

Age can also be expressed without using words. In the following headline, the number 6, separated from the text by commas, gives the boy's age:

Boy, 6, killed by 18-wheeler

The second number expression, 18-wheeler, is an informal term for a truck with 18 wheels.

In the Sports section, numbers *are* the news. They give the scores, or points, that a team or individual made.

RED SOX BEAT YANKEES, 4–3

was even a front-page headline. The Red Sox, Boston's baseball team, scored 4 points and won. The New York Yankees scored only 3 points and lost.

Ordinal numbers (first, second, third, fourth, fifth, etc.) are usually printed as numerals followed by the last two letters of the word. They thus become 1st, 2nd, 3rd, 4th, 5th, etc., as in:

Strike enters 4th day at Wire Belt Co. [p. 164]

(*Second* and *third* can also appear as 2d and 3d, respectively.)

When numerals are used after the dollar sign ($), their meaning is clear: an amount of money. Sometimes a letter—B, G, or M—follows the number. These letters refer to a billion (=1,000,000,000), a thousand (a *grand* is an informal word for a thousand dollars), and a million. Example:

Storm damage estimated at $2.5m

(Note that the "$" is in front of the numeral in writing; but in spoken English we say it after the number, as in "two and a half million dollars.")

3.6 Fun With Words

You have now worked through a lot of detailed explanations about vocabulary, syntax, and punctuation in headlines. Your teacher does not expect you to memorize how to *produce* all this information yourself. Instead, it was presented so that you can begin to *recognize* these details and thus understand headlines. Let us finish with something different. Headline writers do not always just follow rules and conventions. Sometimes they have fun with words.

Alliteration, for example, is easy to appreciate (even if you do not know all the vocabulary in a headline). Look at the following examples; the first is about eating and fitness (health), and the second about two baseball teams.

Get fat as a pig & feel fit as a fiddle ... *say experts*

SAD SOX BATTLE BRONX BOMBERS

If you read them aloud, the repetition of one beginning sound—*f,* or *s* and *b*—becomes clear; this repetition is called *alliteration.* Both editors could have chosen other words, but the alliteration makes these headlines more interesting and fun to read.

Now read aloud the following *USA Today* headline about two champion basketball teams, one from Los Angeles and one from Detroit.

L.A. in huff over Detroit rough stuff

Did you hear the rhyming words "huff–rough–stuff"? ("In a huff" is an idiom[5] that means "angry." "Over" in this context means "about." And "rough stuff" here means a "rough or rowdy style of playing.")

USA Today and the *Herald* also enjoy creating new words. Sometimes words are shortened, such as "fab" for "fabulous" (meaning "wonderful"). Other times they are created out of two existing words; for example, "JetCapade" (*USA Today*) from "jet" and "escapade" (= "adventure"), and "Dukenomics" (*Herald*) for Dukakis' economic plan. The latter is based on the older term "Reaganomics", meaning President Reagan's economic plan.

So, as you see, understanding American headlines is a many-sided learning adventure! The exercises in the last section of this chapter will help you practice your understanding of particular points.

EXERCISES

VV Valuable Vocabulary

1. Recognizing Verbs

Headlines are written either in sentence form, with a noun subject and a verb, or in the form of a noun phrase without a verb.

A. Say whether the following headlines are like a sentence (S) or a noun phrase (N). Circle the verb in a sentence headline (S).

_____ 1. **Police want Chuck Berry**

_____ 2. **YANKEES BEAT RED SOX**

_____ 3. **Jackson: Time to Pause**

_____ 4. **Rich and poor together**

Some words can be either a noun or a verb, such as *export, ban*, or even *rocket*. Verbs must, of course, agree with their noun subjects. A **singular** subject generally has a verb with an -*s* ending: CAR BURNS. A **plural** subject is followed by the base form of the verb (no -*s*): CARS BURN. (You have probably noticed by now that the noun *news*, although it ends in an -*s*, is singular; we say "The news *is* good.") Look for this agreement when you are trying to decide if a word is a verb or not.

B. For the following headlines write S (for sentence) or N (for noun phrase), and circle all the verbs you can find.

_____ 1. **President pushes new law through Congress**

_____ 2. **INSIDE PUSH ON NORIEGA**

_____ 3. **Shortage of Fuel for Rockets**

_____ 4. **Deficit rockets to $400M**

_____ 5. **Trade Deficit Grows**

_____ 6. **Big firms export paperwork**

_____ 7. **EXPORTS ARE UP**

_____ 8. **VP search continues** [VP = Vice President]

_____ 9. **Coast Guard searches yacht**

_____ 10. **Ban on New Chemical**

_____ 11. **Congress bans new chemical**

2. Names

A. Who is the President of the United States? Who is Vice President? Name some state Governors.

B. See II.1, if appropriate.

C. *Extra-credit Exercise.* Some cities in the United States have nicknames. Can you match each nickname on the left with the correct city on the right? Give a reason for each match-up. (*Hint*: Think of culture, geography, economy.)

_____ 1. Boston	a. Beantown
_____ 2. Chicago	b. Big Apple
	c. Jazz Capital
_____ 3. Detroit	d. L.A.
_____ 4. Los Angeles	e. Motortown
_____ 5. Minneapolis and St. Paul	f. Twin cities
	g. Windy City
_____ 6. New Orleans	
_____ 7. New York City	

D. *Optional, Extra-credit Exercise.* Ice hockey and baseball are favorite winter and summer sports, respectively, in the U.S.A. and Canada. Team names are often in the headlines in the Sports section. Using the map on p. 41 and what you know about the culture and economic base of each city listed below, match it with its team's name on the right. (These represent only a selection of the professional teams in each sport.)

Major League Hockey

_____ 1. Edmonton (Alberta, Canada)	a. Capitals
_____ 2. Hartford (Connecticut, U.S.A.)	b. Islanders
	c. Maple Leafs
_____ 3. New York	d. Nordiques
_____ 4. Quebec	e. Oilers
_____ 5. Toronto	f. Whalers
_____ 6. Washington, D.C.	

Baseball: American League (1–3)
National League (4–7)

_____ 1. Milwaukee (Wisconsin)	a. Astros
_____ 2. Minnesota	b. Brewers
	c. Expos
_____ 3. New York	d. Padres
_____ 4. Houston	e. Phillies
_____ 5. Montreal	f. Twins
	g. Yankees
_____ 6. Philadelphia	
_____ 7. San Diego (California)	

THE UNITED STATES OF AMERICA

CANADA

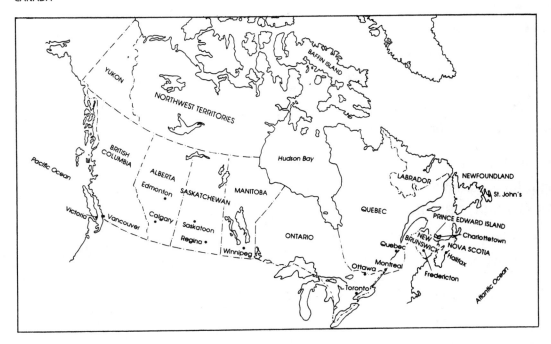

CC Conversation with a Classmate

Local or regional sports news is a common topic of conversation in some workplaces and at parties. Are you a sports fan? What sports are in the headlines at this time? Do you read about them in the Sports section? Tell your classmate(s) which sports you enjoy as a spectator (watching) and as a participant (doing).

CH. 3 UNDERSTANDING HEADLINES **41**

Purposeful Practice: The Passive Voice

The passive voice is formed by the verb *to be*—namely, *is* or *are* in the present tense, *was* or *were* in the past tense—and the past participle of the main verb. Here is an example of an active sentence and a passive sentence with the same main verb:

	Subject	(be)	Main Verb	Completion
Active:	Someone		saw	the Mayor at the casino.
Passive:	The Mayor	*was*	seen	(*by* someone) at the casino.

In both sentences the *agent* (person or thing doing the action) is "someone." In a passive sentence, the agent is named in the "*by* . . ." phrase. Usually the agent is omitted in a passive sentence if it is unknown or unimportant, such as "someone" or "people."

Remember: In headlines the verb *to be* is often omitted, too.

1. Learn to recognize the passive voice in headlines. Mark P for passive, A for active.

   1. **Local girl wins scholarship**
   2. **Scholarship Won by Local Girl**
   3. **Bomb threat—airport closed**
   4. **Bomb Threat Closes Airport**
   5. **NEW CURE FOR CANCER FOUND**
   6. **Earthquake in Peru; 7 Americans reported dead**

2. The following passive forms are elliptical: One part of the verb has been omitted. Insert the missing word in the correct place.

   1. **Local Teenager Murdered by Boyfriend**
   2. **Couple sought for questioning**
   3. **NEW RISKS SEEN FOR SMOKERS**
   4. **Nancy Reagan said to seek astrologer's advice**
   5. **Iran said to want peace**

3. Now check your understanding of headlines in the passive voice. Rewrite them in the active voice.

   1. **Local teenager murdered by girlfriend**
   2. **Concorde Jet Hijacked**
   3. **LOTTERY WON BY MILLIONAIRE!**
   4. **Town pool closed for repairs**
   5. **Couple Sought for Questioning**

RR A Review of the Reading

1. Answer the following general comprehension questions:

   1. What is a *subheadline?* Find some examples in Part Two.

   2. What tense do headline writers usually use? Why?

2. Look into the following details:

   1. Give two reasons why the passive voice may be used in a headline.

   2. How can journalists and editors report things they are not completely sure of? What special words can they use?

   3. An editor may want to quote a person in a headline. What two ways can he or she choose to do this? Consider punctuation.

3. Use what you have learned about headlines to respond to the following:

   A. Check your understanding of the following elliptical headlines by changing them to normal sentences. Insert the missing words into them. (Don't forget the articles *a* and *the; the* for a specific noun, and *a* for a general noun or a nonspecific one of a class.)

      1. **Food Price Rise Seen For '89**

      2. **Lottery winners buy Cadillac, yacht, home**

      3. **Fire kills 3, injures 7**

      4. **BOY, 9, WORLD'S YOUNGEST PILOT**

      5. **Student pres: I expect '99%' of votes**   [pres = president]

      6. **Glibbles: America's Favorite New Toy**

   B. Comment on this headline:

      SUMMER STORM SURPRISES SWIMMERS, SAILORS

1. Have you been to any of the cities listed in VV.2? Describe your impressions and/or experiences there. [For discussion or writing.]

2. Discuss the headlines in an English-language newspaper. How do they attract the reader's interest? (Review the categories in Section 3.1.) If possible, the class should divide into groups with several different papers so that differences between them can be discussed. Write the headlines in the space below. (If no English-language papers are available, discuss the interesting elements of the headlines in Exercises PP.2 and RR.3.)

_____

_____

_____

_____

_____

_____

_____

_____

_____

_____

_____

_____

_____

_____

_____

_____

_____

3. The headlines in Exercise PP.2 are in the passive voice. Give a possible reason why an editor might have chosen it rather than the active voice.

4. *Optional Topics for Discussion or Essay Writing.* Comment on James Carey's beliefs:

   a. that American journalists want to find a representative individual for every group (Do you know of any examples?); and

   b. that "the world is the way it is because individuals want it that way." Do you think this is a particularly *American* point of view?

II Intercultural Issues

1. You and your classmates can help each other to recognize the names of some world leaders. Make a list on the blackboard of the names of (your) countries' leaders.

2. Does your hometown have a nickname? If so, explain it to the class. *Option*: Write a composition describing your hometown (or favorite city) in your native country.

3. Compare headlines of papers from different countries on the same day. Are there any international (or national) stories that appear in all the papers?

CHAPTER 4

Analyzing Lead Sentences

1. Do you believe all the headlines you read?

2. When do you think today's news stories were written?

3. Who are Nelson and Winnie Mandela?

4.1 The Purpose of the Lead

The headline of a newspaper article states its *topic* (subject) in about four to ten words. The *lead* follows the headline; it is the first (leading) paragraph of the article. There are two kinds of leads.

The news lead, also called a *summary* lead, restates the topic and gives the most important facts about it. It usually consists of the *dateline* (see Section 4.2) and one sentence, the lead sentence.

Look at the following example (on the left) of a summary lead from a front-page article. It describes the visit of South African leader Nelson Mandela to Boston in 1990. To the right is a lead from a story in the metropolitan section of the same paper on the same day. How is this second lead different?

SUNDAY, JUNE 24, 1990

Mandela and Boston embrace in a daylong celebration of unity

250,000 rally on Esplanade

By Peter J. Howe
and Diane E. Lewis
GLOBE STAFF

Nelson R. Mandela, the living legend of the international campaign to end South African apartheid, swept through Boston yesterday on an exuberant daylong visit, saluting local heroes from the Revolutionary War through the Kennedy dynasty as inspirations to his freedom quest.

Reprinted courtesy of The Boston Globe.

JUNE 24, 1990

ROXBURY GREETS MANDELA

Appearance brings tears of joy from Madison Park crowd

By Diego Ribadeneira
GLOBE STAFF

It was a roar that started somewhere deep within the souls of the people crowded into Madison Park High School and burst forth in a torrent of emotion that swept across the steamy gymnasium and enveloped Nelson Mandela like the arms of a loving relative.

The purpose of the second lead cannot be to give factual details of a news story, because it does not. Instead, its purpose is to catch readers' interest and thus invite them to read more. It is called an *interest* lead. Interest leads usually accompany feature articles, human interest stories, or editorials. [Ex. RR.1, DD.2]

4.2 The Dateline

In the past, news traveled only as fast as couriers or the mail service. A report could be several days old by the time it was printed. News articles began with a *dateline:* the place and the date of the correspondent's report.

Since the telegraph and, recently, since satellites have been used to transmit news, it is now rare that a story is more than one day old. In fact, it is even possible for Thursday morning's events in Beijing, for example, to reach New York on Wednesday! Therefore, most newspapers no longer print the full dateline before an article; they print only the name of the city—in capital letters—from which the correspondent reported. The actual date is assumed to be the day before the reader gets the story. Adverbs such as "yesterday," "last night," or the name of a weekday appear then in the lead sentence. Only the *Times* still uses the traditional dateline, which states both city and date.

Some articles have no dateline; there are three general reasons for omitting it. (1) Usually these stories are written in the home office, such as Metropolitan-section articles, or sports stories, or most news items in *USA Today* (which are written in the Washington, D.C., office). (2) Sometimes the story does not take place in one city alone; *USA Today*, for example, often reports news about trends across the country. (3) The story may be more or less timeless and placeless, perhaps a Sunday feature story.

Grammar Review: Clauses

A **clause** is a grammatical unit that contains a subject and a verb. Every full sentence is or contains a main, or independent, clause, which states the main idea. Example:

Mayor Cecelia Avi was stabbed in downtown Westchester at 11:50 last night.

A **subordinate clause** (or dependent clause) states a secondary idea and refers to some part of the main clause. It is joined to the main clause by a **subordinate conjunction**, such as *that* or *as*.
Examples:

Mayor Cecilia Avi was stabbed in downtown Westchester late last night *as she was leaving the Milton Hotel after a fund-raising dinner.*

In a statement released by her aides this morning, Mayor Cecilia Avi said *that her campaign for re-election will continue.*

4.3 Syntax: Main and Subordinate Clauses

Journalists know that some readers read only the headline and lead of an article before jumping to another story. Most summary leads, therefore, are long statements, consisting of two or more parts. Interest leads may be long or short statements, or questions.

An analysis of 50 lead sentences from five newspapers[1] showed that only a few of them consisted of only one *clause* (see Grammar Review box). Reporters often need a more complex form to present their information; so most leads contain one or two *subordinate* clauses. Journalists of the *Times* are most likely to use more than one subordinate clause in their leads.

Most leads start with the main clause so the reader gets the main subject (often a person) and verb first, before going on to secondary ideas. The most common subordinate conjunctions in newspaper writing are *that* and *who*. The latter refers to a named person or group of people, such as in the following leads:[2]

ATLANTA – Gov. Michael Dukakis, who has begun putting the final touches on his acceptance speech, will tour the convention hall today. . . . (*Herald*)

BEIT SAHOUR, Israeli-Occupied West Bank (Reuters) – Clashes flared Tuesday between Israeli troops and Palestinians who were angered by the death of a teen-ager. (*Tribune*)

Who (and *which*) almost always refer to the last noun before them in the sentence. So in the second example above, the reader knows that Palestinians, not Israelis, were angry. [Ex. PP]

That is the most general subordinate conjunction. It can refer to a noun or a verb. In newspaper articles, the words " . . . said that" (see Grammar Review box) or " . . . reported that," etc., are common. For example:

PANMUNJOM, Korea – North and South Korea yesterday announced that the prime ministers of the two countries will meet . . . . (*Globe*)

That can also be omitted in many sentences, especially after *said*. The example above could, instead, be written: "North and South Korea yesterday said the prime ministers of the two countries will meet . . . ." Such sentences may look as if they consist of two main clauses. But main clauses in English must always be separated by a conjunction (*and, but*, etc.) or a punctuation mark (semicolon, colon, period, or dash).

In contrast to all the preceding leads, the following one does not begin with the main clause. Can you find it?

NEW YORK – By 1991, 1 in 10 children admitted to USA hospitals may have AIDS, an expert predicts. (*USA Today*)

The main clause is the last one: "an expert predicts." With normal syntax (word order), the sentence would be: "An expert predicts that, by 1991, one in ten children admitted to U.S. hospitals may have AIDS." The subordinate conjunction *that* is omitted when a subordinate clause begins a sentence.

Here is another example:

> WASHINGTON – Personal income and spending rose a strong 0.9 percent in December, the government said yesterday . . . . (Reuters)

The source of the information is the U.S. government. Although the source is important enough to name in the lead, it is not major enough to stand at the beginning of the sentence. Instead, the actual happening itself takes first place there.

4.4 Descriptive Phrases

Names used in headlines are explained in the first sentences of the news story. Sometimes the explanation is a short noun phrase next to the name, as in this lead:

> MOSCOW, Wednesday, July 20 – Mikhail S. Gorbachev, <u>the Soviet leader</u>, was shown on national television Tuesday night. . . . (*Times*)

The grammatical name for this kind of descriptive phrase is *appositive*. An appositive can be enclosed between commas (as in the previous lead) or between dashes (—). The same information could be put into a relative clause—"Mikhail S. Gorbachev, <u>who is the Soviet leader</u>, was shown. . . ." —but using an appositive saves space and words. Many lead sentences have at least one other subordinate clause and too many clauses can become confusing—even for American readers!

Some journalists use *participial phrases* to describe people or things. Participial phrases are formed with the present or past participle of a verb; thus they may look like part of an active or passive verb, but they do not have the role of a main verb. Usually the phrase immediately follows a noun (often the subject), which it describes. For example:

> TOULOUSE, France, July 19 (AP) – A train <u>moving at 30 miles an hour</u> hit another train <u>stopped with mechanical problems</u> today and 15 people were reported wounded. (*Times*)

In this example, the first underlined phrase begins with a present participle (<u>moving</u>), and the second starts with a past participle (<u>stopped</u>).

Like the appositive, participial phrases provide a short way to write a subordinate clause. The previous example could be rewritten as: "A train <u>which was</u> moving at 30 miles an hour hit another train <u>which had</u> stopped with mechanical problems. . . ."

Sometimes the participial phrase is farther away from its noun, as in the following example. The basic participial phrases are underlined. Can you find the noun(s) to which they refer?

> MOSCOW, Wednesday, July 20 – Mikhail S. Gorbachev, the Soviet leader, was shown on national television Tuesday night <u>taking the side of hardline conservatives</u> and <u>rejecting demands for territorial changes</u> in the ethnic dispute between two southern republics. (*Times*)

The *Globe, Times,* and *Herald* all use participial phrases in at least half of their lead sentences. In this respect, the *Tribune* and *USA Today* are easier to read; their reporters rarely use participial phrases, preferring a simpler syntax.

Chapter Summary

Armed with these hints about the structure of typical lead sentences, you should now be able to analyze just about any lead you find. Remember to:

- Look for the main clause. It is usually, but not always, at the beginning of the sentence.

- Decide whether there are any subordinate clauses. (The word *that* may be omitted.) What do they refer to?

- If there seem to be too many verbs in the sentence, check whether some belong to participial phrases. What/Whom do they describe?

- Rethink the sentence. Cut it into several shorter sentences, separating the clauses, if necessary.   [Ex. RR.3]

Exercises

A Review of the Reading

1. What is the purpose of a summary lead? An interest lead?

2. Look into the following details:

   a. Why is there a dateline before some lead sentences? Why don't all leads begin with a dateline?

   b. Do most lead sentences begin with a main clause?

   c. What are two kinds of phrases that describe a noun subject?

3. Reprinted below are the headlines and lead sentences of two newspapers the day after the presidential election of 1988. Do they both contain the same information?
   Review the Chapter Summary (p. 52). Then analyze the following leads; simplify the long sentences by making short (one-clause) statements about Bush, Dukakis, and other people on the basis of the information in each headline and lead.

   BUSH: 'WE'LL MOVE AGAIN'
   Reaches out to Congress

   George Bush was elected the 41st President of the United States Tuesday by a large margin—but without the mandate enjoyed by Ronald Reagan. *(USA Today)*

   IT'S BUSH!
   Victorious veep pledges, 'I'll be the president of all the people'

   Vice President George Bush was elected the 41st president of the United States last night in a sweeping victory, turning back a gallant closing surge by Gov. Michael Dukakis. *(Herald)*

   [veep = Vice President (informal)]

PP Purposeful Practice: Restrictive and Nonrestrictive Clauses

In a sentence with a relative clause (a clause introduced by the subordinate conjunction *who*, *which*, or *that*), it is important to note whether a comma precedes the conjunction or not. A comma before the subordinate conjunction influences the meaning of the sentence.

> If a comma separates a relative clause from the rest of the sentence, then the relative clause contains only secondary information about a noun that has already been defined. That noun is called an *antecedent* (underlined in the following examples).

An antecedent may be a name, for example, which defines a unique person or place, as in the following:

> ATLANTA – Gov. <u>Michael Dukakis</u>, *who* has begun putting the final touches on his acceptance speech, will tour the convention hall today.... (*Herald*)

Or the antecedent may be someone or something that is known to be unique because of the context. For example,

> <u>My uncle</u>, *who* lives in L.A., just got married.

Because of the comma before (and after) the relative clause, it is clear that I have only one uncle. The fact that he lives in L.A. is only secondary information. Since he is unique in this context (I have only one uncle), his person needs no further definition.

The situation is different for the following sentence (no commas):

> My <u>uncle</u> who lives in L.A. just got married.

In this context it is clear that I have more than one uncle, but I am referring to the only one who lives in L.A. The relative clause *who lives in L.A.* is a necessary part of the definition of the uncle I mean. In other words, the antecedent (*uncle*) alone without the clause would not be completely defined.

> Relative clauses that are separated from the main clause by commas are called *nonrestrictive* clauses. Relative clauses that are not preceded and followed by commas are called *restrictive* clauses because they restrict the meaning of the antecedent.

1. Explain why there are no commas in the following lead:

> BEIT SAHOUR, Israeli-Occupied West Bank (Reuters) – Clashes flared Tuesday between Israeli troops and <u>Palestinians</u> *who* were angered by the death of a teen-ager. *(Tribune)*

2. Underline each antecedent in the following sentences. Then write **R** if the relative clause is restrictive (i.e., a necessary part of the antecedent's definition); or write **N** if the relative clause is nonrestrictive (i.e., the antecedent is unique in that context and fully defined). Add the commas around nonrestrictive clauses. In some sentences both interpretations may be possible.

   a. My husband who is Japanese has never gotten used to living in America.

   b. An adult who is Japanese may never get used to living in the U.S.A.

   c. Henry Kissinger who is no longer Secretary of State is still a respected foreign policy advisor.

   d. The Native Americans who were at the pow-wow are interested in their heritage.

   e. We have a Ford stationwagon; and that car which has traveled almost 100,000 miles has never needed major repairs!

   f. The English book that you are reading was written in 1991.

   g. Why don't you help that man over there who is begging?

3. *Optional Writing Activity*: Your teacher will give you a photograph without a caption. Write your own caption (use your imagination), including a relative clause in the sentence.
   Extra Credit: Include a participial phrase, too!

This chapter explained that leads elaborate on the headline, adding some factual details and explanations. Often some key words are restated in different words. They provide a second chance for the reader to understand—without a dictionary.

1. Finding definitions of key headline words in the lead paragraph or the article itself is a very important skill to have. Practice on the short articles below; do *not* use a dictionary! Circle *a*, *b*, or *c*.

Slayer of 4 women executed in Florida

STARKE, Fla. – Jeffrey Joseph Daugherty, who was convicted in the killings of four women, was executed in the electric chair yesterday minutes after the US Supreme Court refused to hear his appeal. Daugherty, 33, was the 19th person executed in Florida and the 103rd put to death in the nation since the Supreme Court reinstated the death penalty in 1976. (AP)

Inquest set July 24 for N. End shooting

An inquest into the fatal shooting of a North End man by a state trooper during an undercover drug investigation earlier this year has been tentatively scheduled to begin July 24.

Boston Municipal Court Judge John A. Pino has been assigned to preside over the closed-door inquiry into the death of Eric Parziale. Parziale, 19, was sitting in a car double-parked on Hanover Street in the North End when he was shot by Robert J. Monahan, a state trooper. Monahan has told investigators he began firing after Parziale pointed an object at him he believed was a gun. No gun or drugs were found on Parziale, according to investigators.

Winnie Mandela opted for rest

Winnie Mandela did not attend a fund-raiser in her honor at a Boston church Saturday because she wanted to rest, not because of security problems as originally reported, a US State Department official said yesterday.

"Mrs. Mandela told our agent that she was tired, wanted to get some rest and for that reason she didn't want to attend the event at St. Paul's" Cathedral said Andrew Laine, a public affairs officer with the bureau of Diplomatic Security at the State Department.

Organizers reported Saturday that Mandela could not attend the event because of security problems.

YANA DLUGY

In the first headline,

1. **Slayer** means:
   a. an ex-convict
   b. a killer
   c. a lover

2. **executed** means:
   a. seated
   b. killed
   c. became an executive officer

In the second headline,

3. **Inquest** means:
   a. inquiry
   b. trial
   c. request

4. **set** means:
   a. made
   b. began
   c. scheduled

5. **N.** means:
   a. no
   b. north
   c. number

In the third headline,

6. **opted for** means:
   a. chose
   b. refused
   c. looked at

Review Questions:

Which of these three headlines are

7. noun phrases? sentences?

8. in the passive?

The first article reprinted by permission of the Associated Press. The second and third articles reprinted courtesy of The Boston Globe.

2. Match these headlines with their lead paragraphs. Key words will help you. (One headline has no lead.)

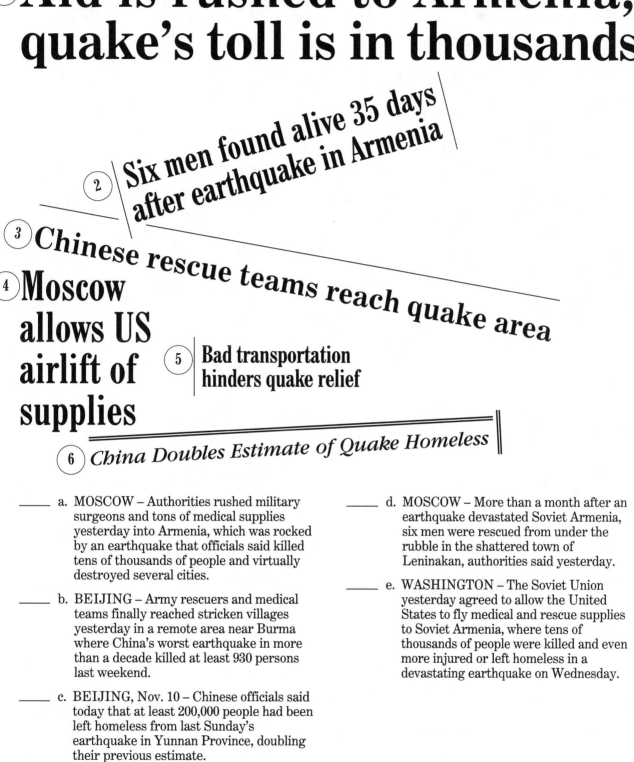

① # Aid is rushed to Armenia; quake's toll is in thousands

② Six men found alive 35 days after earthquake in Armenia

③ Chinese rescue teams reach quake area

④ **Moscow allows US airlift of supplies**

⑤ **Bad transportation hinders quake relief**

⑥ *China Doubles Estimate of Quake Homeless*

_____ a. MOSCOW – Authorities rushed military surgeons and tons of medical supplies yesterday into Armenia, which was rocked by an earthquake that officials said killed tens of thousands of people and virtually destroyed several cities.

_____ b. BEIJING – Army rescuers and medical teams finally reached stricken villages yesterday in a remote area near Burma where China's worst earthquake in more than a decade killed at least 930 persons last weekend.

_____ c. BEIJING, Nov. 10 – Chinese officials said today that at least 200,000 people had been left homeless from last Sunday's earthquake in Yunnan Province, doubling their previous estimate.

_____ d. MOSCOW – More than a month after an earthquake devastated Soviet Armenia, six men were rescued from under the rubble in the shattered town of Leninakan, authorities said yesterday.

_____ e. WASHINGTON – The Soviet Union yesterday agreed to allow the United States to fly medical and rescue supplies to Soviet Armenia, where tens of thousands of people were killed and even more injured or left homeless in a devastating earthquake on Wednesday.

DD For Discussion and Debate

1. Reread the articles in Exercise VV and choose one (or all) to discuss.

   a. *"Slayer . . ."*: Although the death penalty for especially terrible crimes is legal in the U.S.A., many people object to it for practical, philosophical, or religious/ethical reasons. What do you think? Is it legal in your native country?

   b. *"Inquest set . . ."*: A state trooper (police officer) shot and killed a man in Boston while on duty. Is this an example of police brutality in your opinion? Is police brutality a problem in your city? What can be done about it?

   c. *"Winnie Mandela"*: Is she currently in the news? And Nelson Mandela? What is happening in South Africa now?

   d. Have you ever experienced an earthquake? Try to use some of the vocabulary from the previous page: *rescue team, supplies, stricken, rubble.*

2. Have you ever met or seen in person any national leader or internationally famous person? Tell the class about your experience.

3. Look at the front page of the *Weekly World News* at the beginning of this chapter. Discuss the believability of the headlines. Now read the following statement, which can be found inside the paper in small print, and discuss whether it changes your opinion of this newspaper.

   > *Weekly World News is a journal of information, opinion and entertainment published each Tuesday. . . . Articles are drawn from different sources . . . and are published strictly for the enjoyment of our readers.*

4. Reporters write about topics of interest to their local readers. The following two activities concern points of view. Choose *a* or *b* to work on with a partner.

   a. Choose an article about a sports event involving a local team in a local newspaper. Read the headline and the lead. Imagine the point of view of the fans (supporters) of the opposing (nonlocal) team. What might the lead in their local paper contain (different details, names, adverbs and adjectives)?

   b. Choose an article about an international event from a current journal or Chapter 6. After reading the headline and lead, imagine the point of view of one of the countries involved in the event (not the U.S.A.). Do you think the same facts would be mentioned in newspapers from other countries?

   c. *Extra-credit Writing Exercise*: Write the lead that you imagined in *a* or *b* above.

CC | Conversation with a Classmate

1. If you watch any English-language news programs on television—or listen to any on the radio—tell your partner about them. Do you prefer watching the news on TV to reading a newspaper?

2. *Optional Activity:* Choose an article from a current English-language newspaper or from this book. Read the lead sentence with your partner and then analyze it together, breaking it into short, one-clause statements. Then discuss the news content.

II | Intercultural Issues

Compare newspapers from different countries. If some articles deal with the same topic, compare their lead paragraphs (translate where necessary). How is the point of view of each national reporter shown? Which facts are stressed in each lead?

CHAPTER 5

Reading an Article for Information

---------------------- **PREREADING QUESTIONS** ---------------------------

1. What are some of the differences you expect to find between the writing in a novel and in a news article?

2. Do you think newspapers usually publish *bad* news?

3. a. Can American readers express their own opinions about the news or a newspaper and expect the paper to print those opinions?

   b. Is it the same in your native country?

5.1 The Structure of a News Article

The typical news article is written in a form called *the inverted pyramid.* This means that the most important information comes first, at the top of the article, and the information becomes less and less important as the article continues toward its end. In the previous two chapters, we saw that the headline condenses the news story into just a few words; and the lead typically contains the most important facts in a sentence or two. The remainder of the story is called the *body* of the article. It gives supporting facts, quotations from different sources, further descriptions of people, historical context, and so on.

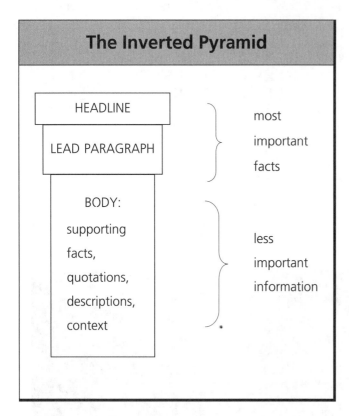

This form of newswriting is helpful to readers because they can get the basic facts quickly, at the beginning of the article. The inverted pyramid is also helpful to editors, who might have to cut the end of a story to fit onto the page. It has some advantages for learners of English as well: Information that is stated briefly in the lead is usually repeated in more detail in a later paragraph. The lead summarizes the story, so the body of the article contains no surprises. Therefore, if you do not fully understand the lead, you can usually find more explanations if you continue reading.

Some stories become quite complex when they are written in the form of an inverted pyramid. To avoid such complexity, one of two other journalistic forms is occasionally used instead: a chronological or a logical order of events.

5.2 The Five W's

Ideally, articles should answer the basic questions of readers. These are called the <u>five W (and an H) questions</u>—namely, <u>w</u>ho, <u>w</u>hat, <u>w</u>hen, <u>w</u>here, <u>w</u>hy, and <u>h</u>ow. Because the answers to these questions provide the most important facts about the topic, reporters try to deal with them in the lead. But, in fact, as most journalists admit, it is rarely possible to answer all six questions in one sentence!

It is often impossible to answer some of these questions at all. "Why" and "how" questions often require an interpretation of events. Theoretically, journalists should not interpret events but only report them. Thus, in order to answer "why" and "how" questions, news writers often ask someone else (a source) for information or opinions. Sources can be a participant, an acquaintance of a participant, an observer (witness), or an expert on the news topic.[1] Quotations from such people usually appear in the body of an article.

The following is a "News in Brief" article from the *Monitor*, Sept. 12, 1988. Let us look for the answers to the Five W (and an H) questions:

Britain's postal strike simmers on

London

An unexpectedly bitter dispute between the Royal Mail and the union of postal workers has kept Britain's postal service closed for two weeks.

Street-corner mail boxes are sealed and international mail suspended until the Union of Communication Workers and post-office management settle their differences over special pay for new recruits.

The strike began as a spotty, 24-hour work stoppage Aug. 31 but was extended last week to include most of the 1,500 Royal Mail offices and more than 100,000 union members. It is the first major disruption of service since 1971, and has prompted discussion of further privatizing postal deliveries. British Prime Minister Margaret Thatcher has said the Royal Mail is one public service that should remain in government hands. But some businessmen have pressed her to expand the market for private courier services to include carrying large volumes of mail.

The pay dispute concerns special bonuses of between $13 and $34 a week for workers in the London area where the cost of living is high and it is difficult to attract new recruits. The Royal Mail is offering the premiums to help alleviate an acute shortage of workers in London but union leaders want the bonuses distributed equally across the country.

The post office has asked other countries to hold all mail deliveries for Britain until the strike is settled, because it is difficult to guarantee security for mail bags piling up at air and seaports.

—Julian Baum

The headline tells us **what** the article is about and **where** it is happening: a strike within the postal service of Great Britain. The lead answers the **who** questions: The Royal Mail and the union of postal workers. It also tells us **when**: for the last two weeks. The question of **how** the postal strike is happening is answered in the second and third paragraphs: mail boxes are sealed (officially closed or locked), international mail is suspended (stopped for a short time), and after all mail work was stopped for 24 hours once, now the work stoppage has continued in most mail offices. The reason for the strike (the **why** question) is also in the second paragraph: special pay for new recruits (newly hired workers). Thus, a very brief answer to all six questions is given in the headline and first two sentences/paragraphs of the article.

This news story follows the form of an inverted pyramid: The body of the article expands on the information at the beginning. It gives further details that answer each of the six questions. For example, one individual, the political leader of the country, is named: Prime Minister Margaret Thatcher. A statement of her views is reported and also an opposing view. In addition, the journalist reports on the consequences of the event: Other countries have been asked not to deliver their mail for Britain. This consequence could directly affect readers of the newspaper.

[Ex. PP]

James W. Carey, professor of communication, writes that daily news coverage is often criticized for not having enough depth.

> This . . . criticism of daily journalism is true as far as it goes . . . What it overlooks is that depth—the how and why—are rarely in any individual story. They are properties of the whole, not the part. . . . But if a story can be kept alive in the news long enough, it can be fleshed out and rounded off. Journalists devote much of their energy to precisely that: keeping significant events afloat long enough so that interpretation, explanation, and thick description can be added as part of ongoing development. Alas, management and the marketing department devote much of their energy to precisely the opposite—making each front page look like a new chapter in human history.[2]

5.3 Journalistic Styles: Journalism of Hope

The "journalism of hope" is an expression that Al Neuharth uses to describe the philosophy of his *USA Today*. Peter Prichard, an editor for *USA Today*, says about it:

> By creating a brand-new publication that fit in no conventional category, Neuharth [was] daring [journalists] to think again about the way they presented news to readers. . . . The new national newspaper, he said, seeks "to cover all of the news, with accuracy, but without anguish, with detail but without despair."[3]

This philosophy, the journalism of hope, Neuharth contrasted with the traditional "old journalism of despair." The latter, he said, leaves readers discouraged or angry. *USA Today*, on the other hand, presents both bad and good news and tries to promote "understanding and unity." The attempt to balance positive and negative news receives both favorable and unfavorable reviews from traditional newspeople.[4]

Along with a nontraditional style of journalism, *USA Today* tends to emphasize different kinds of news from traditional papers. Political scientist Daniel C. Hallin compares its emphasis (focus) with that of the *Times*:

> [The] focus of *USA Today*'s America is very different from that of the *New York Times*. . . . The journalism of *USA Today* is not a journalism of issues and politics, but of symbols and of everyday life . . . defined primarily by the mass culture of leisure and consumption. National political news on the *New York Times* model is concerned with the movers and shakers [leaders in politics and business]; their priorities and concerns define the nation. *USA Today* is concerned with "everyman," . . . with the ways in which ordinary people share, usually through mass culture, in some kind of national life. So in place of national politics, *USA Today* is concerned with: consumption. . . , leisure. . . , television and other forms of entertainment, celebrities and human interest stories, health. . . , consensus values and beliefs ("We Still Believe in the American Dream") . . . [and] sports.[5]

See the boxed articles on p. 65 for an example of these contrasts.

There has been a lot of negative criticism about this emphasis from journalists, editors, and others. But television reporter Charles Kuralt, who travels across the country through small towns, has some praise for the availability of *USA Today*:

> [In] the small towns where I usually wake up in the morning, I can't learn about the weather, the sports, the stock market, or even the important news of the day anywhere else.[6]

U.S. Report Raises Estimate of Smoking Toll

By RICHARD L. BERKE
Special to The New York Times

WASHINGTON, Jan. 10 – Twenty-five years after the Surgeon General of the United States jolted the nation with the first official warning of the health perils of cigarettes, a Federal report has concluded that smoking has caused more death and disease than previously believed.

The first report, published on Jan. 11, 1964, helped encourage millions of Americans to stop smoking and laid the groundwork for Federal efforts to curb smoking. The new report, to be made public at a news conference here Wednesday, reviews the strides that have been made in reducing smoking from 40 percent of adults in 1965 to 29 percent in 1987. But it warned that smoking remains the "single most important preventable cause of death" in the United States.

In the preface, Dr. C. Everett Koop, the Surgeon General says:

"The critical message here is that progress in curtailing smoking must continue, and ideally accelerate, to enable us to turn smoking-related mortality around. Otherwise, the disease impact of smoking will remain high well into the 21st century."

This afternoon Dr. Koop's office released advance copies of the report that were intended for use by newspapers and television on Thursday. But The Christian Science Monitor published key findings of the report today and portions of that article were picked up by The Associated Press.

The report has been long awaited by lobbies on both sides of the issue. Groups that oppose smoking say they will use the 25th anniversary of the first report to redouble their campaigns to discourage smoking. The Tobacco Institute, the major industry lobby, has already begun a national advertising campaign asserting that the rights of smokers are being jeopardized. [Article was shortened]

Anti-smoking efforts will save 3 million

By Kim Painter
USA TODAY

Anti-smoking efforts launched 25 years ago today will extend nearly 3 million lives by the year 2000, Surgeon General C. Everett Koop says in a report out today.

Koop's 1989 report on smoking also says the USA would have 90 million smokers today, instead of 50 million, if not for anti-smoking efforts.

Surgeon General Luther L. Terry first called smoking a health hazard on Jan. 11, 1964.

Anti-smoking efforts added an average of 20 years to 750,000 lives between 1965 and 1985, the report says. By 2000, another 2.1 million smoking-related deaths will be prevented or postponed.

Still, 390,000 people died in 1985 of smoking-linked causes.

"These stats are always coming out and they're always subject to debate," says Gary Miller of the Tobacco Institute in Washington, D.C.

Vocabulary

toll *[noun]*   health cost(s), deaths
Surgeon General *[title]*   highest medical officer of the U.S. government
jolt *[verb]*   to shock or shake
peril *[noun]*   danger
previously *[adv.]*   before
efforts *[noun]*   attempts
curb *[verb]*   to reduce or control
launch *[verb]*   to start
extend *[verb]*   to make longer
hazard *[noun]*   danger

Questions

1. a. Which article represents the journalism of hope?
   b. Why do you think so?
   c. Where in that article are optimistic or hopeful facts or opinions reported?
   d. Is there any hopeful news in the other article?
2. Which article would you rather read in the newspaper? Why?
3. Is either article biased? How?

5.4 Journalistic Styles: Journalism of Policy vs. Journalism of Experience

Ideally, news stories report more than just bare facts about a single event. They should be able to show the larger context of the immediate facts and thus give them a wider significance. But some newspapers favor the facts of a single event, while others focus on larger, more abstract contexts. Daniel Hallin calls these two styles a "journalism of experience" and a "journalism of policy."

In a city with two newspapers, it is not uncommon to find that each represents one of those two styles. Hallin describes the case in New York City, for example, where the *Daily News* represents a journalism of experience and the *Times* a journalism of policy:

> The *Daily News* reports the experiences of particular individuals or neighborhoods, but provides little analysis of how these experiences are related to larger social processes. The *Times* provides exactly this kind of analysis, often at great length; . . . but also [misses] the human tragedy that [lies] in the failures of policy outlined by the experts it had interviewed.[7]

(Articles from the *Daily News* appear on pp. 136 and 142.)

Such a difference in style also leads to a difference in the selection of news articles to print. Thus, no matter how hard you look for a certain kind of information, it may not appear in every newspaper.

Most newspapers try to combine, or blend, the two styles. For instance, an article may begin with an example of one person's experience and then continue with a broader analysis. Or it may begin with a factual news lead and its significance, then include individual experiences in the body of the story. The story on homelessness in the Exercise section is an example of a blend of styles.   [Ex. DD.1]

It has also become common to label some stories "News Analysis." These articles combine objective facts with a personal analysis of their meaning or significance; they always include the author's byline.

5.5 Features and Opinion Articles

The material in this chapter and the last chapter has dealt with news articles, sometimes called *straight news* or *hard news*. Some examples of journalism of experience, however, border on *soft news*, on human interest stories, for example.

A *human interest story* is one that features a person or group of people. It may begin with a current news event (like a fire) and go on to describe in detail the main people involved (a heroic fireman, the family whose house was damaged, etc.). Their personalities may be described; sometimes other interesting incidents from their lives are told, too. Human interest articles usually report on people in uncommon situations—for example, winners of big lotteries, or the survivor of an accident. But sometimes they are stories of ordinary people with whom the reader can empathize (feel similar to). For example, the *Herald* covered a local public housing event with a front-page story about an old woman who was forced to leave her apartment because she did not want to give up her illegal dog. Human interest stories describe American individuals or groups, typical or unusual. They give the foreign reader some fascinating glimpses of life in America.

Many other articles in American newspapers do not follow the organization and styles of a hard news story. Such articles generally are called *features*. They do not describe the facts about an event that happened very recently, as most straight news does. Instead, they describe something, some place, or somebody in a more timeless and colorful way. The journalist allows his or her personal observations to interpret and flavor the story. The reader is invited to participate in or experience the story as the writer did. Thus, the information in features is different from the analysis of the five W's of a hard news article.

Feature Articles

- human interest stories
- second-day news stories
- background articles
- analyses of trends
- entertaining and educational descriptions

Besides human interest stories, other kinds of features are: (1) second-day news stories, which, as James Carey says, offer interpretation, explanation, and description of a news event of the day before; (2) background stories, which explain the context of a recent or future event; (3) analyses of trends taking place over a long period of time; and (4) entertaining and educational descriptions of lifestyles, people, places, and products. Features often occur in newspaper sections called "Home," "Health," "Ideas," or "Travel." A large part of Sunday papers consists of features.

Another kind of newspaper article that does not conform to the rules of objective writing is the *opinion article*—for example, editorials. *Editorials* are direct expressions of the opinions of the publishers of a newspaper. Like features, editorials are not written in an inverted pyramid style. They may begin with some facts about a news event, but they usually start with an interest lead because their purpose is to lead convincingly to an opinion or judgment. Instead of offering less important information after the lead, the editorial becomes more convincing as it progresses. The end paragraph is very important; it contains the decisive arguments and conclusions.

Opinion Articles

- editorials
- columns
- reviews

Editorials often criticize political trends or decisions and sometimes offer an alternative solution to a problem. They can also interpret events or decisions and explore the consequences. Thus, it is here that publishers show their preference for candidates for political office. In a city with two newspapers, the two publishers usually represent different political sides. In the 1988 presidential election, for example, the *Globe* endorsed Dukakis while the *Herald* supported Bush. Occasionally an editorial praises a person or event or, in a lighter tone, comments on a happening or trend in an entertaining way.

On the same page as editorials are letters from readers and other people (usually experts on the topic being discussed). On the opposite page, the Op-Ed page, *columnists* offer their views. A columnist is a person who writes regularly for the press; his or her article usually takes up one vertical column of print and is sometimes accompanied by a small photograph of the writer. Some columnists' work is *syndicated*; that means it appears in many newspapers across the country on the same day.

Columnists specialize in a certain topic or kind of writing: Some offer advice, some are humorous, some comment particularly on business or social events, and some write from a political point of view. *Columns* appear on the Op-Ed page and in other appropriate sections of the newspaper. [Ex. DD.2]

A third kind of opinion article is a *review*. In a review the writer gives his or her opinion of a media or artistic event. Movies, plays, television shows, books, records, restaurants, fashion shows, and art exhibits can be reviewed. The writer first tells about the content of what he or she saw (or tasted, etc.) and then makes a judgment about how good or worthwhile it was. Reviews are often summarized briefly by a number of stars: One star means it was not good; four (or five) stars mean it was excellent.

In expressing personal observations or opinions, a reporter often uses adverbs, adjectives, and strong, colorful verbs and sometimes colloquialisms (informal expressions used in speaking) as well. Such words tell the reader that the article does not intend to be a straight news story. Vocabulary, form, and style of the article do not follow the rules for objective hard news.

EXERCISES

RR | **Review of the Reading Through Valuable Vocabulary and Concepts**

1. The key words and ideas of this chapter are expressed in the five subheadings:

    The Structure of a News Article
    The Five W's
    Journalistic Styles: Journalism of Hope
    Journalistic Styles: Journalism of Policy vs. of Experience
    Features and Opinion Articles

    Review in your mind the contents of each section. If you have trouble summarizing one, read it again. Then write some notes, important words or phrases, about each section. (*Option*: Write a complete paragraph.)

2. Match each of the following kinds of articles (1–5) with the correct definition. If possible, find an example in a current newspaper.

    _____ 1. **a feature article**
    _____ 2. **a human interest story**
    _____ 3. **an editorial**
    _____ 4. **a column**
    _____ 5. **a review**

    a. an opinion of the editor(s)
    b. an opinion about a movie, book, etc.
    c. "soft news" story (but not opinion)
    d. "soft news" about people
    e. an opinion article by an expert or other writer, usually appearing regularly

PP | **Purposeful Practice: Finding Answers to Your Questions**

The Five W's (and an H) are information questions that journalists try to answer at the beginning of their articles. Generally the questions are like the following:

> *What* happened? or *What* object is involved?
> *Who* is involved? or *Who* did it?
> *Where* did it happen?
> *When* did it happen?
> *Why* did it happen? or *Why* was it done?
> *How* did it happen? or *How* was it achieved?

1. Earlier you read this headline:

    Six men found alive 35 days after earthquake in Armenia

    a. Write the six questions—and any other questions you may have—for the article. What questions would you like to have answered?

    b. Now turn back to p. 57 and read lead sentence *d.* How many of your questions are answered in it?

    c. More of the body of the rescue article appears in the box on p. 70. Try to find the answers to the rest of your questions. Then discuss your results with your classmates.

The news agency Tass said in a dispatch from Yerevan, the capital of the Armenian republic, that the six were freed on Wednesday, 35 days after the earthquake devastated the region. It said the men survived on canned food.

The six were pulled from the rubble of a nine-story apartment building in Leninakan, which is near the border with Turkey. It was one of the cities hit hardest by the quake.

A 50-year-old survivor, Atkaz Akopyan, was quoted as saying that on Dec. 7, the day of the quake, he had asked five neighbors to help him carry two wooden kegs into the building's basement for storage. . . .

"We lost track of time completely," he said. "But we did not doubt for a minute that we would be found and rescued."

After their rescue, the six were reported hospitalized in satisfactory condition.

By Charles P. Wallace
Los Angeles Times

2. Now read the headline of the article on p. 71. Write some information questions about the topic. Can you find the answers in the lead? If not, in which paragraphs do you find the answers to the Five W's (and an H)?

DD **For Discussion and Debate**

1. a. Reread the article on homelessness (p. 71). What kind of article is it? For example: What kind of lead does it begin with? Are personal experiences told? Is there a general analysis of the problem of homelessness?
   b. Is homelessness a problem where you live? What can/should be done about it?

2. In this chapter some other kinds of stories besides hard news were described—for example, opinion pieces.
   a. Read an opinion column in an English-language newspaper. What is it about?
   b. Find the editorials in the paper. What are they about?
   Option: Write a letter to the editor telling your opinion about the same topic(s).
   c. *Extra-credit Exercise*: Analyze further a column and/or editorial that you found. Choose one to read thoroughly. Define its topic and the writer's opinion. Find reasons that the writer gives to support his or her opinion. Do you agree with the conclusion of the article?
   Option: Write your own "editorial" or column about a similar topic.

3. Do/Would you prefer to read articles based on a journalism of experience or a journalism of policy? Why?

4. *Optional Debate*: What do you think of Mr. Neuharth's journalism of hope? The class should divide into two groups: (1) those students opposed to a journalism of hope as a basic policy for a newspaper, and (2) those for (in favor of) it. (Undecided students may act as a third group, of judges, if desired.) Each group should write down as many supporting arguments as it can and then select one or two group speakers. The speakers should then debate the issue: First each team gives arguments for the group position; then each rebuts/answers the other's arguments. Finally, the judges, if any, summarize the most convincing positions.

Homeless man found frozen to death in Hub

By KATHRYN MARCHOCKI,
L. KIM TAN and DOREEN IUDICA

1 THE FIERCE cold claimed its first Boston victim yesterday when the frozen body of an apparently homeless man was found on a Jamaica Plain street by passers-by.

2 Meanwhile, in Scituate, the frigid conditions may have claimed a second person—a 22-year-old Boston man found behind a bus shelter on First Parish Road.

3 The first victim was found on the quiet, dead-end St. Mark's Road in Jamaica Plain, where residents found the body of a man, described as white and in his 40s or 50s, lying near a garbage dumpster with his face in a paper bag. Authorities have not identified the victim.

4 Dr. Stanton Kessler, a Suffolk County medical examiner, said the man—who is believed to be homeless—died of hypothermia, the first victim to succumb to the effects of the sub-freezing temperatures that have enveloped the Hub the last few days.

5 The victim was found at about 8 a.m. by a couple and their children who live on nearby South Street.

6 The mother said she could tell the victim was homeless from "the way he dressed"—an old baseball hat, a tattered rose-colored parka, beige pants, argyle socks and sneakers.

7 "He was lying there, not moving," said the woman, who did not want to be named.

8 "My husband went over to him, and he could see that he was dead. He had his face in a paper bag instead of a pillow."

9 City officials said last night they couldn't confirm that the victim was one of the Hub's estimated 5,000 homeless people.

10 But Arthur Jones, Mayor Ray Flynn's press secretary, said, "But it does point out the need, under these severe weather conditions, for people to seek assistance for shelter and the need for residents who see people in distress to alert officials to their conditions."

11 Police said residents who see homeless persons in trouble may call 911, and cruisers will be dispatched to transport those in distress to appropriate shelters.

12 Investigators in Scituate said there were no signs of foul play in the death of the man found behind the bus shelter there.

13 Through a piece of paper found in the man's pocket, authorities identified the victim as Eric Barrows of Boston.

14 Police said it appeared as if the body was dropped at the shelter. The victim's last known address was on Tremont Street, and had no apparent reason to be in Scituate, police said.

15 The body was frozen and slightly dusted with snow when found around 7:15 a.m. by a man arriving to catch a bus, indicating it probably had been behind the bus shelter for two days.

16 The frigid weather took its toll all over the region in the past few days. Boston City Hospital reported several cases of mild hypothermia and about 300 Boston tenants turned to the city for help in getting heat turned on in their apartments, said Gerry Cuddyer, who runs the Mayor's Office of Neighborhood Services' "No Heat Hotline."

17 Meanwhile, low- and moderate-income people will find less help available this winter to pay fuel bills. Cutbacks in the federally-funded fuel assistance program has reduced the maximum benefit from $750 per household to $675, said Edward McCauley, who manages Boston's program.

18 "It's really a tragic comment on national priorities when families and elderly may have to choose between food and heating fuel," said Don Gillis, director of the Mayor's Office of Neighborhood Services.

19 Freezing temperatures were accompanied by record-breaking energy demand of 19,596 megawatts Tuesday night, the New England Power Pool reported.

Conversation With a Classmate

Optional Activity: Find an advice column (in which a reader asks for advice on a personal subject) in an English-language newspaper. Choose one letter in the column to read with your partner. Tape the article in the space below (or write a summary of your conversation).

1. *Before you read the columnist's advice*, discuss with your partner how **you** each would answer that letter. Then compare your answers with the columnist's.

2. If your answer is not similar to the columnist's (or your partner's) answer, do you think that cultural views are the cause of the differences?

Intercultural Issues

Discuss the following issues in small groups (of various nationalities, if possible), using some of the advanced-level vocabulary that appeared in the articles in this chapter. (*Option*: Write about the issues.)

1. Are strikes common in your country? In your discussion use some of these words (from p. 63): *dispute, union, suspend, work stoppage.*

2. Is smoking popular in your country? How concerned are people about the health hazards of smoking? Try to use some of these words (from p. 65): *previous(ly), curb, extend, hazard, efforts.*

PART TWO

Introduction

In the remainder of the book, you will find samples of real newspaper articles. They are organized according to the arrangement of sections in a typical metropolitan daily: international news, national news, and business news.

The articles were chosen on the basis of their subject matter; they include many issues of the 1990s. They all use vocabulary that is essential for the understanding of each topic. The goal of this book is to enable you, after you practice with such sample articles and understand important words, to go on and read current English-language newspapers wherever you are.

The emphasis is on straight news stories. Standardized news stories from wire services, as well as more colorful writing from local journalists, are represented.

Study Tips

Before you read the articles in each section, do the Essential Vocabulary exercise at the beginning of the section. It will introduce you to the basic, key vocabulary that you must know in order to understand the articles that follow.

There are two ways to effectively read the articles in each section.

1. Read the news story itself first, guessing or reading quickly over words that you do not know; then study the vocabulary for that article; and then reread the story with the knowledge of the vocabulary fresh in your mind (three steps).

OR

2. Study the vocabulary list first; then read the article; refresh your memory of the new words; and finally reread the article (four steps).

Advanced students will probably want to try the first method, which approximates reading a real newspaper most closely. Intermediate students may enjoy the articles more if they have studied some vocabulary first via the second method.

After reading each article, answer the questions as your teacher directs. If you are studying independently, write your answers and then check them with the Answer Key at the back of the book. May you all learn from your reading and go on to enjoy reading a newspaper regularly!

CHAPTER 6

International News

Introduction: The World Through American Eyes

People from other countries are sometimes disappointed that they cannot find news about their lands in U.S. newspapers. Certainly there is no lack of events taking place there. Does the lack of reports from so many diverse countries *reflect* the indifference of the American public? Or does it *create* an ignorance about other nations?

Recent studies have shown that citizens of the United States do not learn much geography in school and are indeed quite ignorant about other countries (compared with other industrialized nations). Television and newspaper reporters often assume that their audiences know little or nothing about international topics and are not interested in them.[1] Polls have shown that Americans say "their first interest is local news, then national news."[2] International news is last. Dan Rather, a well-known television news editor and anchorman, protests such poll results as being a "misleading mixture of half-truths and no truths."[3] But he admits that they influence how much foreign news is produced—the trend is decreasing—and how it is presented.

In order to generate interest for their foreign stories, reporters sometimes begin with dramatic interest leads. In some cases the events are personalized: The report focuses on individual victims or terrorists, for example. This is true especially for papers that favor a journalism of experience, not for papers like the *New York Times*, which emphasizes a journalism of policy (see Section 5.4, p. 66).

In most articles the news is presented so that it has direct relevance or importance to an average person in the United States. Daniel Hallin[4] writes that, from the 1960s to the 1980s, the main American view of the world was fairly simple. It was the free world versus Communism. The 1960s were a time of the Cold War between the Soviet Union and the United States. During the 1970s, President Carter's emphasis on human rights opened up a new perspective. Each country was looked at more individually, instead of as a part of the Western or the Communist bloc or the Third World. Since the 1980s, the Reagan era, another element has been added to the geopolitical view: the element of irrational (and noncommunist) terrorism directed against the United States. The attitude of some reports has been to describe what "they" are doing to "us." And some readers have responded with the same view in letters to the editor.

Thus, in U.S. newspapers you are likely to read reports from other countries as they affect the United States. (Such ethnocentrism is not limited exclusively to American journalism, of course.) War, conferences, and elections may affect the U.S. political position in the world. International trade and debts may affect the country economically. Hunger and natural disasters are human issues to which readers can relate on a more personal level.

Hallin writes that American journals actually cover foreign events quite well:

> A typical edition of the *New York Times* will contain, in the front section alone, news from about thirty cities in fifteen to twenty countries around the world.... A major metropolitan newspaper contains, in fact, far more information about the world around it than most people can possibly consume.[5]

But, he concludes, journalists need to be more aware of their wider roles. They do not simply relate facts. They teach readers about the world around them, and they help readers to define who they, as citizens of their country, are.

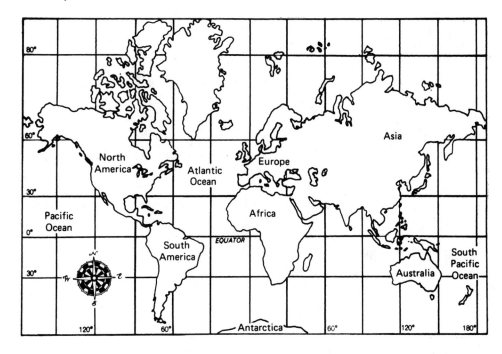

Essential Vocabulary and Sample Articles

Essential Vocabulary

Disasters that affect several countries are usually front-page news. The vocabulary used in the stories depends on the type of catastrophe, but some words occur regularly in many articles. Essential vocabulary you need to know when you read about disasters includes:

blame on	official
blaze	strike [struck, stricken]
century	threaten
devastate	toll
evacuate	wake
off	

and their forms. (You will recognize some words from the readings on earthquakes, pp. 57 and 70.) These words are used in the following practice story.

PLANE CRASH TOLL RISES

The death **toll** reached 4 today as two more victims of last night's plane crash died of burns and multiple injuries. The pilot and one passenger are still reported to be in critical condition at City Hospital. The plane had been carrying mostly Japanese tourists.

The crash is **blamed on** mechanical failure, airline **officials** said, although exact details are not known yet. They said the pilot had reported having problems while the plane was still several miles **off** the coast. As it approached the airport, radio contact was lost.

The plane exploded several minutes after it **struck** the ground, but most passengers had been **evacuated** by then.

Fire **threatened** rescue workers as well as still escaping passengers and crew. Fire Chief Edward Mueller, in charge of putting out the **blaze**, said it was lucky not more people were injured.

"And if it had landed just a mile farther north, it would have **devastated** the Old Church and left a lot more damage in its **wake**," Mueller said. The Old Church, a historic landmark, was built at the turn of the **century**.

Now restate the following phrases from the article. Use your *own* words instead of the Essential Vocabulary words shown in boldface (thick letters).

1. the death **toll**: _____

2. the crash is **blamed on** mechanical failure: _____

3. airline **officials**: _____

4. several miles **off** the coast: _____

5. **struck** the ground: _____

6. passengers had been **evacuated**: _____

7. Fire **threatened** rescue workers: _____

8. the **blaze**: _____

9. **devastated** the church: _____

10. in its **wake**: _____

11. at the turn of the **century**: _____

SUNDAY, APRIL 14, 1991

Blasts rock oil tanker off Italy as government declares emergency

REUTERS

1 GENOA, Italy – A series of explosions rocked a blazing supertanker off northwestern Italy yesterday, as workers battled an oil spill threatening ecological disaster in the Mediterranean.

2 The blasts engulfed the 109,000-ton Haven in a cloak of flames and smoke while experts fought to stop it from spewing a million barrels of Iranian crude oil.

3 The government declared a national state of emergency, said by aides to be the first since the end of World War II.

4 "It means we are mobilizing all the resources we have got—navy, police, everything—because if this wretched oil does get out, it threatens not just Italy, but the whole Mediterranean," said Pio Mastrobuoni, a spokesman for Prime Minister Giulio Andreotti.

5 Police evacuated a seafront shopping district at the small nearby port of Arenzano. Port officials said the explosions sent more flaming oil into shallow waters in the Bay of Genoa.

6 The already polluted Mediterranean is threatened with its worst oil spill if the Haven discharges its full cargo off the Italian Riviera.

GLOBE STAFF MAP / JIM KARAIAN

Nearby fishing areas have already been ruined.

7 "There was a series of explosions throughout the morning," an official at Arenzano said.

8 Witnesses said the blasts appeared to cause the Cypriot-registered tanker Haven to sink even faster in the spot about 2 miles offshore from where it was towed after a first explosion Thursday.

9 "It's a situation of total uncertainty. We can't even see the ship through the smoke. It's difficult to see if it's still floating or sunk," said an official of the Merchant Navy Ministry.

'We are mobilizing all the resources we have. . . . If this wretched oil does get out, it threatens not just Italy, but the whole Mediterranean.'

PIO MASTROBUONI
Prime minister's spokesman

10 Three of the tanker's crew were killed and three others are still reported missing in Thursday's explosion set off by a fire on the 17-year-old Haven.

11 Shipping sources said the tanker, owned by Cypriot-registered Troodos Shipping, was on charter to the National Iranian Tanker Co.

12 The Iranian crude cargo has a high sulfur content, which makes it particularly thick and syrupy, environmental groups said.

13 Europe's worst oil spill was in March 1978 when the Amoco Cadiz emptied 1.6 million barrels onto France's Brittany coast.

Reprinted by permission of Reuters. Map reprinted courtesy of The Boston Globe.

Vocabulary

Head   **blast** *[noun]*   shock waves from an explosion

        rock *[verb]*   to move back and forth rhythmically like a <u>rock</u>ing chair

        tanker   ship that holds large quantities of gas or liquid

¶1   **ecological**   concerning the <u>eco</u>system (the relationship of plants, animals, humans, and their environment)

¶2   **engulf**   to cover or hide something, usually by huge waves

        spew   to spit out or vomit

        crude oil   unprocessed petroleum

¶3   **aides**   assistants/helpers, especially of a government official

¶4   **resources** *[plural]*   goods and money; also *[singular]* something helpful/supportive

        wretched   [here] causing a problem; also, miserable

¶6   **polluted**   unclean, unfit for human use

        discharge   to let go/leave, or to send out

¶8   **Cypriot**   from Cyprus

        towed   pulled

¶10   **set off**   to begin/start a chain of events

Reading for Information

Skim (look quickly through) Sample Article 6.1-1 for the answers to these information questions. Write short answers (a sentence is not necessary), and include the numbers of the paragraphs in which you find each answer.

1. What is the name of the tanker?

2. What company owns the tanker?

3. What is the death toll?

4. What area has been ruined?

5. What area is threatened?

6. When was Europe's worst oil spill?

Questions for Discussion

1. What are the blasts blamed on?

2. Has an oil spill ever threatened your country's coastline?

3. Are there any similar disasters in the news now?

4. *Optional Work:* Read Sample Articles 7.5-2 and 7.5-3, stories about the oil spill off Alaska in 1989 (pp. 154 and 156). Answer the questions in *Reading for Information* above for the Alaska articles. (Change item 6 to: When was the *U.S.A.'s* worst oil spill?) Discuss the differences and similarities between the two cases. Include an analysis of each government's handling of the situation.

THURSDAY, SEPTEMBER 15, 1988

Killer 'cane!

Thousands flee onslaught of 'Gilbert,' storm of the century

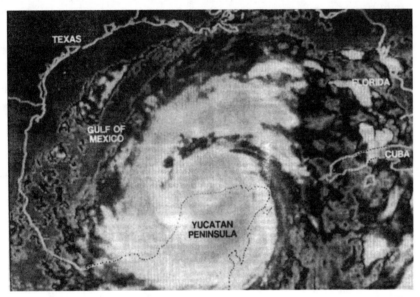

EYE ON THE STORM: A special satellite photo of Hurricane Gilbert last night shows the 'eye' moving off the Yucatan Peninsula in a northwest direction. Forecasters said the monster storm should continue churning through the Gulf toward Texas.

By DAVID ARMSTRONG

1   GALVESTON, Texas – Hurricane Gilbert—the most powerful storm of the century—took dead aim at the Texas Gulf coast this morning after its 200-plus mph winds and towering 15-foot waves left a wake of death and destruction along Mexico's Yucatan Peninsula.

2   The killer hurricane flattened slum areas in the Mexican coastal resort city of Cancun and forced thousands of residents and tourists to flee. Looters reportedly roamed the deserted streets.

3   Forecasters said the monster storm, with winds last night clocked at 160 mph, should continue churning through the Gulf of Mexico, regain strength and smash into the south Texas coast early tomorrow.

4   Officials said a direct hit on Texas would cause "catastrophic damage."

5   Galveston officials said 15 percent of the island's 65,000 residents already have been evacuated. All residents were asked to be off the island by 1 p.m. today.

6   "The sound of the wind outside is horrible," said receptionist Pablo Torres at the Hotel Carrillos in Cancun in a telephone interview as the storm approached. "You couldn't leave even if you wanted to."

7   At least 20 deaths in Jamaica and the Dominican Republic have been blamed on the storm. The Jamaican Embassy in Washington said the storm left more than 500,000 people homeless in that island nation.

Vocabulary

Head **flee**   to hurry away to escape something

         onslaught   a violent attack

¶1   **take dead aim** *[idiom]*   to point or direct itself exactly toward

         towering   very high (like a tower)

         peninsula   a thin piece of land surrounded on three sides by water

¶2   **slum areas**   very poor (and dirty) city areas

         looters   thieves who take things from empty stores or houses

         roam   to wander around without a goal

         deserted   empty

¶3   **forecasters**   weather officials who tell what the weather will probably be

         clocked   timed (with a clock)

         churn   to move violently (in a circular motion)

Caption **(to have/keep an) eye on** *[idiom]*   to watch

         the "eye" of a hurricane   the center

         move off   to move away from

Questions

1. Explain the headline.

2. a. Where was the reporter when he wrote this article?

   b. What countries besides the U.S.A. are mentioned?

3. The reporter uses many colorful adjectives in his writing—for example, *killer* and *towering*.

   a. List the other adjectives you can find. What nouns do they refer to?

   b. What effect do these adjectives have on the reader?

   c. Can you find any strong, colorful verbs?

   d. Is it good journalism to use such adjectives and verbs?

4. Have you ever experienced a hurricane? (Use some words from the Essential Vocabulary, such as: *devastate, threaten, wake.*)

5. Are hurricanes or other wind storms common in your country?

See the next page for a report on the consequences of Hurricane Gilbert for Jamaica.

Note: Hurricanes are given forenames (like "Gilbert" or "Gloria") to make them easier to identify and discuss. Originally they were given women's names only, but in the 1980s it was decided to alternate men's and women's names. The first such storm of the season, which begins June 1st, gets a name beginning with "A", the second with "B", and so on. "Gilbert" was therefore the seventh storm of 1988.

MONDAY, SEPTEMBER 19, 1988

Jamaica seeks aid for hurricane damage

Kingston, Jamaica

Officials from international lending agencies and donor countries were expected to arrive in Jamaica over the weekend to aid in the island's long-term economic recovery in the wake of Hurricane Gilbert.

Prime Minister Edward Seaga initially estimated Jamaica would need $400 million to rebuild. But the official Jampress news agency later quoted him as saying the recovery process would require $8 billion. The hurricane left about half a million of the nation's 2.3 million people homeless and 36 people dead.

Vocabulary

seek   to try to get, to ask for
aid *[noun, verb]*   help
donor   person/country that gives/donates something
initially   at first

Questions

1. Where did the report come from? Can you find the place on the world map below?

2. This article is about the *effects of* Hurricane Gilbert.

   a. How many days after Sample Article 6.1-2 did it appear?

   b. Do the two articles agree on the facts about the number of deaths and homeless people?

3. Does this article contain colorful verbs or adjectives?

4. Has your native country donated aid to any devastated area recently?

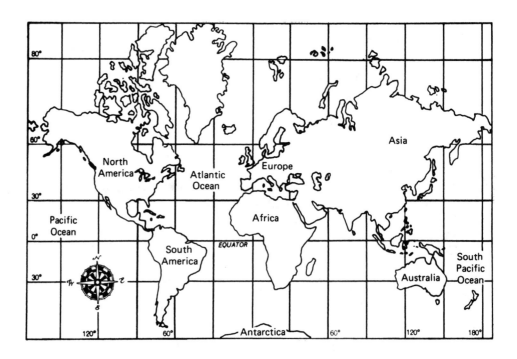

MARCH 22, 1991

Peru's cholera toll now stands at 535

LIMA – The death toll in Peru's two-month-old cholera epidemic has jumped past 500, the Health Ministry said yesterday, the day after the Argentine foreign minister said the outbreak is threatening all of Latin America. The ministry said cholera had struck 89,000 people and killed 535 since the epidemic, the worst in Latin America in a century, began in northern Peru in January. Guido di Tella, the Argentine foreign minister, said Wednesday during a visit to Lima, "There is no country in Latin America that can say it is free from this potential problem." (Reuters)

Reprinted by permission of Reuters.

Vocabulary

cholera   infectious disease of the digestive system, often deadly

epidemic   (development of) a great occurrence of a disease in an area

outbreak   sudden development or start of a disease, etc.

Questions

1. When did the cholera epidemic start?

2. How many people have gotten sick with cholera?

3. What is the death toll?

4. Are other countries besides Peru threatened?

5. Is there any epidemic in the news now?

Essential Vocabulary

A. The following 14 words are essential for the understanding of articles about war, conflicts, and demonstrations. Match each word on the left with the correct definition on the right. Write the corresponding letter in the blank to the left of each number. How many did you know without using a dictionary? _____

_____ 1. **anti-**

_____ 2. **arms/armed**

_____ 3. **arrest**

_____ 4. **civilian**

_____ 5. **clash**

_____ 6. **confrontation**

_____ 7. **defiant**

_____ 8. **disperse**

_____ 9. **fire**

_____ 10. **massive**

_____ 11. **protest**

_____ 12. **rally**

_____ 13. **troops**

_____ 14. **wounded**

a. a large, public meeting
b. showing no fear or respect for authority, challenging
c. shoot(ing) with guns (verb, noun)
d. bold, face-to-face opposition
e. expression of (or to express) opposition
f. organized group(s) of soldiers
g. nonmilitary (person), or citizen
h. against, opposed to
i. (to) fight
j. the taking of (or to seize/take) someone by police
k. weapons of war or having weapons
l. to scatter in different directions
m. (seriously) hurt by a weapon
n. very large and also strong, powerful

B. Classify these 14 vocabulary words into groups: nouns, verbs, adjectives, and prefix. Be careful: Some words belong in more than one category!

C. Fill in the blanks with vocabulary from the list (opposite page). After the blank the word group is given (*n* = noun; *v* = verb; *a* = adjective).

Violent Protest Against Food Shortages

Government troops _____ (*v*) with

_____ (*a*) protesters in the capital yesterday. About 2,000

townspeople had gathered in the main square to _____ (*v*)

the shortage of meat and other foods. Some began to throw rocks at

store windows, and the situation quickly became violent. Police and

_____ (*n*) arrived a few minutes later and began to

_____ (*v*) the crowd with tear gas. A few

_____ (*a*) demonstrators, _____ (*a/v*) with

rocks, resisted. The army _____ (*v*) rubber bullets back.

The _____ (*n*) lasted about 20 minutes. No one was

killed, but about 25 protesters were _____ (*a/v*), according

to official reports.

SUNDAY, JUNE 4, 1989

Troops kill hundreds of protesters in massive crackdown in Beijing

Bloody pandemonium as tanks roll into square

By Colin Nickerson
Globe Staff

1 BEIJING – Chinese troops massacred unarmed civilians this morning, cutting a bloody swath through Beijing and rolling into student-occupied Tiananmen Square with tanks and armored personnel carriers. Hundreds of people were killed and hundreds wounded as the military put a violent end to a peaceful protest.

2 In an attack that began in the middle of the night and was still under way at dawn (around 7 p.m. EST), security forces drove student protesters from the historic square that they had occupied for nearly three weeks.

3 Witnesses and hospital officials said 176 persons were killed and

Associated Press, Globe staff map/Jim Karaian

464 wounded, according to United Press International, while the Associated Press reported that a hospital doctor estimated that 500 people were killed. There was no way to confirm the casualty reports.

4 At least 75 battle tanks and . . . thousands of troops set up positions all around the square. Throughout the night security forces turned intensive fire on hundreds of thousands of citizens thronging the streets in support of the students, who are demanding a more democratic society.

Violence began at 2 p.m.

5 The violence began at 2 p.m. yesterday when security forces fired volleys of tear gas at demonstrators. Later, crowds confronted several thousand soldiers massed outside the Great Hall of the People, China's capitol, and overturned a military jeep.

6 There were continual broadcasts on government-run television urging people to stay off the streets and telling all foreign reporters to leave the area. . . .

7 It was a night of blood, pandemonium and defiance as tracer rounds flashed over the Statue of Liberty erected by demonstrators in the square. . . .

8 Security forces fired directly into the crowds. At 3:30 a.m. on the avenue near the Forbidden City, the ancient center for the Chinese government adjoining Tiananmen Square, several hundred soldiers knelt and fired hundreds of rounds into a great mass of demonstrators who had been driven about a hundred yards down the main artery. This reporter saw at least eight persons killed and dozens wounded in the intense fusillade, which lasted more than five minutes. Most of the wounds were in the chest and stomach. . . .

9 Several people were crushed to death by armored vehicles that roared toward the square. Soldiers were also killed by the vehicles. . . .

10 The protest rallies began in mid-April with students making a single demand: a public dialogue with China's hard-line Communist leadership to discuss political reform. They had vowed to continue their occupation until June 20, when the ruling body of the Parliament meets. . . .

11 Twice before security forces sought to recapture Tiananmen Square but were turned back by peaceful crowds using persuasion.

Reprinted courtesy of The Boston Globe.

Vocabulary

Head **crackdown** the taking of severe disciplinary action by authorities; [here] the ending of the protest by force

Subhead **pandemonium** wild confusion or disorder

tank a heavy, armored, military vehicle with a machine gun on top, which has metal belts instead of wheels

¶1 **massacre** to murder large numbers of unarmed or defenseless people

swath path

armored personnel carriers heavy, protective cars carrying (military) people [also called: *APC*]

¶2 **security forces** the army, police, etc.

¶3 **witness** someone who saw the event himself/herself

officials people who hold an office, or high-level employees, of the government or a large organization

confirm to prove, make sure of

casualty a person hurt or killed in an accident or war

¶4 **thronging** crowding (into), moving together in groups or crowds

¶5 **volley** some, a number (of)

¶6 **urge** to strongly encourage or give advice

¶7 **tracer rounds** shots, bullets that make their path visible with fire

erect to put up/stand up something tall

¶8 **adjoining** next to

knelt past tense of *kneel*: to be on one's knees (not feet)

artery [here] big street

fusillade shooting

¶10 **hard-line** inflexible, unwilling to move from a fixed position

vow to promise solemnly

¶11 **sought** past tense of *seek*: [here] to try/want

persuasion the act of using words (arguing, reasoning, etc.) to convince somebody to do something

Questions

1. The reporter uses many descriptive adjectives and strong verbs in his article. For example, find:

   a. two adjectives + nouns describing protesters:

   _____

   b. two adjectives + nouns describing the shooting:

   _____

   c. two strong verbs meaning *to kill:*

   _____

2. What do you think of the reporter's style of writing and choice of words?

3. Was the reporter a witness to the events? How do you know?

4. Besides a description of the crackdown, does the reporter offer any background information to the event? Where is that information written?

5. Was this an international event? How many countries were involved?

6. a. Do you remember hearing about the crackdown? What was your reaction?

   b. What was your country's official response?

7. What is happening in China now?

OCTOBER 12, 1988

West Bank, Gaza quiet on uprising anniversary

By Curtis Wilkie
Globe Staff

1 NABLUS, Israeli-occupied West Bank – The first anniversary of the Palestinian uprising in the occupied territories passed without a deadly clash yesterday because of the combination of a heavy Israeli military presence, curfews and a Palestinian strike. . . .

2 . . . there were only scattered confrontations in the territories where the intifadah began on Dec. 9, 1987.

3 At least four Palestinians were reported wounded by Israeli army gunfire in the West Bank during demonstrations after weekly Moslem prayer services yesterday. There were also reports of defiant gestures by the Palestinians, who have lived under occupation for more than 21 years.

4 Tires were burned, makeshift roadblocks were thrown up and the outlawed green, white, orange and black colors of the Palestinian flag were flown, but compared with the strife that has claimed an estimated 320 Palestinian and 11 Israeli lives and left hundreds wounded and imprisoned, it was a relatively quiet day.

5 Activity in the Gaza Strip, the scene of the first battles a year ago between the civilian Palestinian population and Israel's army of occupation, was shut down by a curfew imposed by Israeli authorities Thursday night. Violence had erupted in Gaza earlier Thursday, and one youth was shot to death by soldiers during a disturbance.

6 Because of the Palestinians' tendency to observe significant anniversaries with demonstrations, the Israeli army also deployed additional units across the West Bank. . . .

7 A commercial strike, called by the underground leadership of the intifadah, was honored by virtually all of the Arab merchants in East Jerusalem and the territories. . . . Streets were practically empty.

8 Protesters in Nablus welcomed two American reporters who circumvented an Israeli roadblock by parking their car on a side street and reaching the commercial center on foot. Speaking in Arabic and broken English, the Nablus youths said they were proud of their fight against the Israeli army and determined to continue it. . . .

9 One young man, named Wahel, offered the reporters shelter in his home. At one point, he clasped his hands together and held them to his head as if he was ready for a nap. "Wahad sanna," he said. One year. The intifadah was one year old. He was tired, he said, but not yet ready to rest.

Reprinted courtesy of The Boston Globe.

Vocabulary

Head: **uprising**   revolt, rebellion [from the verb: *to rise up*]

¶1   **curfew**   (a military rule stating) a time when people must be indoors

¶2   **scattered**   in a few different places

¶4   **makeshift**   made quickly from any available materials, temporary

outlawed   unlawful, illegal (from: <u>out</u>side the <u>law</u>)

strife   conflict, fight

an estimated 320   about 320

¶5   **erupt**   to begin suddenly, like the explosion of a volcano

¶6   **tendency**   readiness

deploy   to arrange for military action

¶7   **virtually all**   almost all, very nearly all

¶8   **circumvent**   to go or get around something

¶9   **shelter**   a protection

nap   a short sleep during the daytime

Questions

1. Where is the West Bank? Where is Gaza?

2. The headline says that the West Bank and Gaza areas are "quiet." Does the article include more references to peace/quiet or to conflict? How many nouns in the article refer to peace? How many nouns express conflict? Make two lists.

   Peace: _____

   Conflict: _____

3. The dateline tells us where the reporter was. What other information in the article shows the reader that the reporter was present in the area?

4. What is the status of the Israeli–Palestinian conflict now?

APRIL 26, 1987

Protests mark Chernobyl anniversary in Europe

Associated Press

1 Thousands of demonstrators crowded antinuclear rallies in Europe yesterday, donning gas masks in West Germany and blockading a nuclear power plant in the Netherlands on the first anniversary of the Chernobyl nuclear power plant disaster.

2 Protests turned violent in Switzerland, where police used tear gas to break up an illegal march, and in the Netherlands as police swinging batons dispersed club-wielding protesters outside an aluminum plant.

3 Today is the anniversary of the April 26, 1986, explosion and fire that engulfed a reactor at Chernobyl power plant in the Soviet Ukraine, releasing a cloud of radioactive material that traveled around the world. Soviet authorities did not publicize the accident for three days. Later they said it killed 31 persons and injured hundreds.

Violence in Bern

4 A protest organizer, Peter Zuber, said 18 persons were hurt when Swiss police fired tear gas and rubber bullets to disperse thousands of protesters who broke away from the official march route in Bern. Demonstrators smashed bank windows, tossed firecrackers in the air and damaged a fence around a construction site, he said.

5 Bern police spokesman Stefan Kaspar declined to confirm the injury reports but confirmed that "several ambulances" were sent to the scene.

6 The . . . demonstrators left an antinuclear rally that drew at least 10,000 people, according to estimates from police and demonstration organizers.

7 A poll released yesterday by the Berner Zeitung newspaper indicated that 55 percent of 527 Swiss questioned about nuclear energy opposed it.

Confrontation in Holland

8 In the Netherlands, about 200 demonstrators with clubs tried to blockade the entrance to the Pechiney aluminum firm near the southern town of Borssele . . . At least one police officer and one demonstrator were injured. No arrests were reported.

9 Police said the protesters came from a rally at a nuclear plant in Borssele and apparently targeted the aluminum firm because of its heavy use of electricity produced by nuclear power.

10 Last week, a Leiden University opinion poll indicated that 53 percent of the Dutch oppose nuclear power, and 87 percent oppose its expansion in the Netherlands.

West German protests

11 In West Germany, demonstrators staged rallies and marches in Berlin, Bonn, Hamburg, Munich and Stuttgart.

12 Police said about 5,000 protesters marched through West Berlin's downtown area, wearing gas masks . . . in a peaceful demonstration. . . . No arrests were reported.

13 The crowd in Hamburg was estimated by police at 6,000.

Parade in London

14 Thousands of British protesters paraded through London yesterday, led by Glenys Kinnock, wife of Labor Party leader Neil Kinnock. They observed a minute of silence as a siren sounded, symbolizing a nuclear warning.

15 Organizers estimated the crowd at just over 100,000, but Scotland Yard, the police headquarters, put the number at 48,000. Police described the march as peaceful and said there were only three arrests, all for drunkenness. . . .

Vocabulary

¶1 **don** to put on (clothes)
blockade to block (especially by the army/navy) so that people can not move to and from a place [*also a noun*]
plant a factory

¶2 **baton** a rod like a small club
club-wielding holding clubs

¶3 **engulf** to destroy by swallowing up
reactor [here] a large machine that produces nuclear power

¶4 **break away from** to separate and go in a different direction from
firecracker a small explosive used (in celebrations) to make a noise

¶5 **decline to** to refuse to
confirm to support, to give proof of

¶6 **drew** [here] attracted

¶7 **poll** the results of questioning many people in an organized way
indicate to show

¶9 **target** to aim at, to make into a target (a mark to shoot at)

¶11 **stage rallies** to organize large, public meetings

¶14 **parade** [*noun and verb*] a/to march in a ceremony
siren a machine that makes a loud sound as a warning

¶15 **drunkenness** the state of being drunk (having had too many alcoholic drinks)

Questions

1. In what countries were there demonstrations?

2. What were the demonstrations about?

3. Which demonstrations caused unrest? What words give that information?

4. Compare the results of these protests.

   a. For each country, find the number of protesters, arrests, and injuries. Which seems to have been the most violent protest?

   b. Who is the source of each statistic given? Are sources important?

   c. *Extra Credit:* Write a summary comparing the different protests; then add your own thoughts about nuclear power. Include some of the Essential Vocabulary, such as: *anti-, civilian, clash, confrontation, defiant, protest, rally.*

5. Was your country affected by Chernobyl? How? or Why not?

6. Is the issue of nuclear power still in the news today? In what way? Can you read about it in your local or metropolitan newspaper?

The following headlines reported unrest in 1988 through 1991:

a. # Ethnic Clashes in Soviet Azerbaijan

b. ## Prague police beat protesters, crush rally

c. ### CHINESE STUDENTS DEFY MARTIAL LAW

d. ### Zulus, Political Rivals Clash over Natal Province

e. *Baker*: Attack on Iraq would be fast, massive*

f. ANTIWAR PROTESTS GROW IN CITIES AROUND THE WORLD

*U.S. Secretary of State James A. Baker III.

Questions

1. Circle the verbs in the headlines. (Which headline is a noun phrase?) Are the verbs in the active or passive voice? Discuss.

2. Write each headline as a sentence.

3. Analyze the headlines according to their content. Which of the five W (and an H) questions (who, what, when, where, why, how) are answered most often? Discuss your conclusions.

4. Have you been to any of the places named in the headlines above? When? Tell the class about your experiences there. *Extra Credit:* Discuss with a classmate (or write out) the location of each place of unrest. (If you are uncertain, ask your teacher for the name of the country involved and then consult an atlas.)

5. Find some headlines about unrest in a current newspaper. Discuss (in groups) the vocabulary and content of each one.

6.3 SUMMITS AND TALKS

Essential Vocabulary

The following 14 words are found in articles about talks and meetings. Each one is used in a typical sentence or headline. In the blanks write a synonym or phrase for the underlined word. How many can you write without using a dictionary? _____

1. **accord** Officials from East and West signed an <u>accord</u> to begin talks.

   _____

2. **agenda** The <u>agenda</u> for this first talk consists of just two topics.

   _____

3. **breakthrough** The talks ended without a <u>breakthrough</u>; the leaders refused to soften their positions.

   _____

4. **concession** He made too many <u>concessions</u> and left the meeting in a weaker position.

   _____

5. **issue** They could not even agree on which <u>issue</u> to discuss first.

   _____

6. **joint** The <u>joint</u> efforts of all seven members finally brought success.

   _____

7. **negotiate** The mood here is hopeful as the two leaders sit down to <u>negotiate</u> an agreement.

   _____

8. **pact** BOGOTA AND REBELS SIGN PEACE <u>PACT</u> _____

9. **seek** With good intentions they <u>sought</u> to reach an agreement but could not.

   _____

10. **settlement** They have made progress toward reaching a <u>settlement</u> of their differences.

    _____

11. **spokesman/spokesperson** Her <u>spokesman</u> presented her views to reporters.

    _____

12. **summit** CLINTON AND YELTSIN PLANNING <u>SUMMIT</u> "SOON" _____

13. **ties** Her <u>ties</u> to her homeland remain strong. _____

14. **truce** Tired of fighting, they agreed on a 14-day <u>truce</u>.

    _____

WEDNESDAY, JULY 17, 1991

Breakthrough not likely as Gorbachev arrives at summit

By Michael Kranish
GLOBE STAFF

1   LONDON – Amid US promises that he will not return to his economically ailing nation empty-handed, Soviet President Mikhail S. Gorbachev holds a historic meeting today with the leaders of the world's wealthiest democracies, [the Group of Seven].

2   But on two key issues, aid to the Soviet economy and strategic arms reduction, the Bush administration yesterday expressed doubt that major progress would be made.

3   President Bush's top aides yesterday rejected the idea of a $12 billion stabilization fund for the ruble, the virtually worthless Soviet currency. And Secretary of State James A. Baker 3d, at a news conference last night, sought to play down speculation that Bush and Gorbachev would reach agreement on the Strategic Arms Reduction Treaty....

4   The inability to resolve START creates an awkward background for today's long-anticipated presentation by Gorbachev of his economic reform plan. In addition to calling for a $12 billion Western contribution to a fund to stabilize the ruble, Gorbachev is expected to say that the Soviet Union intends to turn 80 percent of its defense plants to commercial use.

5   Bush's aides have made clear that they do not like what they have heard about Gorbachev's intention to request the $12 billion.

6   "This would not be a wise thing to do at this stage," the undersecretary of the Treasury, David Mulford, said at a news conference. He said that the United States would consider contributing to the fund only "much, much later," after the Soviets have put economic reforms into place.

7   The Bush administration is generally supported by Japan, Britain and Canada in this position, but the countries closer to the Soviet Union — Germany, France and Italy — are more inclined to give aid to the Soviet Union immediately. The nearby nations fear that without aid, massive numbers of poor emigres would move into their countries.

8   Baker seemed eager to dispel the idea that the US rebuff on the stabilization fund would mean that Gorbachev would fail to get anything out of his meeting here with the Group of Seven.

9   "He won't go home empty-handed," Baker said, noting that Gorbachev has benefited by being allowed to address the democratic leaders and that he will gain an associate membership in the International Monetary Fund for the Soviet Union.

10   Soviet officials also tried to play down the disagreement over the ruble stabilization fund. Soviet Foreign Ministry spokesman Vitaly Churkin said that Gorbachev's meeting here marks "the beginning of a historic process of integration of the Soviet economy in the world economy."

11   Indeed, all the summit participants have made clear that they do not want their meeting with Gorbachev to result in failure. The leaders generally support Gorbachev and want to help him politically even if they do not provide aid to his country immediately....

12   Gorbachev's arrival here has overshadowed the original purpose of the summit, which was to try to conclude a free-trade agreement. Although Bush had wanted to finalize that pact here, his efforts appear to have failed, largely because of Japanese objections.

13   As a result of that failure, the summit partners did not seem unhappy that Gorbachev's arrival has obscured the original agenda.

14   Gorbachev is scheduled to meet with the seven leaders as a group and will also have a private luncheon with Bush, after which Bush and Gorbachev are scheduled to have a joint news conference....

Reprinted courtesy of The Boston Globe.

Note: This article appeared near the end of a summit of the Group of Seven, after several days of reports on the Group's meetings. For that reason the reporter assumes that the readers are somewhat familiar with the participants and happenings at the summit; he does not explain in the lead or in detail in the body of the article the "who" and "where" of it.

Vocabulary

Head   **likely**   probable
¶1   **amid**   with (literally: in the mid̲dle of)
     ailing   not healthy
¶2   **aid to**   help for
     strategic arms   long-range weapons, such as missiles, that can reach enemy
         land
¶3   **aide**   assistant
     stabilization fund   [here] sum of money for the purpose of making the ruble
         stable/firm
     virtually   almost completely
     currency   money (of a country)
     news conference   meeting with reporters
     play down   to make something seem unimportant
     speculation   guessing/guesses/thoughts without firm supporting facts
     treaty   formal agreement between countries
¶4   **resolve**   to settle
     awkward   [here] inelegant/difficult, almost embarrassing
     long-anticiapted   expected for a long time
     plant   [here] factory
¶7   **are inclined to**   favor, lean toward
     massive   huge (and powerful)
     emigres   emigrants, people leaving their country to live elsewhere
¶8   **dispel**   to make something disappear, to scatter
     rebuff   refusal, an answer of "No"
¶9   **monetary**   adjective form of *money*
¶12   **overshadow**   to be more important than
¶13   **obscure** *[verb]*   to make obscure/unclear, to hide

Questions

1. a. Who participated in the summit?

    b. Is Gorbachev a member of the Group of Seven?

2. Which of the following are *not* major issues of discussion with Gorbachev: money, weapons, emigration, free trade?

3. List the countries (and their reasons) that are in favor of giving aid to the Soviets immediately, and those against it.

4. According to the article, which original issue of the summit could not be agreed upon? Why not?

5. Is there any news about the economies of the former Soviet republics in your current newspaper?

JULY 4, 1990

Prime ministers of two Koreas agree to meet

Talks could start as early as August; some observers are still skeptical

By John Gittelsohn
SPECIAL TO THE GLOBE

1 PANMUNJOM, Korea – North and South Korea yesterday announced that the prime ministers of the two countries will meet, signaling a possible break in tensions in one of the world's last Cold War fronts.

2 The meeting, which could take place in Seoul as early as next month, would be the highest level contacts between communist North Korea and capitalist South Korea since the war 40 years ago. Nearly 2 million soldiers, including 43,000 Americans, still face each other across the demilitarized zone that cuts across the waist of the peninsula.

3 Negotiators from both sides hailed the tentative agreement as a major breakthrough in relations. But many analysts remain skeptical that the prime ministers will even meet, noting that nothing has been put on paper and that previous negotiations have collapsed over minor details.

4 "The day the two prime ministers actually sit down and talk is the day I'll be impressed," said a West European diplomat in Seoul.

5 Still, the talks at this border truce village that led to the agreement were remarkable for their conviviality and absence of acrimony. About a third of the meeting time was spent discussing the heavy monsoon rains that have drenched both Koreas in recent weeks.

6 "This is a milestone on the road to reunification of Korea," said Paik Nam Jun, North Korea's chief delegate to the preliminary talks.

7 North and South Koreans agreed that changing world conditions, particularly the unification of Germany, have made the time ripe for easing tensions here. President Roh Tae Woo's summit with the Soviet president, Mikhail Gorbachev, in San Francisco last month also appears to have played a key role, giving South Korea more confidence and leaving North Korea worried that it may be losing important allies.

8 South Korean officials claimed credit for the breakthrough after conceding on the North's demand that military issues top the agenda. The South had previously demanded that the prime ministers focus on economic and humanitarian topics as confidence-building measures between the two nations.

9 North Korea has long called for the withdrawal of 43,000 US troops and their nuclear weapons from the South. With military issues at the top of the agenda, some analysts have said North Korea could sabotage the prime ministerial meeting by pressing for demands unacceptable to the South.

10 But officials in Seoul say the risks are worth taking. They are confident of benefiting from the symbolism of the talks, just as South Korea profited from Roh's meeting with Gorbachev. The mere establishment of high-level contacts, they say, would lay the groundwork for future talks.

11 Despite changes sweeping through Eastern Europe and the Soviet Union this year, relations between the two Koreas have remained frozen in a Cold War standoff. All unauthorized mail, phone calls and personal exchanges between citizens in the two Koreas are strictly forbidden. In the last year, North–South Red Cross talks on reuniting divided families, sports talks on fielding a joint team to this summer's Asia Games in Beijing and discussions to arrange an inter-Korean parliamentary meeting have failed. Prior to yesterday's talks, North Korea had suspended meetings with the South for five months to protest joint US–South Korean military maneuvers.

12 South Korean officials see themselves negotiating from a position of strength. North Korea's economy is in ruins. The communist country finds itself increasingly isolated diplomatically as its allies seek to broaden trade ties with Seoul. . . .

13 Negotiations on the prime ministerial meeting will resume Friday with a July 26 deadline to sign a written statement covering travel arrangements and a specific agenda for the talks. Under an agreement reached during previous discussions between the two sides, the prime ministers would meet within a month of the signing of the agreement.

14 Prime Minister Kang Young Hoon of South Korea is his nation's No. 2 official. Prime Minister Yon Hyung Muk is ranked fourth in North Korea's government hierarchy. North Korea has refused to respond to the South's repeated calls for a summit between Presidents Roh and Kim.

Vocabulary

Subhead **skeptical**   not believing everything

¶1   **tension**   anxious feelings

¶2   **peninsula**   a thin piece of land that is surrounded on three sides by water

¶3   **hail** *[verb]*   [here] to recognize (gladly)

   tentative   not definite/certain, only suggested

   collapse   to break down, to fall apart

¶5   **conviviality**   friendliness

   acrimony   bitter words, blaming

   drench   to make completely wet

¶7   **ease** *[verb]*   to do something gently/carefully

¶8   **credit**   [here] praise for something achieved

   concede   to yield or agree to someone's conditions or arguments [verb form of *concession*]

   top *[verb]*   to be at the top; [here] to have first priority

   measure   action

¶9   **call for**   to demand, to request strongly

   withdrawal   removal, taking away

   sabotage   to destroy or damage secretly

   press for   to demand, to continue to ask for

¶10   **mere**   [here] simple

¶11   **standoff**   stalemate; both participants equal and not moving [informal]

   prior to   before

   suspend   to postpone or to stop for a period of time

¶13   **deadline**   date by which something must be done/accomplished

Questions

1. Is this article about a summit meeting that has just taken place, will take place, or might take place? Explain your answer.

2. What three events influenced leaders of the two Koreas to get together?

3. Name two topics that the delegates discussed.

4. What issue are the two prime ministers going to talk about?

5. What else might they discuss?

6. What is the status of contacts between the two Koreas now? Is there any news about them in your current newspaper?

FEBRUARY 24, 1988

Spain Cites Progress In Talks With ETA

By Sarah Nicholson
Special to the Herald Tribune

1 MADRID – The Spanish government says it remains hopeful that talks in Algiers with the Basque separatist group ETA could eventually lead to a truce with the guerrillas.

2 A state security press spokesman, Agustin Valladolid, said the talks had made progress toward a settlement to end nearly 21 years of separatist violence that has taken more than 600 lives.

3 "It will not happen overnight, and there will be many phases," he said. "But on a scale of 0 to 10, I believe we have now advanced to four."

4 The Algiers talks are widely viewed as the most determined effort to date by the government of Prime Minister Felipe González to reach an agreement with ETA, a Basque acronym for Basque Homeland and Liberty. Security preparations for 1992, when Spain hosts the Summer Olympics in Barcelona and a World's Fair in Seville, have given added urgency to ending the separatist threat.

5 Algeria, a onetime training base for Basque guerrillas, announced a year ago that it no longer considered the group a national liberation movement. It reportedly ordered an ETA leader, Eugenio Etxeveste, who had been living in exile in Algeria, to sit down to talks or to leave the country.

6 The Madrid government stresses that the Algiers talks are aimed solely at setting up what it calls a "framework of dialogue" and involves no political concessions.

7 "No government can negotiate politically with terrorists," Mr. Valladolid said.

8 In recent weeks, even conservative members of the legislature have given the government a vote of confidence in the talks, explicitly accepting that an accord could produce a pardon for most of the 520 Basques serving terms for terrorist activities.

Vocabulary

Head **cite** to mention; also, to quote

¶1 **separatist** (person) wanting to separate from the main government

eventually after a (long) time, sometime in the future

guerrillas group of fighters (not regular army) that attacks suddenly

¶2 **take lives** to kill, leave dead (humans)

¶4 **determined** firm

effort *[noun]* attempt, try

to date until now

acronym short name made from initials of words in the long name

urgency importance

¶5 **onetime** at one time, once, former

in exile away from his own country for political reasons

¶6 **aim solely at** to have as a limited goal, direct only toward

framework (just a) structure

¶8 **legislature** law-making body of the government

explicitly clearly expressed

serving terms [here] in prison as punishment for crimes

Reading for Information

1. Who or what is ETA? Where did you find the answer?

2. Have the talks ended?

3. What does the Spanish government want?

4. What does ETA want?

5. Which of the following might be a result of a truce?
   a. more deaths
   b. Basques get out of prison
   c. violence at the Olympics

6. Did you attend the last Summer Olympics or watch them on TV? What do you remember?

7. Have you ever been to a World's Fair? If so, what did you see and do there?

Essential Vocabulary

The following 12 sentences use words that are essential for the understanding of articles on world trade and international finances. You will find them in general articles in any metropolitan or national newspaper. Match each essential word (in boldface) with the correct definition on the right. Write the corresponding letter in the blank to the left of each number.

_____ 1. President Bush **banned** the sale of some foreign guns, but American guns can still be sold.

_____ 2. Her **concern** is for our safety.

_____ 3. Many **consumers** buy whatever is the cheapest.

_____ 4. My **debt** to Tom is not large; I borrowed only $30.00 from him.

_____ 5. The government **deficit** this year adds to the national debt next year.

_____ 6. **Domestic** wines are good, but European wines are more popular.

_____ 7. **Global** talks are needed to discuss world hunger.

_____ 8. Countries have been accused of **protectionism** when they do not open their markets to imports.

_____ 9. The U.S.A. established economic **sanctions** against Cuba, stopping all trade with that country.

_____ 10. Committee members held a party with the **surplus** in the account.

_____ 11. The **tariff** on imported shoes makes them more expensive.

_____ 12. Foreign **trade** has made many more products available in every land.

a. people who buy and use (_consume_) things
b. the result of spending more money than is taken in
c. worry [noun]
d. to forbid/prohibit/stop officially [also a noun: _ban_]
e. action(s) taken by a government against a country that has broken a rule or law
f. commerce, buying and selling [also a verb]
g. [here] from one's own country, not foreign
h. [here] extra money left over after debts have been paid
i. what is owed (has been borrowed) and must be repaid
j. a tax on imported products
k. the act of protecting a domestic industry (unfairly) by restricting imports
l. of or concerning the whole world/_globe_/planet

JANUARY 3, 1989

Asians Seek Regional Solution

By Michael Richardson
International Herald Tribune

1 SINGAPORE – Asian concern at what is seen as protectionist inclinations in the United States and Europe is leading Western Pacific nations to intensify a search for new regional economic and political cooperation.

2 Officials and analysts in the area say that while most of these proposals are intended to strengthen multilateral negotiations on free trade, they could also serve as alternative arrangements if the global talks fail.

3 The most recent round of multilateral negotiations, in Montreal last month under the auspices of GATT, the General Agreement on Tariffs and Trade, failed to make progress because of a deadlock between the United States and Europe over farm trade.

4 At Tokyo's suggestion, officials from Australia and Japan recently began a study of the U.S.–Canadian free trade agreement and the unified European market planned by the end

Protectionism / Free Trade

One of an occasional series

of 1992. The free trade agreement, which took effect Sunday, will phase out almost all tariffs between the two countries over the next 10 years.

5 Both arrangements are regarded as potentially exclusive by Asian and Australian officials, and many officials have expressed concern about them. The Tokyo–Canberra study will consider the effect on international trade and the economic health of the Western Pacific, officials said.

6 Singapore's prime minister, Lee Kuan Yew, said in November, "It is in the interest of Asia and Australasia to increase our economic relations if for no other reason than to be in a better bargaining position against the Europeans and the Americans."

7 The same month, economic ministers of ASEAN, the Association of South East Asian Nations — Brunei, Indonesia, Malaysia, Philippines, Singapore and Thailand — agreed that South Korea should hold regular talks with ASEAN as a "sectoral partner."

8 On a visit to Indonesia, South Korea's foreign minister, Kwang Soo Choi, asserted that East Asia was "too much dependent on the industrialized countries."

9 Mr. Kwang's deputy, Hong Soon Yong, said it was "time to think about the possibility of getting the region organized into a community."

10 Japan and the newly industrialized countries of East Asia — South Korea, Taiwan, Hong Kong and Singapore — accounted for 15 percent of world gross national product in 1987 and 17 percent of global trade.

11 But officials said that East Asia's economic growth continued to rely heavily on export sales to the United States and the European Community.

12 Prime Minister Lee noted that, until recently, Japan, South Korea, Taiwan, Hong Kong and Singapore were able to export relatively freely to the United States and Europe.

13 "Today, both the U.S. and European markets are less open," he said. "The trends are towards more restrictions."

14 There are no alternative markets as large as the United States and the EC, Mr. Lee said, so economic growth in East Asia will slow.

15 Singapore officials said last week that they expected Japan's economy to expand by 4.5 percent in 1989 compared with 5.75 percent this year.

Vocabulary

¶1   **inclinations** *[noun]*   liking
            intensify   to make more intense/stronger
            search *[noun]*   look(ing) for; also a verb: to *search*

¶2   **proposal**   a plan
            multilateral   many-sided; [here] international
            serve as   be (useful as)

¶3   **under the auspices of**   with the help/support of
            deadlock   stalemate, situation in which no agreement can be reached

¶4   **phase out**   to remove gradually

¶5   **regarded as**   viewed as, seen to be, considered
            potentially   possibly in the future
            exclusive   excluding/leaving out some people or countries

¶6   **bargaining position**   position of strength from which one can bargain, do
                   business/trade

¶7   **sectoral**   of or from a sector/district [unusual]

¶9   **deputy**   person second in rank, representative

¶10   **accounted for** ~ were responsible for
            gross national product (GNP)   total of all products and services of a
                   nation/country

¶11   **rely on**   depend on
            heavily   mostly, to a great extent

Questions

1. *Skim* (read quickly, scan) the article to identify the following people. Which paragraphs contain that information?

   a. Lee Kuan Yew: (¶____) _____

   b. Kwang Soo Choi: (¶____) _____

   c. Hong Soon Yong: (¶____) _____

   d. Were all the names explained in an *appositive* phrase (see Sec. 4.4, p. 51)?

2. Skim the article again to find the full names for these abbreviations:

   a. GATT: (¶____) _____

   b. ASEAN: (¶____) _____

   c. EC: (¶____) _____

   d. Were they explained with appositives?

3. Explain the headline. "Solution" means that there is a problem. *What* is the problem that the Asians want to solve? What may be their solution?

4. a. There are many countries named in this article, but only a few cities. What is meant by the "Tokyo–Canberra study" in ¶5?

   b. How many of the countries have you visited?

JANUARY 19, 1989

Trade gap surges 21% in November

By Mark Memmott
USA TODAY

1 The nation's trade deficit ballooned to $12.5 billion in November, up 21% from October.

2 The surprisingly high figure didn't disturb Wall Street. But economists say the report confirms that the nation's monthly gap between imports and exports has stopped shrinking.

3 "We've got a very sticky trade imbalance and it's not coming off," says Wayne Gantt, economist at SunTrust Banks in Atlanta.

4 The deficit widened from October's $10.3 billion because:

5 ▶ Imports grew by 4.2% from October, to their second-highest total ever: $39.7 billion. Leading the way were imports of computers and other capital goods, which rose $1.1 billion.

6 ▶ Exports dropped 2.2%, to $27.2 billion. Even though November was the fifth-best month on record, the decline in exports "is very disturbing," says Robert Brusca, chief economist at Nikko Securities.

7 His concern is that demand for our exports may be weakening. That would be the opposite of what the Federal Reserve has been trying to achieve in raising interest rates since summer. The Fed wants domestic demand to drop, and exports to stay strong.

8 Since July, when the deficit slipped to a four-year low of $9.5 billion,

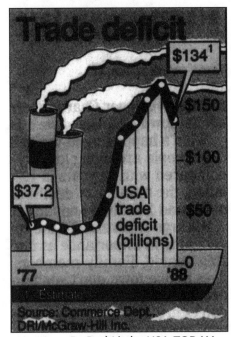

Trade deficit

$134[1]

$37.2

USA trade deficit (billions)

$150
$100
$50
0

'77   '88

[1] Estimate

Source: Commerce Dept., DRI/McGraw-Hill Inc.

By Rod Little, USA TODAY

monthly gaps have averaged $11.5 billion.

9 Also Wednesday: Japan said its global trade surplus jumped to $9.65 billion in December, vs. $6.56 billion in November.

10 With the U.S. alone, Japan's 1988 surplus totaled $47.6 billion, down from $52.1 billion in 1987. But the rise in the December global surplus doesn't bode well for the U.S. trade report for December.

Vocabulary

Head **gap**   an empty space between two things; [here] between imports and exports

      surge   to move strongly forward; [here] to move strongly upward

¶1   **balloon** *[verb]*   to become bigger (a balloon expands as it is blown up)

      up 21% from   21% higher than

¶2   **disturb**   to bother or to make nervous

      Wall Street   the stock market or financial district of New York City

      confirm   to prove, give (additional) evidence

      shrinking   becoming smaller

¶3   **sticky** ´ [here] difficult [informal]

      coming off   showing success [informal]

¶5   **capital goods** *[plural noun]*   equipment, machines, etc., used in the production of goods/products

¶6   **securities** *[plural noun]*   stocks and bonds (etc.)

¶7   **Federal Reserve/the Fed**   the central bank of the United States

¶8   **slip**   to fall (accidentally)

      low *[noun]*   low point/amount

¶10 **bode well**   to be a good sign (for future developments)

Questions

1. Explain the headline.

2. a. According to the article, how often are trade figures reported?

   b. In what month can you read about the report for December?

3. Does the article report good news or bad news for U.S. businesses?
   What words helped you decide? _____

   _____

4. Find all the verbs that represent an upward/bigger or downward/smaller movement and list them here:

   ↑ _____
   ↓ _____

   You should find 11 verbs in all.
   Note: These same verbs can also be used to describe movements of interest rates, wages, prices, etc., in the Business Section.

5. Compare these figures to those in a current paper. Is the trend good—for the U.S.A.? for your country?

JANUARY 2, 1989

US hits EC with trade sanctions

By Nelson Graves
Reuters

1   WASHINGTON – Without fanfare, the United States yesterday slapped $100 million in trade sanctions against the European Community in retaliation for an EC ban on imports of hormone-treated American meat.

2   The move, effective with the stroke of the New Year, imposes 100 percent duties on seven types of specialty products imported from the European Community.

3   The hit list, valued at $100 million a year, was Washington's retaliation to the EC's decision to ban all imports of meat from animals treated with growth hormones.

4   European consumers say the hormones, legal in the United States, could be harmful, while the US administration claims there is no scientific evidence of danger.

5   To punish the EC for its ban, the United States doubled the prices of the specialty products.

6   Included on the list are canned tomatoes and tomato sauce (Italy, Spain), wine coolers and wine beverages (Italy), instant coffee (West Germany, Netherlands), some fruit juices (West Germany, Netherlands), pet food (West Germany, Britain), boned beef (Denmark) and high-quality preserved pork (West Germany).

7   As usual in a trade war, producers and consumers in the opposing countries share the cost of the reprisals.

8   Producers in Italy and West Germany, singled out because they have strongly supported the ban, will bear the brunt — two-thirds — of the sanctions.

9   Virtually untouched will be France, Belgium and Portugal.

10   The US move will hurt America's own specialty shops and importers. . . .

11   Eugenio Pozzolini, one of the owners of Dean and Deluca Imports Inc. of New York, said his firm would lose $2 million in sales of Pumate sun-dried tomatoes, which he called a "hot hit" among wealthy customers.

12   "This is not a tariff, it's a ban," said Pozzolini. "Twenty-five percent of my business is gone." . . .

13   "This is going to hit every single pizza parlor in the US," said Pozzolini. "These are everyday people."

14   The new duty increases will price many of the EC products out of the US market, giving domestic producers a chance to expand sales.

15   "People aren't going to stop buying tomatoes. It's too big an item," . . . said Louis Balducci, general manager of Balducci's, a specialty food store in New York. . . . "This is going to force us to look for another, domestic tomato."

16   Pozzolini said the new duties on tomatoes would help Israel and Brazil, but also California growers, who he said now would be able to "dictate the price they want."

Vocabulary

Head **hit** [here] to attack; also, to strike (with a hand); used in headlines because it is short

¶1   **fanfare** [here] a lot of ceremony or noise

       slap (a thing) against (someone) to hit someone with something

       retaliation answering a bad deed with a (different) bad deed

       hormone-treated injected or fed with hormones (biological substances that
            produce change [here: greater growth and weight])

¶2   **the stroke of** the beginning of [from: *at the stroke* (sound) of the clock]

       impose to establish

       duty [here] a tax on imports

       specialty fine *[adjective]* or luxury *[noun]*

¶3   **hit list** list of things (or people) to be attacked

¶4   **administration** government (officials)

       claim to argue or state as a fact

¶6   **wine cooler** a drink made from wine and fruit juices

       preserved [here] canned, kept from spoiling by processing

¶7   **reprisal** act of retaliation

¶8   **single out** to choose from a group for special treatment

       bear the brunt to accept or suffer most

¶9   **virtually** almost/very nearly completely

¶11   **hot hit** popular favorite, best-selling success [informal] (NOT the same "hit" as in the headline)

¶13   **pizza parlor** (small) pizza restaurant

¶14   **price out of** to make something too expensive for

¶15   **item** one thing in a list (such as a shopping list)

Reading for Information

1. Explain the headline. What does "EC" stand for?

2. Which happened first? a. The U.S.A. imposed duties on specialties.

                         b. The EC banned hormone-treated meat.

3. Does the reporter tell us: a. how much the U.S. action will cost the EC?

                         b. how much the EC ban will cost U.S. firms?

4. Why are most of the foods on the hit list from West Germany and Italy?

Questions for Discussion

1. The sanctions apply to specialty foods (see ¶6 and ¶11).

   a. Which of the listed foods do you enjoy?

   b. Have you ever tried sun-dried tomatoes? How much do they cost?

   c. Why did Mr. Pozzolini say the sanctions would "hit every . . . pizza parlor"?

2. The EC banned the importation of hormone-treated meat from the U.S.A.

   a. Do you know whether the meat you eat is hormone-treated or not? Is it important to you?

   b. Is this issue still in the news today?

MARCH 6, 1989

Sting on the jungle

■ British rock star *Sting*, who has said he will lead a campaign to preserve the Amazon rain forest, says the destruction of the jungle is tied to Brazil's $121-billion foreign debt. The Brazilian government contends it must develop the Amazon to pay off its huge debt. But development equals environmental destruction, critics say. "The truth is that the world is in debt to Brazil, not the contrary," Sting said in an interview in the Jornal do Brasil newspaper. "The United States and Europe produce more dollars and Brazil produces more air. It's a question of how you value things. I personally value air more."

Reprinted courtesy of The Boston Globe.

Vocabulary

Head **on**   [here] talks about, gives his opinion *on*

rock star   popular singer of rock music

campaign   a series of activities directed toward a goal

preserve   to protect/keep (the forest) as it is

tied to   related to

contend   to state firmly

develop *[land]*   to prepare it for human activities/use

pay off   to pay the whole debt

environmental   of the environment; [here] of our natural surroundings

Amazon River

SOUTH
AMERICA

Questions

1. This article describes two opposing opinions about the development of the Amazon rain forests. Whose opinions are given? And what are they?

   a. _Sting_____ says that _____.

   b. _____ says that _____.

2. What do you think of the concluding quotation by Sting (the last three sentences of the article)?

3. Discuss with your classmates where you might find current articles on:

   a. third world debt

   b. the Amazon rain forest

   c. life in Brazil

   d. rock stars

   Then scan an English-language newspaper to see if you can find any articles on these topics.

You can find more articles on the environment in Section 7.5.

National News

Introduction: Elections, American-Style

Most of the issues that are presented in the national news section of an American newspaper can also be found to some extent in the international section. For example, crimes, drug problems, and scientific progress occur all over the world; they are not topics specific to the United States. There is one area, however, that requires special knowledge to understand: American elections. The following background on elections in the United States can help you understand the articles in this book and in your current newspapers.

Presidential Elections

National Election Day is always the first Tuesday after the first Monday in November. There may be several names or questions on the ballot (voting paper) that each voter marks, but the most important names are those of the candidates for the presidency.

The road to the presidency is long (see the political cartoon on p. 112). Candidates may begin to campaign unofficially as early as 1½ to 2 years before the election takes place. They usually announce officially that they are running for President at least a year before that November Tuesday. The following numbered paragraphs describe the four main stages of a campaign. Campaigns for other offices and at lower levels go through a similar but shorter process.

1. Between February and June of the election year, each political party* has to decide on a candidate to represent it. There may be as many as seven or eight people who would like to be that candidate. So the parties hold ***primary elections*** in the states; they are called *primaries* or

---

*Since 1854 the elected President has been from either the Democratic or the Republican party. Third or fourth political parties have always been very small and short-lived. In 1992 Ross Perot, a billionaire businessman, ran for President without any official party. Although he was unsuccessful, he attracted 19% of the popular vote and created real interest in the election process.

caucuses, depending on the exact method used. In most states, voters who are registered as a member of a party may select their choice for the presidential candidate of that party. In other words, registered Democrats vote for one of the several candidates who are Democrats; registered Republicans choose a Republican.

The first state to hold such a primary vote is Iowa (it has the caucus system); the second is New Hampshire. The winners of those primaries, who get special attention from the media, then try to convince the voters of other states to join their supporters. Their opponents try to win whatever primary is next. By early summer there are only a few men left to compete, as those who lost one or more primaries gradually give up. Up through 1993 there have been no women who have made it to this point.

Sample Article 7.1-1 describes a local primary election; in this case it is a primary to decide on a candidate for Mayor of Chicago. Sample Article 7.1-3 describes the primaries for a Florida Representative to Congress.

2. After each state party has chosen its preferred candidate, the **national conventions** are held. The Democratic and Republican national conventions take place separately, in July or August. Each state sends a certain number of party delegates, who then take the final vote on the official candidate for that party. In recent elections, the choice has been clear, because one candidate has already won a majority of primaries, and thus delegates; so the conventions have not been exciting news. The winning candidate is officially nominated to run for the presidency; he becomes the nominee.

The nominee then chooses a vice-presidential running mate (person to campaign with him). The convention votes on his suggestion. Sometimes the selection of the running mate is really news, such as when Walter Mondale chose the first woman candidate, Geraldine Ferraro, in 1984, or when George Bush surprised most people by choosing the relatively unknown junior Senator, Dan Quayle. Running mates are usually picked because they come from another part of the country than the nominee and/or they attract a different kind of voter. For example, Mondale is from the Midwest, Ferraro from the populous state of New York; Bush is from Texas, and Quayle, from Indiana, is a generation younger. Bill Clinton did not follow the trend in 1992 when he chose Al Gore, a man of similar age from a neighboring state, to be his vice-president.

3. In August or September, the competition between the parties really begins. The members of each party generally unite behind their candidate, although some may not be sure of their vote until the last day. Many voters, however, are not registered members of any party, and much of the candidates' efforts are directed toward attracting these votes. The two nominees spend millions of dollars, travel throughout the country, and try to appear in the media as often and as favorably as possible. They attack the platform (plans and ideas) of the other party; and sometimes the parties also participate in verbal "mud-throwing" when they spread negative information about the opposing candidate's personal life. Usually there are one or more nationally televised debates between the candidates. There are many paid advertisements for—or against—one nominee or the other, too.

The conclusion of the campaign is **Election Day** in November. Unfortunately, not many more than one-half of the adults in the U.S.A. actually vote.

Vocabulary

caucus   a meeting to choose a party's candidate (like a primary)

joint   together

convention   big meeting with members from across the U.S.A.

flier   pamphlet, or advertisement on one or more sheets of paper

square one   the beginning [literally: in a board game like "Monopoly" the first square to move onto]

(See also the Essential Vocabulary in Section 7.1.)

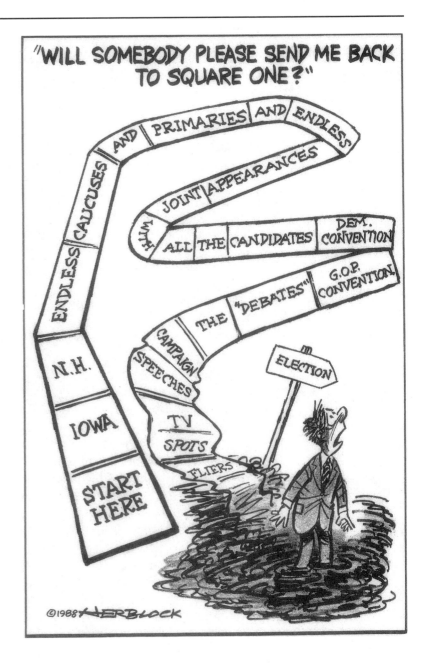

Cartoon copyright 1988 by HERBLOCK in the Washington Post.

4. The United States does not have a true "one-man-one-vote" system. Instead, according to the Constitution, the president actually must be chosen by the **Electoral College**. (The word "College" here has nothing to do with studies or university.) It is a group of electors from all states and the District of Columbia (Washington, D.C., the capital), who vote, in December, as the citizens of their state did in November. In all the states except Maine, the chosen nominee in each state gets all of the elector's votes for that state. The number of electors from each state, like the Representatives in Congress, is determined by population. But the population of a district can vary from under 450,000 to about 750,000; so not all districts are equally well represented in the Electoral College. In close elections it is possible for a candidate to receive the majority of popular votes but lose in the Electoral College. This has happened three times in American history; the last president to win election without a majority of popular votes was Benjamin Harrison in 1888.

Sample Article 7.1-2 mentions the importance of the electoral votes of the large state of California (¶2).

The new President takes office on January 20 after the vote of the Electoral College. His term is for four years, and he may serve two terms if he can get re-elected four years later.

State and Local Elections

In addition to the presidential and vice-presidential nominees, some other names or some questions may appear on the ballots. Voters may be asked to:

- choose a Senator,

- choose a Representative,

- choose candidates for state or local offices, or

- vote for or against a referendum.

Two *Senators* are elected per state in the U.S.A., so there are 100 members in the Senate. The Senate is part of Congress, the legislative (law-making) branch of the national government. Each Senator is elected for a 6-year term; every two years one-third of them are up for re-election. (The two Senators of one state are never both up for re-election in the same year.) Because their terms in office are relatively long, they enjoy relative security and prestige. In addition to making laws, they have the power to ratify (agree to) international treaties that the President has set up, and they have the responsibility of approving, or not, the President's choices of Cabinet members, ambassadors, and federal judges.

Representatives are elected to Congress for only two years. The reason for their short term is to keep them in close touch with the wishes of the constituents (the people they represent) in their district. There are 435 districts—and Representatives—in the country. The size of each district is based on population, so all states do not have the same number

of Representatives. These elected officials serve in the House of Representatives, often called "the House," the second part of Congress. In addition to making laws, they have the important function of approving, or not, the federal budget (financial plan). See Sample Article 7.1-3 for an article about a special primary election for a Florida Representative.

The Senators and Representatives in Congress make up the legislative branch of the national government. They represent the people of their states when decisions about national policies are made.

At the state government level, there is also a legislative branch, to which state senators and representatives are elected. These law-makers represent the people from all parts (districts) of their state. They meet in the state capital along with the executive branch, which is headed by a governor. The voting for state government officials usually takes place on Election Day in November with the national elections.

Elections for city, town, or county officials are held regularly as well, but not necessarily in the month of November. Sample Article 7.1-1 describes the primary in the election of the mayor, the head of the city government, in Chicago.

Also on the ballot may be some questions called *referenda*, or propositions or initiatives, on local or state issues. These are questions that the voting public may decide directly, not through elected representatives. There are several ways for a referendum question to get on a ballot; it is usually a long process. And there are several reasons why such questions go directly to the people. For example, a group of people or organizations may disagree with a law that has been passed by a local or state government; they may force the government to let the citizens decide the issue directly. In recent years this has been the case in some states where many residents were unhappy with the amount of state or local (real-estate) taxes they had to pay. Through a referendum question, the majority of citizens forced the government to limit taxes; government growth and services were then also limited. Another cause for a referendum may be that law-makers want to know the opinions of the people before they debate a new law or vote on a budget. Referenda, and local elections, can occur at any time of the year.

Essential Vocabulary and Sample Articles

Essential Vocabulary

A. The following 15 words are essential for the understanding of articles about elections in the U.S.A. Many of these words are explained or used in the Introduction to Chapter 7, which you should read before doing this exercise. Match each word with the correct definition on the right.

_____ 1. **base** [*noun*]

_____ 2. **campaign**

_____ 3. **candidate**

_____ 4. **Dems**

_____ 5. **GOP**

_____ 6. **incumbent**

_____ 7. **lead**

_____ 8. **lean (toward)**

_____ 9. **nomination**

_____ 10. **poll**

_____ 11. **polls**

_____ 12. **primary**

_____ 13. **run**

_____ 14. **turnout**

_____ 15. **(TV) spot**

a. Democrats [short word for headlines]
b. (to be in) the front/winning position
c. (person) holding a position/office currently
d. place(s) to vote
e. a person who wants to be elected
f. center of support [here: supporting voters]
g. a survey, the results of questioning many people in an organized way
h. an advertisement on TV
i. Grand Old Party, nickname for Republicans
j. (the act of) being nominated/named as the official candidate for election
k. an election by members of a political party to choose the candidate of that party
l. an organized set of actions presenting a candidate for election
m. to compete in a race/election/contest
n. the number of people who attend an event
o. [here] to favor

B. Now fill in the blanks below, using 11 of the Essential Vocabulary words.

Poll: Brown Leads in Primary

The latest _____ surprised political analysts yesterday, showing
        1

that Tiffany Brown has taken the _____ and is leaving her opponent,
        2

Herbert Walker, behind. Ms. Brown, who entered the _____
        3

just a month ago, has a substantial _____ of supporters in the state
        4

capital, where she has been politically active since 1982. She is

_____*ing* for public office for the first time.
    5

The survey found that many people saw and remembered the TV

advertisements featuring Ms. Brown and her work, while the _____
        6

about Mr. Walker did not leave much of an impression.

Another strength of Ms. Brown's _____ is the
        7

hundreds of students from local colleges who have volunteered to help.

"There is no doubt that our _____ should win the
        8

_____," said Lincoln Smith, leader of "Students for Tiffany
    9

Brown".

The poll also shows that both young and elderly voters favor Ms.

Brown, while mid-life men _____ toward Mr. Walker.
        10

The _____ , Jamie Smythe, is not seeking re-election.
    11

FEBRUARY 28, 1989

Campaign sniping ends as Chicagoans go to polls

By Curtis Wilkie
Globe Staff

More than 1 million Chicago residents will vote today, according to the Board of Election Commissioners. The size of the turnout will probably determine the outcome of the Democratic primary, which traditionally produces the mayor.

1 CHICAGO – Primary campaigning in the special election for mayor of Chicago ended yesterday in a cross-fire of sniping commercials between the Democratic candidates while there was almost silence among the Republicans.

2 More than 1 million Chicago residents will vote today, according to an estimate by the city's Board of Election Commissioners. The size of the turnout will probably determine the outcome of the Democratic primary, which traditionally produces the mayor.

3 Virtually all of the votes cast will be in the Democratic primary, but there is interest in the Republican primary. Edward R. Vrdolyak, a leading political figure here for more than a decade, is trying to win the GOP nomination as a write-in candidate.

4 The winners of the two primaries will meet in a general election April 4, when they will be joined by Timothy C. Evans, a popular black alderman running as an independent. The ultimate victor will serve the remaining two years of the late Mayor Harold Washington's term.

5 If turnout today is no higher than the predicted 68 percent of the city's registered voters, then Richard M. Daley is expected to win. Daley is state attorney for Cook County and a scion of the city's First Family for more than two decades.

6 But an outpouring of black votes for the acting mayor, Eugene Sawyer, who was appointed by the City Council to replace Washington in December 1987, could upset Daley's equations.

7 Many Jewish voters . . . were troubled by Sawyer's slowness last year in firing an aide, Steve Cokely, for making anti-Semitic remarks. Many are supporting Daley.

8 Sawyer's ads accuse "Big Spender" Daley, who raised more than $4 million from business interests, of permitting them to "buy access to City Hall." . . .

9 Daley countered with a spot questioning the propriety of a $30,000 "finder's fee" Sawyer accepted when he was an alderman from a . . . lawyer.

10 In the Republican race, where as few as 15,000 voters could participate, Vrdolyak is challenging Dr. Herbert Sohn, the candidate chosen by the party leadership.

Reprinted courtesy of The Boston Globe.

Vocabulary

Head **sniping**   nasty attacks/attacking

¶1 **mayor**   the head of a city government

cross-fire   an exchange of shooting [here: exchange of verbal attacks]

commercial [*noun*]   any advertisement on TV or radio

¶2 **resident**   a person living there [here: in Chicago]

Board of Election Commissioners   a group of officials who oversee elections

determine   to decide

outcome   result [what *comes out* of a situation]

¶3 **virtually all**   almost all, very nearly all

cast (a vote)   to vote, to complete a voting ballot

write-in candidate   a candidate whose name is not preprinted on the official ballot (voting paper); voters may *write* any name *in* a blank on the ballot

¶4   **alderman**   member of a city government

          ultimate   final

          the late (mayor)   the deceased (dead) (mayor), the (mayor) who recently died

¶5   **attorney**   lawyer

          county   unit of government including several towns

          scion   descendant [here: son]

          First Family   family of the leader of government

¶6   **outpouring**   coming/*pouring out [noun]* like a flood [unusual word]

          acting mayor   an appointed substitute mayor who serves until a mayor can be elected

          appointed   named, chosen (not elected by the public)

          upset *[verb]*   to disturb, cause to change

          equation   [here] calculated plans

¶7   **fire**   [here] to dismiss from a job

¶8   **ad**   advertisement

          "Big Spender"   person who likes to spend a lot of money

          raise (money)   to ask for and receive; to collect

          access   entrance

¶9   **propriety**   moral or ethical properness/rightness

Questions

1. What kind of *voting* is taking place?

    a. a local primary   b. a local general election

    c. a national general election   d. none

2. The lead paragraph gives essential information about the race but no names. Who is running? List the five candidates' names and parties:

    a. _____   b. _____

    c. _____   d. _____

    e. _____

3. What is especially interesting about Timothy Evans' role in this race?

4. Does the reporter give information on:

    a. Who is expected to win today?

    b. Who is expected to become mayor on April 4?

5. Does race play a part in this election?

6. The lead paragraph mentions "sniping commercials." Does the reader find out any details about those TV ads? If so, in what paragraph?

SEPTEMBER 22, 1988

Keys to the election
Candidates battle for 'four states' of California

By John Dillin
Staff writer of The Christian Science Monitor

Anaheim, Calif.

1 Democrats and Republicans agree: The key to the 1988 presidential election is California.

2 The Golden State will be absolutely essential for the Democrats, they say. Michael Dukakis can't put together enough electoral votes for a nationwide victory without it.

3 The state will be nearly as important for Republicans, though George Bush might squeak into office even without California, both sides concur.

4 From July to September, Vice-President Bush cut Mr. Dukakis's huge 16-percent lead in the state down to a contest that is now almost even. In one recent poll, Governor Dukakis led by one point, in another by four points.

5 Even so, Dukakis probably has the best shot at California by a Democrat since the 1960s — primarily with the help of northern California and a potentially large vote out of Los Angeles.

6 Dukakis will try to build new momentum here by attacking Bush on the environment and illegal drugs. . . .

7 Bill Lacy, the California coordinator for Bush, says September is being devoted to shoring up the vice-president's base among conservative and Republican voters, like those here in Orange County. In October, Bush will go after independent voters and swing Democrats, who will hold the balance of power, Mr. Lacy says.

8 On a recent campaign swing through the state, Lacy noted that strategists talk about "the four states of California." Bush has set goals in all four areas.

9 Pivotal to Bush hopes is the first "state," the Republican heartland, from Orange County down to San Diego. In that area, Bush needs to get a strong majority of votes. . . .

10 The other strong Republican area is the central valley — the fertile basin of California agriculture — where Bush also needs nearly 60 percent of the votes.

11 The other two "states" lean Democratic. But Bush is targeting both.

12 In northern California, dominated by the San Francisco Bay area, the vice-president must capture at least 40 to 42 percent of the vote.

13 In Los Angeles, where Democrats also hold sway, Bush needs about 45 percent of the vote to carry the state.

14 It will be touch and go for both campaigns, and the winner could be decided in the final few days before the Nov. 8 vote. . . .

15 Some insiders here say the race is so close that the winner could eventually be the candidate who can avoid making a serious mistake on the eve of the election.

Vocabulary

Head **key** something that explains; an important solution

¶2 **electoral votes** votes of the Electoral College

¶3 **squeak into** to be just barely successful (almost fail) [informal]
concur to agree

¶4 **even** *[adj.]* equal
point [here] percent (in a poll)

¶5 **best shot at** best chance (to win) in
primarily mainly
potentially possibly (in the future), undeveloped and not yet actual

¶6 **momentum** forward movement
environment [here] issues of the natural surroundings (pollution, etc.)

¶7　**devoted to**　spent in, set apart for

　　shore up　to strengthen/support

　　go after　[here] to try to win against

　　swing (voters)　(voters) who do not support one party steadily but may vote for a different party in each election

　　balance of power　position in which (political) power is evenly balanced on both sides

¶8　**(campaign) swing through**　quick (campaign) trip through

　　note [verb]　to remark/mention

　　strategist　person who plans (a war, campaign, etc.)

¶9　**pivotal**　like a *pivot* (a point from which something can turn in any direction)

　　heartland　an area that dominates the surrounding areas, which in turn support it economically [geopolitical term]

¶10　**fertile**　productive/fruitful

　　basin　in geography, a circular or oval-shaped valley

¶11　**target** [verb]　to aim at, make into a *target* (a mark to shoot at)

¶13　**hold sway**　to have power, rule, have influence

　　carry　[here] to win the support of

¶14　**touch and go**　uncertain (or dangerous) situation

¶15　**insider**　someone in a group with special knowledge about that group's field of interest

　　close　decided by a very small difference

　　eventually　in the future

　　eve of　evening before

Questions

1. What are the "four states" of California (¶8–13)? Toward which candidate is each one leaning?

2. Why is California so essential for each candidate? (The answer may not be explicitly stated in the article.)

3. Who is likely to carry the state, according to the article?

4. *Looking at Language:* The reporter uses some strong, colorful *verbs* and *verb phrases*, such as **squeak into** (¶3) and **shore up** (¶7). Can you find a verb phrase and three verbs that come from military vocabulary?

5. a. Who is the U.S. President now, and when was he elected?

　 b. When will the next national election take place? When do you expect people to announce their candidacy? (See the Introduction to Chapter 7.)

6. How is the top national leader in your native country chosen?

JUNE 20, 1989

Florida race fuels Cuban-American pride

By Chris Black
Globe Staff

1   MIAMI – After waiting 15 years for a chance to run for Congress, Democratic state Sen. Jack D. Gordon finally reached for the mantle of the late Rep. Claude Pepper last week. Just 48 hours later he withdrew from the race, saying he could not stomach a negative campaign that pits Jews, Cubans and blacks against one another.

2   His withdrawal sent an early signal that the race to succeed Pepper, who was Congress' oldest member and a champion of the nation's elderly, is certain to fuel high emotions as Miami's Cuban Americans get their first opportunity to send one of their own to Congress.

3   Gordon's rapid retreat came a day after Republican National Committee chairman Lee Atwater said his priority was to see the seat filled by a Cuban American. Gordon denounced Atwater's statement as "inflammatory, outrageous, irresponsible."

4   The fiery nature of politics in Florida's 18th congressional district reflects the intense anti-Castro sentiment of the large Cuban population in Greater Miami.

5   During Pepper's 27-year tenure, the district shifted from being overwhelmingly Jewish, liberal and a safe Democratic seat, to heavily Cuban, conservative and a prime Republican target.

6   In 1959, the year Castro came to power on the island 90 miles off the US coast, only 70,000 Cuban-born natives lived in the United States. Today, about one million live in southern Florida, where peer approval is more important than assimilation into American culture.

7   As a result, exile politics will be a powerful undercurrent in this congressional race.

8   "Ethnicity is an undeniable factor," said Lincoln Diaz-Balart, a 34-year-old Republican state representative who came to the United States from Cuba at the age of 4.

9   One survey shows Hispanics make up as much as 44 percent of the district's voters. Local pollster Robert L. Joffee said Cuban-American turnout is routinely 5 to 20 percent above non-Cuban voter turnout.

10   "The Cuban American knows how important the vote is," said Ileana Ros-Lehtinen, the probable Republican nominee. "We take it a lot more seriously than others because we lost our homeland."

11   This means the next member of Congress from the 18th district will likely be a Cuban American—the first ever elected to Congress. That prospect is expected to fire Latin pride, and with it Cuban-American voter turnout in the Aug. 29 special election. Overall turnout is expected to be low for a special election held during the steamiest month of the year.

12   "There is a natural inclination among all groups to lean towards someone they can identify with," said Simon Ferro, a Cuban American who became chairman of the Florida Democratic Party a week ago.

13   The likely Republican nominee, Ros-Lehtinen, a 36-year-old Havana-born state senator . . . has been a legislator since 1982. She faces token opposition from another native Cuban, businessman and former banana importer Carlos Perez whose extreme conservatism makes the conservative Ros-Lehtinen appear moderate by comparison, and David Fleischer, an insurance executive who got into the race last weekend.

14   Although there are several prominent and popular Democratic Cuban Americans who would be strong general election candidates, . . . Democratic primaries generally favor non-Cuban candidates. . . .

15   Prospective Democratic candidates include JoAnn Pepper, a federal probation officer who is the niece of the late congressman, and Marvin Dunn, a black academic who made an unsuccessful run for mayor of Miami in 1985.

Vocabulary

Head **fuel** [verb]   to provide *fuel* for; to feed, strengthen

¶1   **mantle**   [here] position [literally: cloak/cape] [unusual word]

      the late   deceased, who died recently

      Rep.   Representative in Congress [*not* Republican!]

      withdraw   to take away or remove

      stomach [verb]   to bear, accept without displeasure [used in negative
            sentences]

      pit (X) against (Y)   to set (X) against (Y) in a fight

¶2   **succeed**   to follow (in his position), to be his successor

¶3   **priority**   first goal, primary consideration

      seat   [here] position, office

      denounce   to speak (or write) against

      outrageous   very offensive, in bad taste

¶4   **sentiment**   feeling [noun]

¶5   **tenure**   [here] length of time in a position/office

      overwhelmingly   for the most part, almost completely

      prime   main; also, of good quality

      target   a goal to achieve [literally: a mark to shoot at]

¶6   **off**   [here] away from, in the ocean near

      peer   person who is one's equal in age or social status, etc.

      assimilation   becoming part of

¶8   **ethnicity**   belonging to or classification by cultural groups [more usual is the
            adjective *ethnic*: of a cultural group or background]

      undeniable factor   a clear/certain condition or influence

¶9   **Hispanic**   person in the U.S.A. who comes from a Spanish-speaking culture or
            country

¶11   **fire**   [here] to stir or fuel/strengthen

¶12   **inclination**   liking [noun]

¶13   **likely**   probable

      legislator   member of the [state] legislature, law-making politician

      token [adj.]   unimportant, not serious/dangerous

¶14   **prominent**   well-known, important

¶15   **prospective**   potential/likely

      probation officer   supervisor of criminals when they get out of jail

Questions

1. What kind of election is this article about? Circle one of the following:

   a. election of a state senator in Florida

   b. election of a Florida Senator in the U.S. Congress

   c. election of a Florida Representative in the U.S. Congress

   d. none of the above

2. Skim (read quickly, scan) Sample Article 7.1-3 for the answers to the following questions. In skimming, you only need to look quickly for the name or date in the question; when you find it, note the information about it. When answering the questions, use your own words. Do not copy sentences from the article.

a. Who is Claude Pepper? _____

_____

b. Who is Ileana Ros-Lehtinen? _____

_____

c. What happened in 1959? _____

_____

d. What will happen August 29 (1989)? _____

_____

3. a. The first paragraph mentions two names. Are those men participating in the election?

b. List all of the people who are running and their parties:

_____

_____

_____

_____

4. Does the reporter suggest who will win the August election?

5. Does race play a role in this election?

6. *Looking at Language:* The journalist uses the images of "fire" and "fuel" several times in the article, beginning in the headline. Find four more examples of these images in the article and circle them.
   Extra Credit: In one paragraph the reporter uses a word (a noun) that brings to mind an image very different from "fire." Can you find that noun?

7. Are there similar primary elections for national offices in your native country? Or do party leaders alone choose their candidate? Explain.

Follow-up Note: Ileana Ros-Lehtinen won the election.

Essential Vocabulary

A. The following 13 sentences contain words that are commonly used in economic news articles. Match each essential word (in boldface) with the correct definition on the right.

_____ 1. The President said his **administration** would not raise taxes.

_____ 2. Our family **budget** does not include an expensive vacation this year.

_____ 3. They used some of their **capital** to expand the business.

_____ 4. The mayor said there was not enough money to pay all the police officers next year unless their pay was **cut**.

_____ 5. The U.S.A. has a trade **deficit** with Japan.

_____ 6. **Federal** and state income taxes must be paid by April 15.

_____ 7. The weather **forecast** predicted sunshine; the economic **forecast** was not so good.

_____ 8. During times of **inflation**, prices go up but wages do not always rise as fast.

_____ 9. With **interest rates** at 14%, few people could afford to buy a house.

_____ 10. His **projections** show an impressive profit by next year.

_____ 11. The company closed one of its factories during the **recession**.

_____ 12. She's lost 15 pounds; her **target** weight is 135 lbs.

_____ 13. Many graduates enter the **work force** in June every year.

a. a plan for spending income/earnings

b. to reduce, make less/smaller

c. prediction, saying something about the future

d. national, or relating to the central government

e. workers/employees in general, as a group [also, labor force]

f. a goal to achieve

g. the cost of using borrowed money, figured as a percentage of that money

h. time of little business activity with low production, sales, profits, and employment

i. result of spending more money than is taken in

j. money or stocks, national or individual wealth, used in/by business

k. an estimate of future situations or trends based on a study of present data

l. increase in the amount of money in a country, with a falling value of the money and rising prices

m. government under a specified leadership/president

B. Which three of the Essential Vocabulary words would you expect to find mainly in the context of economic decline?

7/19/89

Washington prediction: slow growth, no recession

By John W. Mashek
Globe Staff

1 WASHINGTON – The Bush administration, in a forecast that even Democrats applauded as "more realistic" than many previous White House projections, predicted yesterday that economic growth would be slower in the year ahead but the nation was in no danger of a recession.

2 Treasury Secretary Nicholas Brady said the US economy was in good health, maintaining that growth will be 2.7 percent this year and will slip slightly to 2.6 percent next year. That forecast is a little more optimistic than the consensus of most economists but it is not considered far off target, as many reviews were considered to be during the Reagan administration.

3 At the same time, Brady and other top economic advisers said the federal budget deficit will be considerably lower than expected and next year's deficit target can be met if Congress restrains itself on spending.

4 "If it has a surprise, it is perhaps that it suggests we may be moving along the path toward deficit reduction," said Budget Director Richard Darman of the administration's report. "We are certainly not racing along the path, but we do at least seem to be moving."

5 Darman announced that the deficit for the fiscal year ending Sept. 30 will be $148.3 billion rather than an earlier figure of $164 billion. Larger than expected tax receipts account for most of the difference, he added.

6 As for the current fiscal year, Darman said the White House was projecting a deficit of $99.2 billion or a shade under the target deadline of $100 billion established by the so-called Gramm-Rudman-Hollings law. Darman emphasized that there was "little margin for slippage or error." Congress, he added later, was "cutting it very, very close."

7 Darman warned that current trends in Congress indicate a budget with a deficit of around $110 billion, which could trigger automatic cuts, including a sizeable reduction in non-defense as well as military programs. The military cuts will be even larger if military personnel are included.

8 Michael Boskin, chairman of the president's Council on Economic Advisers, said inflation would be 4.2 percent for the year and would decrease slightly to 4.1 percent next year.

9 Boskin said the labor force would slow as the generation following the Baby Boomers enters the nation's work place. But he said productivity would continue to improve and offset some slowdown in the growth of the labor force.

10 "Some would argue that the current expansion cannot go on for very much longer and that a recession must occur soon. We reject that view," Boskin told reporters. In fact, he said the economy had done much better than expected over the last two years and "it could outpace expectations once again."

11 Later, Darman appeared before the House Budget Committee and received a generally good response for his report. Chairman Leon Panetta (D-Calif.) applauded Darman for the candor on his projections. During the Reagan era, Panetta and other top Democrats continually challenged the White House on its economic assumptions, accusing Reagan and his aides of cooking the books or coming in with unrealistic figures to support supply side economics.

12 The majority Democrats are still a little wary that the White House is trying to set them up as big spenders and blame them for any deficit that fails to reach the agreed-to targets.

Reprinted courtesy of The Boston Globe.

Vocabulary

¶1   **applaud**   [here] to praise

¶2   **maintain**   to state/assert, defend a position

       consensus   opinion that everyone agrees on

¶3   **restrain**   to control, prevent, hold back

¶4   **reduction**   noun for *reduce*

¶5   **fiscal year**   bookkeeping year, often not a calendar year

¶6   **a shade under**   a little less than

       margin   extra space (or time) above the minimum

       slippage   making a careless mistake

       cut it close   [here] to leave very little money as a reserve, taking a risk that the
                budget might not work without automatic cuts

¶7   **trigger**   to start, especially to start a chain reaction

¶9   **Baby Boomers**   generation of people born soon after World War II, about
                1946–1963 in the U.S.A.

       offset   to balance

¶10   **outpace**   to go faster than, to exceed

¶11   **candor**   honesty in speaking

       assumption   something *assumed*/supposed/believed

       cook the books *[idiom]*   to prepare financial records (*books*) to look favorable

¶12   **wary** cautious

       set them up *[idiom]*   to harm them through a trap or trick, to make them look
                bad when it is not their fault

Reading for Information

First read the beginning of each sentence (1–5) below and circle the correct
sentence-completion answer (*a, b,* or *c*). Then write the number of the
paragraph(s) where you found the information to support your answer.

¶ _____ 1. President Bush is
       a. a Democrat.   b. a Republican.   c. neither a Democrat nor a Republican.

¶ _____ 2. The Bush administration
       a. was generally positive/optimistic about the national economy.
       b. was generally negative about the national economy.
       c. warned of dangerous threats to the national economy.

¶ _____ 3. The Democrats responded to the report
       a. mostly favorably.   b. unfavorably, saying it was far off target.
       c. unfavorably, saying it was full of errors.

¶ _____ 4. The deficit for the fiscal year (ending Sept. 30, 1989)
       a. is larger than expected.   b. is smaller than expected.
       c. is very close to what was expected.

¶ _____ 5. Inflation for the next year (1990) is expected to be
       a. 2.6%.   b. 4.2%.   c. 4.1%.

Questions for Discussion

Are the views of both political parties reported? If so, what are their positions on
the economy and on the administration's prediction?

3/25/91

Brady upbeat on US economy
But urges the Fed to cut rates further

REUTERS

1 WASHINGTON – Treasury Secretary Nicholas Brady yesterday said he was optimistic about the US economic outlook but said the Federal Reserve Board should cut interest rates further to spur growth.

2 "I'm optimistic," he said in a broadcast interview. "I see lowering interest rates, lower oil prices, consumer confidence — the figures that are coming out this next week are going to show a bounce right back to where it was in the mid-80s, and that's very encouraging," Brady said.

3 Brady, appearing on ABC's "This Week With David Brinkley," declined to predict when the recession would end, but noted a number of economists are projecting an upturn this summer.

4 While generally sounding upbeat, Brady said the economy would benefit from lower interest rates.

5 "I've said for some nine months now that there is ample room to lower interest rates. I still think that's the case," he said. "It seems to me inflation is not the worry; the worry is growth."

6 Brady acknowledged that the government's continuing budget deficits totaling hundreds of billions of dollars a year were "alarming" but he expressed confidence that a recent budget agreement reached between the Bush administration and Congress had set the deficits on a downward course.

7 "The fact that it's going down is all-important," he said, adding that he would not say whether the annual deficit would soon reach zero because "it depends a lot on the economy."

8 Brady defended President Bush's repeated call for a cut in the federal tax on income from the sale of capital assets, saying this was a tax break adopted by the other six members of the G-7 group of industrialized nations.

9 "If they think it's a national program that's good for their people, then why not the United States?" he asked.

Vocabulary

Head **upbeat**   optimistic
Subhead **urge**   to try to persuade, encourage strongly
          the Fed   the <u>Fed</u>eral Reserve Board, the central bank of the U.S.A.
¶1   **outlook**   probable future
          spur   to encourage, stimulate
¶2   **broadcast**   television (or radio) program
          bounce   to return to a high position
¶3   **ABC**   one of the three major television networks
          decline to   to decide not to, refuse
          upturn   upward (positive) movement/trend, improvement
¶5   **ample**   lots/plenty of
¶6   **acknowledge**   to admit/agree/accept
          alarming   frightening
¶8   **break**   [here] relief
          G-7   Group of Seven: Britain, Canada, France, Germany, Italy, Japan, U.S.A.

Questions

1. Why is Brady upbeat? Is it because the recession is over?

2. What two things would Brady like to see done to stimulate the economy?
   And who should do them—does the article tell us?

3. Brady represents President Bush's administration. Is the view of the
   opposition, the Democrats, given also?

4. *Optional Discussion*: Read Sample Article 7.2-1 (again). Compare the
   administration's views of the economy in 1989 and 1991.

5. a. Is the U.S.A. in a recession now? Is there inflation? What does your
      current newspaper report about the U.S. economy?

   b. Does the U.S. national economic situation affect your life directly?

6. How is the economy in your native country? (Can you find any news of your
   country's economy in American newspapers?)

JANUARY 31, 1989

Income, spending up sharply

Reuters

1 WASHINGTON – Personal income and spending rose a strong 0.9 percent in December, the government said yesterday, providing further evidence of rapid growth in the economy.

2 The Commerce Department said personal income was up 7.5 percent for all of 1988 over 1987, the largest increase in four years.

3 The gain reflected the large increase in the number of new jobs last year, but economists say gains in personal income and spending should slow as higher interest rates put a damper on economic activity.

4 Despite the overall rise in personal income, weekly paychecks for most Americans have failed to keep pace with inflation and more households are becoming two-earner families, said Cynthia Latta, senior financial economist for Data Resources, a Lexington, Mass., forecasting firm.

5 "For hourly workers, inflation has taken a bite out of spending power. That is why you have seen so many women come into the work force in the last year," she said.

6 The 7.5 percent rise in personal income for all of 1988 was the largest gain since a 9.5 percent increase in 1984, the department said.

7 The 0.9 percent rise in consumer spending came after increases of 0.3 percent in November and 1.0 percent in October.

8 Higher government subsidies to farmers boosted income in December, the department said.

9 Personal savings rose to $158.5 billion in December from $156.5 billion in November.

Reprinted by permission of Reuters.

Vocabulary

¶1 **evidence** proof, proven fact(s)
¶2 **commerce** trade
¶3 **put a damper on** to depress/lessen/diminish
¶4 **despite** in spite of
¶5 **take a bite out of** *[idiom]* to make less, to decrease
¶8 **subsidies** money paid by the government (or an organization) to help support a group of people
boost to raise/improve/increase

Questions

1. What does the headline mean? Write it as a sentence.

2. Which sentences best describe the cause of the rise in income and spending? Circle the correct letters (*a–e*).

   a. Interest rates are higher.

   b. Wages are higher.

   c. More wives are working.

   d. Farmers got more money from the government.

   e. Families are buying more for the December holidays.

3. Which month had the highest rise in spending in 1988: October, November, or December? Which paragraph contained that information?

Essential Vocabulary

The following 18 sentences contain words that are commonly used in articles about drugs and crime. Match each essential word (in boldface) with the correct definition on the right.

_____ 1. She **allegedly** stole the money, but it hasn't been proven yet.

_____ 2. The police **arrested** her and took her to the police station.

_____ 3. His **assault** was deadly; the woman died of head injuries.

_____ 4. The two gangs started shooting at each other, and the one **bystander** ran for his life.

_____ 5. They were **charged** with murder; their lawyer explained the **charges** to them.

_____ 6. Those six crimes were **committed** by a single man.

_____ 7. After her release from jail, the **convicted** thief could not find a job.

_____ 8. The drug **dealer** stands on the auto **dealer**'s used car lot.

_____ 9. **Drug trafficking** is a real business in inner cities.

_____ 10. The **felon** spent many years in jail.

_____ 11. This Latin suffix is used in words like insect**icide**.

_____ 12. She **pleaded** innocent but was found guilty.

_____ 13. The bank **robbery** was filmed by hidden video cameras and the robber was soon caught.

_____ 14. The judge **sentenced** him to 100 hours of community service.

_____ 15. Gunman **Slays** Stranger in Train

_____ 16. The **suspect** was seen hurrying away from the scene of the crime.

_____ 17. TV cameras were allowed in the courtroom during the **trial**.

_____ 18. In many inner cities, both the killer and his **victim** are young African-American males.

a. attack [usually noun, also verb]
b. proven/found guilty in a court of law
c. person who has been found guilty of a serious crime
d. person in a stated type of business
e. person who is standing nearby but is not involved
f. person who suffers from a crime (or misfortune)
g. person who probably did a crime
h. killing
i. legal process of determining guilt or innocence in court
j. to put a person under police control/custody because of an unlawful act and (usually) put him/her in jail (temporarily)
k. buying and selling drugs
l. done (a crime)
m. to declare the punishment, said by the judge after a trial
n. to declare officially that one is innocent, guilty, insane, etc.
o. supposedly, according to someone's statement but unproven
p. accused of; the accusation
q. to kill violently
r. stealing something from a place or person, usually with violence

Gunman slays 5 at Calif. school

SAMPLE ARTICLE 7.3-1

JANUARY 19, 1989

Rifle cheap and easy to buy

By Steve Marshall
USA TODAY

1 The AK-47 assault rifle is a "super Saturday Night Special" that is cheap and easy to buy in the USA, experts say.

2 One of the Soviet-designed, semi-automatic weapons was used in Tuesday's Stockton, Calif., school massacre.

3 The rifles are "considered like dad's hunting rifle so there are no restrictions," says National Coalition to Ban Handguns president Michael Beard.

4 Stockton killer Patrick Purdy — whose criminal record included firearms violations — paid $147 for his.

5 The semi-automatic AK-47 fires single rounds as fast as the shooter

pulls the trigger. It doesn't fall under the same tight federal controls as automatic rifles and machine guns, which fire continuously when the trigger is held down.

6 Federal laws on semi-automatic weapons require only that the buyer be at least 18, and not a felon or court-declared mental incompetent.

Vocabulary

¶1   **special** [*noun*]   special, low price; sale, bargain

¶2   **massacre**   killing of large numbers of defenseless people

¶3   **coalition**   a group of people from several smaller groups (or political parties) who are united for a certain reason or cause

¶4   **record**   [here] known facts about someone's past

       firearm   gun

       violation   unlawful action

¶5   **fire** [*verb*]   to shoot

       trigger   small tongue-like piece of a gun that the finger presses down (or pulls) to fire

       fall under   to come within the scope/range of [here: of federal controls]

¶6   **incompetent** [*noun*]   person not able to function well mentally and thus not able legally to sign contracts, etc.

Questions

1. Is *massacre* (¶2) an appropriate word to describe the shooting at the Stockton school?

2. Four kinds of guns are mentioned in the article. Match the pairs that are considered equal under the law:

   assault rifle   *automatic rifle*   *hunting rifle*   *machine gun*

3. About how much did an AK-47 cost in 1989? Do you think it's expensive?

4. Are guns or gun laws in the news in the U.S.A. now? Scan a newspaper.

5. Do you own a gun? Do you think it is a good idea to have one for protection? (If there are two opinions about this topic, have a debate.)

5. Compare the costs and laws about guns in America with those in your country, if you know them. In your discussion try to include words from the Essential Vocabulary list, such as: *felon, slay, victim*.

Note: Attention became focused on the AK-47 assault rifle after a man used one to shoot at schoolchildren in Stockton, California. The headlines and article refer to that terrible event. (The gunman shot himself after firing into the schoolyard, so he could not be questioned about his reasons for the crime, and there was no trial.)

JUNE 20, 1989

WAR ON DRUGS

Inner-City Teen Talks About Drugs

By Robert P. Hey
Staff writer of The Christian Science Monitor

=== WASHINGTON ===

Eighteen-year-old woman testifies at congressional hearing about life in housing project

1 The contrast with business-as-usual is extraordinary, at this congressional hearing [of the House Select Committee on Children, Youth, and Families] that is examining the related issues of youth, guns, crime, and drugs.

2 Members of Congress usually learn about these issues from adult witnesses who know second-hand. This day they instead are raptly listening to a self-assured 18-year-old tell about what she knows firsthand: youth, guns, crime, and drugs.

3 They are all related, says the 18-year-old, identified only as Detra J. She lives in a low-income housing project in Washington, D.C. Detra explains that drug dealers have fancy cars and clothes. They serve as role models for many poor youth.

4 Girls think it is "cute" to go out with boys who work for drug dealers, and who have lots of money; thus boys work for drug dealers to gain money, respect from their peers, and popularity among the girls.

5 The money in drug selling is certainly good; even teen-agers can make "$1,000 a night," Detra says. By comparison, wages of legal activities, whether $3.50 an hour or $10, look paltry.

6 Finally, gun dealers supply guns to the boys who work for them, often called runners. The weapons provide both protection and social status, Detra says.

7 Detra also says that youths who have guns often use them against other youths. "Eight people who I know have been killed by guns," she says. The shootings were over trivial reasons: "Most of the ones, they die for no reason."

8 Others have been shot and have recovered, she says without giving a number. All the shootings are drug related, she adds. They were either people involved in drug selling, or bystanders shot by people who were involved. . . .

9 Throughout her testimony and the questioning by committee members, drug trafficking is repeatedly referred to as "the trade" or "the business."

10 Experts say that drug trafficking has indeed become a business in poor urban neighborhoods, and that it reflects considerable, albeit illegal, entrepreneurial skill by residents involved.

11 One challenge that is confronting society is how to redirect such entrepreneurial abilities into legal channels of business activity, they add. . . .

12 "No question that we've got a serious problem" with guns and drugs, says Rep. Ron Packard (R) of California. There is great divergence during the committee hearing, as in American society in general, on what to do about it. Some of the ideas are very difficult to carry out. . . .

13 Rep. Lamar Smith (R) of Texas . . . recommends strengthening American families and ending drug traffic.

14 Rep. Barbara Boxer (D) of California says one part of the solution is providing more positive role models.

15 Rep. George Miller, a California Democrat who is the committee chairman, urges that some attractive activity, like recreation programs, be provided in inner-city neighborhoods.

16 Detra herself suggests more programs to help disadvantaged youth, more communication between parents and children, and "more jobs that offer more money."

17 What if youths used guns anyway? Her reply is straight out of the law-and-order school: "Lock 'em up."

Vocabulary

Subhead **testify**   to make true statements during a trial or hearing

congressional   of the U.S. *Congress* (legislative branch of the government)

hearing   a meeting to listen to arguments on an issue

housing project   apartment or townhouse buildings for people with little or no earned income

¶1   **House**   House of Representatives, part of the U.S. Congress

issue *[noun]*   important topic or subject (that is not easy to solve)

youth   young people or young person

¶2   **witness**   person who testifies about what he/she has seen/experienced

secondhand   from someone else, not belonging originally to oneself

raptly   with complete attention

¶4   **go out with**   to date

peers   people of the same age, social status, etc.

¶5   **paltry**   unimportant and very small (number)

¶7   **trivial**   unimportant

¶8   **recover**   [here] to get well again, become healthy again

¶9   **testimony**   testified statement (at court or a congressional hearing)

trade   buying and selling, commerce

¶10   **urban**   of the city

albeit   although, even though [formal]

entrepreneurial   business [as an adjective]

¶11   **confront**   to face, to challenge

¶12   **divergence**   differences

¶15   **urge**   to argue strongly for; to stress/emphasize

¶16   **disadvantaged**   without any advantages, poor and with little education

¶17   **"Lock 'em up."**   "Put th<u>em</u> in jail/prison." [informal]

Questions:

1. Is this a news or a feature article? Give reasons for your answer.

2. Four people suggest solutions to the drug issue. List the suggestions:

_____

_____

_____

_____

3. Are drugs an issue in your city?

4. Does Detra give reasons for young boys to traffic in drugs? If so, what are they?

5. Does Detra give reasons for *taking* drugs? If so, what are they?

6. The following headline and *excerpt* (short piece cut out of a whole) concern drugs in the suburbs instead of the city. What reason is given by Michael Dundas, a teen from a "comfortable suburb," for taking drugs?

Substance Abuse Worries Suburbs

. . . . Cases such as Dundas' are chilling to suburbanites. Most alarming, perhaps, are the reasons he gives for doing drugs, reasons that have no apparent family or sociological underpinnings.

"Because it was fun . . . it was awesome . . . it's better than real life . . ."

In suburban towns, the law enforcement march against alcohol and drugs intensifies. And few are willing to suggest that any suburban youth is immune from drug troubles.

Reprinted courtesy of The Boston Globe.

SATURDAY, JULY 15, 1989

Junkie: I'll take test
Okays AIDS check for sake of firefighter

BY PATRICK CLARK
Daily News Staff Writer

1   A convicted junkie and suspected thief accused of jabbing a Manhattan firefighter with a hypodermic needle last week agreed yesterday to submit to an AIDS test in a gesture of goodwill.

2   Carlos Colon, 38, will receive a blood test sometime next week at the Rikers Island hospital unit, according to Robert Sullivan, attorney for firefighter Dan Rowan.

3   "I'm nervous and shaky, but relieved that he agreed to cooperate," Rowan, 33, said after a Manhattan Criminal Court hearing.

4   "I'm hoping for the best," said his wife, Georgine, 26, who is four weeks from the delivery of their first child. "I'm very happy for the decision, for Danny, for my unborn baby and myself."

5   Sullivan said test results will be confidential and not used as evidence against Colon as part of the arrangement.

6   "He did it for my client's peace of mind," Sullivan declared. Such tests cannot be compelled by court order.

7   Judge Paula Omansky ordered Colon held on $20,000 bail after his indictment on robbery, assault, weapons and drug-implement possession charges was disclosed. He pleaded innocent. He faces up to 15 years if convicted.

8   Colon, a reputed heroin addict, allegedly stabbed Rowan last Saturday night after a car break-in near the firehouse on Great Jones St. in lower Manhattan.

9   Authorities said the suspect served a month in jail last year for misdemeanor drug possession.

10   Rowan received shots to prevent hepatitis and tetanus. He returns to duty tomorrow.

11   "I want to get back to what I do best," said Rowan. "Fighting fires and helping people."

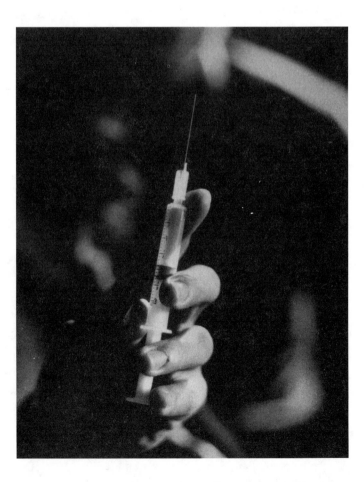

Vocabulary

Head **junkie** drug addict [slang]

okay to agree/approve, to say *OK* [informal]

for (the) sake of in order to benefit, for the good of

¶1 **jabbing** quick pricking or pushing (of something into someone)

hypodermic needle needle used to give injections

submit to [here] to have

¶2 **attorney** lawyer [American]

¶3 **relieved** feeling less tense/worried, comforted

hearing [here] a listening to arguments in a court of law

¶4 **delivery of (a) child** birth of a child

¶5 **confidential** secret

¶6 **client** customer of a professional (especially of a lawyer)

compelled forced

¶7 **bail** money given as an assurance that a suspect not kept in jail will return to court for a trial at a later date

indictment formal accusation/charge

implement tool/device

disclosed made public

face [verb] must expect

¶8 **reputed** having the reputation of

¶9 **misdemeanor** less serious crime

Questions

1. a. Who allegedly committed a crime?

   b. Where is he now (at the time the article was written)?

2. What crime(s) has/have allegedly been committed?

3. Why did Carlos Colon plead innocent?

4. Why should Colon take an AIDS test? (The answer may not be directly stated in the story.)

5. This is an example of journalism of experience. What are some of the ways the reporter tries to help readers experience the event on a personal or emotional level?

6. Do you have a car? Has it ever been broken into?

7. Did this article interest you? If so, look through a current newspaper for similar stories and discuss them with your classmates.

More articles about AIDS appear in Section 7.4 (pp. 148–150).

DECEMBER 28, 1988

Boston homicide rate up 36%

By Sean Murphy
Globe Staff

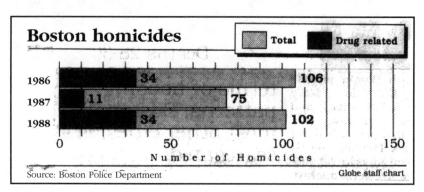

Boston homicides

Total | Drug related

1986	34	106
1987	11	75
1988	34	102

0   50   100   150

N u m b e r o f H o m i c i d e s

Source: Boston Police Department   **Globe staff chart**

1 At least one-third of the 102 killings recorded in Boston to date in 1988 were drug-related, helping to push the homicide rate to its second-highest level in 13 years, according to Boston Police Department data.

2 "The drug dealers are killing each other," said Boston police Superintendent Joseph V. Saia, Jr., the department's chief of detectives.

3 The 1988 homicide rate is about 36 percent higher than last year's rate, when 75 killings were committed, the smallest number in the 1980s, police data said. More than 60 percent of this year's victims were black males, according to police data.

4 By the end of November, Boston police had made 6,700 drug-related arrests, compared to 5,200 for the same period in 1987 and 4,500 in 1986, police data said. . . . More than 100 pounds of cocaine has been seized this year, a 25 percent increase over last year, Saia said.

5 "That amount of cocaine seized represents millions and millions of dollars," he said.

Bystanders victimized, too

6 But drug-related violence was not confined to buyers and sellers.

7 Sherman Griffiths, 36, of Milton, a police detective and father of two, was shot to death in February while attempting to search a Dorchester apartment for drugs. Darlene Tiffany Moore, 11, was killed in Roxbury by a stray bullet in a drug-related shooting.

8 "You're never going to say, 'Yeah, it was a great year, only 100 homicides,' because one homicide is bad enough, but when the innocent bystander gets hit or the cop doing his job, those are the ones that stick with you," Saia said.

9 Suspects in the Griffiths and Moore killings are awaiting trial.

10 Saia said arrests were made in 60 of the 102 killings. Arrest warrants were issued for suspects in six other slayings, he said.

11 According to police data, 24 killings were classified as resulting from arguments between acquaintances or strangers; 15 as family-related; seven as robbery-related, and six as gang-related; . . . and there were no racially motivated homicides in 1988.

12 More than half of the killings in 1988 were committed by a handgun or shotgun, the third-highest percentage of total killings since 1973, police data said. Stabbing deaths ranked second, at 25 percent, while there were 13 killings by beating, two by strangulation and seven slayings not specified by means, police data said.

Reprinted courtesy of The Boston Globe.

Are there any articles about these kinds of violent crimes in your current newspaper?

Vocabulary

Head **(is) up 36%**   has increased by 36%

¶4   **seize**   [here] to take by the police

Subhead **victimized**   made into or caused to become a *victim*

¶6   **confined to**   limited to

¶7   **search**   to look through (or examine) in order to find something

   stray   undirected, random

   bullet   what is fired from a gun

¶8   **yeah**   yes [informal, colloquial]

   innocent   without blame, not guilty of wrongdoing

   cop   policeman or -woman [informal]

   that stick with you *[idiom]*   that stay with you (in your memory)

¶10   **warrant**   an official written order

   issued *[verb]*   given out, provided

¶11   **gang**   [here] an organized group of (trouble-making) youths

   motivated   having a reason to happen

¶12   **shotgun**   a gun that fires small balls (*shot*) for close-range shooting

   stabbing   killing with a knife or similar sharp object

   strangulation   killing by pressing on the throat so that the victim cannot
            breathe

   specified   named specifically

   means   method

Questions

1. Do all homicide cases come to trial, according to the article? If not, what do you think is the reason?

2. Does the article give information on the most common type of:

   a. victim? _____

   b. killer? _____

   c. weapon used in homicides? _____

   d. reason/motivation for homicide? _____

   e. Would the answers be the same for your culture?

3. Do you know the homicide statistics for your city? Do you feel safe where you live? In your discussion try to use some of the Essential Vocabulary, such as: *commit, drug trafficking, assault, victim, bystander, arrest, convict, sentence.*

a. **LaRouche gets 15-year term for IRS fraud, loan default**

b. **Barnoski found guilty in McDermott slaying**

c. **North will be sentenced today by judge known for toughness**

d. **Otsuki found guilty of murder**

e. **Doctor Guilty of Infanticide**

f. **Officer cleared in death of motorcyclist**

g. *Just 2 years for 'beauty queen' thief*

h. **Killer gets 1½ years**

Vocabulary

verdict   judge's or jury's decision at the end of a trial
IRS   Internal Revenue Service, U.S. tax-collecting agency
default   failure to repay a debt
clear   [here] declare innocent, free from blame

Questions

1. Which headlines are in the active voice? _____

   Passive voice? _____ Which is a noun phrase? _____

2. a. Which cases involved deaths? _____

   b. Which headline tells about someone who is *not* guilty of a crime? _____

3. *Looking at Names.*

   a. The names in headlines *a–d* are evidence of the variety of cultural heritages (backgrounds) of American citizens. Can you guess which name comes from each of the following cultures?

   French: _____ ; Irish: _____ ;

   Japanese: _____ ; Polish: _____ ; English: _____

   b. Why are there two names in headline *b*?

4. Explain headlines *g* and *h*.

5. Look through your current newspaper for headlines about trials and verdicts. Explain each headline. Can you find all the facts needed for an explanation in the lead?

Essential Vocabulary   The following puzzle includes all of the 13 words that you need to know when reading articles about medical crises or health policies. (Of course, other words will be important, too, depending on the subject of the news story.) Clues for Essential Vocabulary words are marked with an asterisk (*).
Challenge: Cover the bottom right corner of the page, and try to solve the puzzle first without looking at the Essential Vocabulary list.

A C R O S S

*1. doctor

*3. moral (adjective)

5. <u>h</u>uman <u>i</u>mmunodeficiency <u>v</u>irus, which causes AIDS

*8. in/into a vein

10. abbreviation for "specimen" (a sample of something that is to be studied or tested, such as a blood specimen)

*11. (to set up) an amount of money for a specific purpose

12. something medicine cannot cure: old ____

*14. to try to cure/heal with medicine

16. *fund = a ____ of money for a specific purpose

*17. illness

18. abbreviation for "Registered Nurse," a university degree

D O W N

*1. to keep or stop something from happening

2. sick

*4. protection through insurance

*6. organism that can cause illnesses—for example, the flu

*7. authority/power to apply policies; also, to require

*8. having an illness caused by bacteria or a virus

*9. a man who officially speaks for a group, government, or other person

*13. <u>A</u>cquired <u>I</u>mmune <u>D</u>eficiency <u>S</u>yndrome

15. small, narrow glass vial for liquids, used in scientific tests and research: ____ tube

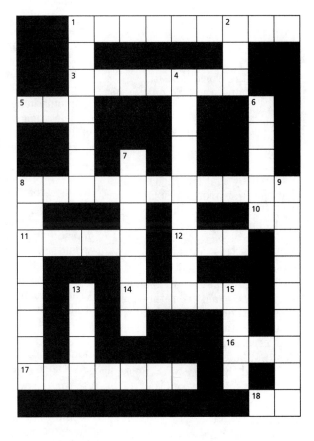

Essential Vocabulary

AIDS
coverage
disease
ethical
fund
infected
intravenous(ly)
mandate
physician
prevent
spokesperson
treat
virus

SATURDAY, JUNE 11, 1988

Liver boy has chance

1st transplant done for rare disease

By FRANK McKEOWN

1 Richard Michael Grecco was born 24 days ago with a liver disease so rare that no more than 20 people in the world have it.

2 Little hope was held out for his survival.

3 Thanks to medical technology — and the generosity of a grieving family — the infant has a chance at life.

4 The baby's father, Richard, said that the first liver transplant ever performed for the disease, urea cycle enzymatic deficiency, was completed successfully June 2 at Children's Hospital in Pittsburgh when his son was 16 days old.

5 "Now the kid's got a shot at life," Grecco said from the hospital, where he and his wife, Sabrina, have been staying with their son.

6 Grecco, 26, a route salesman for Hostess Bakeries in Saddle Brook, N.J., said his son was born a month prematurely on May 17 in Staten Island Hospital.

More tests

7 Like other preemies, the child was placed in an "isolette" (incubator) and fed intravenously.

8 The day after Richie was born, he stopped breathing. He was put on a respirator.

9 "He was unconscious for the rest of the week," Grecco said. "They did more tests and the last found that he had high levels of ammonia in his blood."

10 The diagnosis was that the child's liver was not producing an enzyme that broke down the toxic ammonia. . . .

11 Doctors said most children suffering from the disease died in their first year.

12 Mount Sinai physicians determined that a liver transplant would give the child a better chance at life, Grecco said.

13 Mount Sinai contacted Children's Hospital, which is accredited for liver transplants.

14 Almost miraculously, physicians in Pittsburgh learned of a donation from the parents of a child born brain-dead.

'Very generous'

15 "They were very generous," a hospital spokeswoman said. "And the Greccos are extremely grateful." The donor family was not identified.

16 The spokeswoman said other youngsters might benefit from the experimental surgery because doctors could study Richie's liver.

17 She said there probably were only about 12, certainly no more than 20, persons in the world with the disease.

18 Richie was in critical but stable condition, still far from out of danger.

Expensive drugs

19 He must remain in the hospital for at least two months and be treated with expensive drugs.

20 Transplant costs — from $250,000 to $500,000 — are covered by Grecco's insurance, the spokeswoman said.

21 There are additional expenses, including drugs. One of these, Cyclosporine, costs $150 for two ounces.

22 Mary Ann Bruccoleri, Grecco's sister, said a fund had been established to defray medical expenses.

23 Contributions may be sent to the Richard Michael Grecco Liver Fund, Post Office Box ------, Staten Island, N.Y. 10314.

Vocabulary

Subhead **transplant**   replacing a sick organ in one body with a healthy one from another body

¶5   **a shot**   a chance to succeed [informal]

¶7   **preemie**   baby born prematurely, before the natural time [informal]

¶9   **unconscious**   not mentally awake, not aware of one's surroundings

¶10   **toxic**   poisonous

¶14   **miraculously**   like a *miracle*/wonder

¶16   **surgery**   medical operation(s)

¶18   **stable**   unchanging

¶19   **drugs**   medicines

¶22   **defray**   to provide money to pay

Questions

1. Is this article about a famous baby? an unusual baby?

2. Was the transplant successful?

3. Who donated the healthy liver?

4. Is Richard Grecco at home now, according to the article?

5. a. Does the Grecco family have to pay hospital costs themselves ("out of their own pockets")?

    b. How about the cost of medicine?

    c. Do you think their situation is typical of an American family in a medical crisis?

6. How do people feel about organ transplants in your native country? Discuss this issue with your classmates. Try to use some of the Essential Vocabulary words, such as: *ethical, physician, coverage, prevent, treat*.

7. Are there any stories of medical crises in your current newspaper?

6/12/91

Hatch opposes aspect of health bill

By Renu Sehgal
CONTRIBUTING REPORTER

1 WASHINGTON – Despite a consensus on Capitol Hill that the nation needs major health care reform, differences remain over its eventual shape. Opposition stirred yesterday over Democratic legislation in the Senate to create a universal health care system.

2 "At a time when Eastern Europe is emerging from the yoke of centralized price and wage planning, why would we choose to adopt it?," asked Republican Sen. Orrin Hatch of Utah, the ranking Republican on the Senate Labor and Human Resources Committee, which is holding hearings on the bill.

3 Hatch is opposed mainly to the "play or pay" aspect of the legislation, under which employers either would offer health insurance or would pay a 6 to 8 percent payroll tax to fund the government program.

4 "The play-or-pay mechanism makes this legislation a job-loss bill, not an enhanced-access-to-care bill," Hatch said.

5 He termed the measure "a mandate on the backs of American workers. What they get is loss of jobs, loss of flexibility, and loss of wages."

6 Hatch cited an estimate by the Partnership on Health Care and Employment that up to 3.5 million jobs could be lost as a result of the mandates because some small businesses would not have the money.

7 But proponents see the plan as helping middle-class workers, who are being increasingly hard hit by soaring health costs and insurance rates as employers cut back benefits and coverage.

8 "The plan . . . is not a government takeover of the nation's health care system," said Sen. Edward M. Kennedy [Democrat from Massachusetts].

9 "But it is designed to eliminate the worst faults of the current system, while preserving its most essential aspect: the public-private partnership."

10 Elliot L. Richardson, secretary of health, education and welfare in the Nixon administration, said, "We have imposed other costs on business: workmen's compensation, minimum wage, Social Security, Medicare," in arguing that the proposal would not impose a larger burden on businesses.

Reprinted courtesy of The Boston Globe.

For more information on employee benefits, see Sample Article 8.1-3 (p. 166).

Vocabulary

Head **aspect** view

 bill proposed law that is to be discussed and voted on

¶1 **consensus** general agreement of all people involved

 Capitol Hill where Congress is situated in Washington, D.C.

 eventual final (in the future)

 stir [here] to begin to move, to awaken

 legislation [here] discussion of the bill

¶2 **emerge** to come out of, to come away from

 yoke [here] heavy load/burden, symbol of unwilling subjection to something

 ranking highest in rank, leading member

 hearings meetings to listen to arguments on an issue

¶3 **payroll** list of employees and their wages

¶4 **enhanced** made better/greater

 access to admittance to, freedom/right to have

¶5 **term** *[verb]* to call/name

¶6 **cite** [here] to quote, or to refer to

¶7 **proponent** supporter (opposite of *opponent*)

 soaring rising fast and far

 benefits money or other advantages given to employees by the employer

¶9 **eliminate** to cut out, get rid of, do away with

¶10 **impose . . . on** require . . . of, place/force . . . on

 workmen's compensation insurance for employees injured while working, paid for by the employer

 Social Security national system of insurance for retired (and unemployed or disabled) people, paid for by taxes on businesses and personal income

 Medicare national medical insurance for people over age 65

Questions

1. a. Which political party does Hatch belong to?

   b. Which political party proposes this bill?

2. Is Senator Hatch for or against the bill? Why?

3. Who supports the bill? For what reasons?

4. Has there been any recent news (in American or other newspapers) about universal health care in the United States?

5. Does your native country have universal health care?
    Optional Discussion Topic: Discuss with classmates (from different countries, if possible) what kinds of insurance systems your country has for employees and nonworking people. Compare them to the U.S. systems listed in ¶10 (and to each others' countries).

JUNE 6, 1990

Doc watches as Alzheimer's victim kills self

'Suicide machine' takes first life

1 HOLLY, Mich. – A woman suffering from Alzheimer's disease killed herself by triggering a retired pathologist's "suicide machine" as the doctor who assembled the device watched her die.

2 Dr. Jack Kevorkian, 62, of Royal Oak, said he had done nothing illegal by hooking Janet Adkins, 54, of Portland, Ore., to the device Monday afternoon in his van at a park 50 miles northwest of Detroit.

3 Adkins died five or six minutes after she pressed a button on the machine that released a dose of potassium chloride into her veins.

4 The procedure is similar to that used in some capital punishment cases.

5 Some medical ethicists called the doctor's actions immoral and perhaps illegal. . . .

6 Kevorkian said yesterday: "I feel I haven't broken any laws."

7 But Susan Wolf of the Hastings Center for biomedical research in Briarcliff, N.Y., disagreed.

8 "Physicians should not be killers, even in cases where the patient requests it and there is a compassionate reason behind the act," she said. . . .

9 Oakland County Prosecutor Richard Thompson said he was aware of Adkins' death but declined to comment further pending the outcome of "an ongoing investigation."

10 Gerald Poisson, the county's assistant prosecutor, said the suicide device is not illegal but someone who provided it could be charged with homicide, depending on the facts in the case.

11 Kevorkian said Adkins was the first patient to use the device, which he invented in September. He said Adkins learned of it through the news media.

12 Medical journals have refused to publicize the device, he said.

13 "It simulates exactly the judicial executions that we do now with legal executions, except with this device the person does it himself by pushing a button," Kevorkian, an outspoken advocate of what he calls doctor-assisted suicide, said in a published report Monday.

14 "The last thing Janet Adkins said was, 'You just make my case known.'"

15 After Adkins was dead, Kevorkian immediately called Michigan State Police and the Oakland County Prosecutor's office. When police arrived at the park, they confiscated the van and the suicide device.

16 Kevorkian said Adkins, her husband, Ronald, and a family friend flew to Michigan over the weekend because providing the means to commit suicide is a felony in Oregon.

17 Kevorkian described Adkins as "a remarkable woman" who did not want to live with the ravages of Alzheimer's disease.

18 "She told me she wanted to take her life while she was still clear in her mind and knew what she was doing. She said she wanted to do it before she slipped into a vegetative state."

Follow-up Note: Six months later Dr. Kevorkian was charged with murder by the prosecution. After a short trial, he was found not guilty. In March 1993, the Michigan state legislature made a law against assisting suicide. By that time Dr. Kevorkian had helped 13 people end their lives.

Vocabulary

Head **Alzheimer's** disease that gradually destroys a person's mental ability

     victim person who suffers from a disease (or from a wrongdoing by someone else)

¶1 **trigger** to start

     pathologist doctor who studies dead bodies to determine the cause of death

     suicide killing oneself

     assemble [here] to put together, to construct

     device machine/instrument

¶2 **hook** [verb] to connect

¶3 **dose** measured amount, a dosage

     veins blood vessels that carry blood to the heart

¶4 **capital punishment** legal punishment of death

¶8 **compassionate** merciful, with a feeling of sympathy

¶9 **prosecutor** lawyer for the state

     pending the outcome until the result is known

¶10 **homicide** killing a person

¶13 **simulate** to copy/imitate

     judicial of/from a court of law

     execution legal killing of a person

     outspoken openly saying (and/or writing) what one thinks

¶15 **confiscate** to legally take something away from someone and put it in the custody of police

¶16 **felony** serious crime

¶17 **ravages** destructive effects

¶18 **vegetative state** state of existing without awareness (like a plant)

Questions

1. a. Who built the suicide device? Why?

   b. Who used it? Why?

2. Dr. Kevorkian advocates assisted suicide. Who opposes it and why, according to the article?

3. Have you read any news about Alzheimer's disease recently? Tell your classmates what you know about it.

4. Many Americans advocate an individual's right to commit suicide; others think it is wrong, often for religious or ethical reasons. Do you know if suicide is an issue in other countries too? In your discussion try to use: *ethical, physician, disease, prevent.*

JUNE 6, 1990

AIDS Makes Mark on Sex Education

States adapt curricula out of concern for teens

By Catherine Foster
Staff writer of The Christian Science Monitor

SAN FRANCISCO

1   The push to teach youths how to avoid AIDS is changing the face of traditional sex education in schools across the United States.

2   Three years ago, no states required AIDS education. Today, 33 states do and the rest encourage it. More and more school districts have incorporated education on AIDS (acquired immune deficiency syndrome) into sexuality education, health, family life, and biology classes — even social studies. Many new teaching tools — pamphlets, videos, and even comic books — are being used. And frank discussion about sexual practices and condoms as protection against disease, which would have been unthinkable in younger grades only a few years ago, is becoming common.

3   More states now mandate AIDS education than sex education, and according to a national study, 80 percent of sex education money is spent on AIDS education.

4   While only 1 percent of AIDS cases involve adolescents, many public health officials say teenagers are increasingly at risk of becoming infected because of their experimentation with drugs and sex. Twenty percent of all AIDS cases involve people in their 20s; because of the long incubation period for the AIDS virus, many believe those people contracted the disease in their teens.

5   Since 1981, more than 128,000 cases of AIDS have been reported in the United States, according to the Centers for Disease Control (CDC), the lead federal agency for AIDS prevention. The CDC estimates that as many as 1.5 million Americans may be infected with the human immunodeficiency virus (HIV), which researchers say causes AIDS.

6   Schools have found themselves on the front lines of educating youth about the disease. A recent General Accounting Office report finds that two-thirds of all school districts require AIDS prevention education in some grades, but that teachers lack sufficient training to give such education. It also found that the subject received the least attention in the upper grades, when sexual activity is deemed most likely. . . . A CDC study found that about half of 16-year-olds have had sexual intercourse; by age 19, 70 to 80 percent have. . . .

7   The curriculum also has to be sensitive to the cultural needs of the large Hispanic and Asian populations, educators say.

8   Oklahoma was the first state to require AIDS education, and Oklahoma City has developed teachers' guides that include the origin and history of the virus, correct misconceptions about AIDS, and identify high-risk behaviors.

9   By law, Oklahoma schools must hold a workshop explaining the AIDS curriculum to parents and guardians a month before it is taught. No student is required to participate if his or her parent or guardian objects in writing, says Carolyn Hughes, assistant superintendent of curriculum and program development for the Oklahoma City schools.

10   "The first year, not one parent objected," she says. "They've been very supportive."

Vocabulary

Head   **make (its) mark** *[idiom]*   [here] to influence/affect strongly
Subhead   **curricula**   plural of *curriculum*: course of studies
¶1   **push**   determination/effort
¶2   **social studies**   curriculum that includes geography, history, and sociology, usually taught in the middle grades
       pamphlet   booklet
       frank   honest and open
¶4   **adolescents**   teenagers
       at risk   in danger
       incubation   period of time before a disease becomes active/noticeable
       contract the disease   to get/catch the disease/illness
¶6   **lack**   to not have, or to have not enough of something
       deemed   thought/believed/considered
¶7   **Hispanic**   person in the U.S.A. who comes from a Spanish-speaking country or culture
¶8   **misconception**   wrong idea, misunderstanding
¶9   **workshop**   class or meeting in which all members participate (*work*) actively
       guardian   person, not a parent, who has legal responsibility for a child

Questions

1. a. Is AIDS education mandatory in schools in the United States?

    b. And sex education?

2. *True or false?* Write T or F in the blanks on the left.

    _____ a. AIDS education is taught mostly to teenagers in upper grades.

    _____ b. Classes about AIDS are mandatory for all students in Oklahoma.

    _____ c. Most teachers are not well trained to teach about AIDS.

    _____ d. In Oklahoma teachers can receive information about AIDS.

    _____ e. In some schools comic books are used to teach about AIDS.

    _____ f. Parents do not like schools to offer AIDS prevention classes.

    _____ g. About 1½ million Americans have AIDS (at the time the article was published).

    _____ h. More teenagers have AIDS than people in their twenties, because adolescents have high-risk behavior.

3. Is AIDS a problem in your native country? Do schools in your native country have education programs about AIDS? Should they?

APRIL 28, 1989

FDA allows a new AIDS drug to be tested in humans in May

Associated Press

1 WASHINGTON – The Food and Drug Administration said yesterday it will allow a potentially promising new AIDS drug to be tested on people infected with the deadly virus.

2 Researchers say the drug, known as GLQ223, is unique because it appears to kill only those immune system cells that are infected with the AIDS virus, leaving others alone.

3 However, they cautioned that the drug so far has been tested only in the laboratory.

4 "I'm very optimistic because of the test tube results, but there's always the possibility it could have unpredictable side effects, or when given to humans the drug may not be able to get to all the infected cells," said Dr. Michael McGrath of the University of California in San Francisco and San Francisco General Hospital.

5 McGrath led a team of scientists from the University of California, the Chinese University of Hong Kong and Genelabs of Redwood City, Calif., that developed GLQ223.

6 The drug is a highly purified form of the plant protein trichosanthin, which is derived from the root of a Chinese cucumber plant. The plant extract has been used in China to induce abortions.

7 In the laboratory, the drug has been found to work on two different types of cells crucial to the normal functioning of the immune system: T-cells and macrophage cells, which act as a reservoir for the virus.

8 AZT, the only drug now licensed for treatment of AIDS, only prevents the virus from replicating in T-cells. Other drugs like it work the same way.

9 David Corkery, a spokesman for the American Foundation for AIDS Research, called the drug "very promising," and said he is "cautiously optimistic" about its prospects.

10 Genelabs said yesterday the clinical trials are expected to begin in May at San Francisco General Hospital.

Reprinted by permission of the Associated Press.

Vocabulary

Note: Some technical and medical terms are used in ¶6–7. It is not necessary to know their exact meaning to understand the story in general.

¶1   **promising**   giving hope of future excellence; likely to do well

¶4   **test tube results**   results in the laboratory

   side effects   secondary or unplanned effects

¶6   **induce**   to make happen, to produce

¶7   **crucial**   all-important

   reservoir   place where something is collected and stored

¶8   **replicating**   [here] duplicating/copying itself

Questions

1. Two abbreviations are used in the headline: FDA and AIDS. Are both explained in the article? Why, or why not?

2. How is this new drug, GLQ223, different from the known drugs like AZT?

3. Was the new drug developed at a university or a private company?

4. Could people buy GLQ223 at the time of the article?

5. Have you read about any further advances in AIDS medicines recently?

Essential Vocabulary

A. The following 13 words are essential for the understanding of articles about environmental issues. Match each word on the left with the correct definition on the right. How many can you match without using a dictionary? _____

_____ 1. **cleanup**
_____ 2. **consumer**
_____ 3. **effort**
_____ 4. **emission**
_____ 5. **environment**
_____ 6. **invent**
_____ 7. **pollute**
_____ 8. **potential**
_____ 9. **preserve**
_____ 10. **proceed**
_____ 11. **recycle**
_____ 12. **toxic/toxin**
_____ 13. **waste**

a. to create or design something never made before
b. to go ahead, continue
c. to use something a second time instead of throwing it away; or to treat it for reuse
d. to make part of our environment impure/unclean/unfit for human use
e. our natural surroundings (air, rivers, oceans, forests, tundra, etc.)
f. sending out, expulsion, of a (natural) substance into the environment
g. an attempt, try
h. possibility for future development
i. person who buys and uses (consumes) things
j. poisonous/poison
k. discarded material, garbage
l. making something clean (again)
m. (a special area) to protect/keep a natural environment

B. Fill in the blanks with 12 of the Essential Vocabulary words. In some cases, the form of the word is different from the one listed above.

RIVER CLEANUP CONTINUES TODAY

NOTMYTOWN, USA – The _____ of the polluted Pristine River just outside town
1
here is _____ing_ on schedule, said a representative of the Environmental Protection
2
Agency yesterday. She said the Whyoff Company was cooperating fully in the _____ to
3
make the river clean again by December.

Townspeople were pleased that their complaints about the company, beginning two years ago, had finally resulted in the investigation by the EPA. "The water was so _____d_ you
4
could smell it," said one resident at the site yesterday. "It had to be _____."
5

A Whyoff Company spokesperson said that "people are always calling for a cleaner
_____. But they're all _____s_ of our products." The company produces
6   7
insecticides and mosquito repellents.

Whyoff is now testing a new machine that treats and _____s_ some of the offensive
8
chemicals. It was _____ed_ by a team of Whyoff engineers recently. "It has the
9
_____ to reduce our chemical _____s_ and _____s_ by about
10   11   12
40%," explained the spokesperson. They hope to have it in operation by the end of the year.

AUGUST 8, 1989

4 large corporations will reduce emissions that harm ozone layer

By Kara Swisher
Washington Post

1 WASHINGTON – Four giant corporations, responding to growing consumer and governmental concern about the damage that chlorofluorocarbons do to the earth's protective ozone layer, have announced over the past week that they would voluntarily cut back or end their release of the chemicals.

2 General Motors said that by 1991 it would require its 10,000 car dealers to recycle the chemicals, called CFCs, purged from automobile air conditioners undergoing servicing.

3 Nissan Motors said it would end the use of CFCs entirely in its air conditioners by 1993, replacing the coolant with an alternative that does not attack ozone.

4 American Telephone and Telegraph Co., which uses CFC solvents and coolants in hundreds of manufacturing processes, said it would cut the volume used by 50 percent by 1991 and end it entirely by 1994.

5 And General Electric Co. agreed, after negotiations with Sen. Albert Gore Jr., Democrat of Tennessee, to offset its much-criticized release of 300,000 pounds of CFCs from its nationwide refrigerator repair program by cutting back on releases elsewhere.

6 Although corporations have been slow to respond to the calls of environmentalists to eliminate CFCs, many are now taking their own action, prodded by pending legislation in Congress and several state Legislatures, increasingly organized and vocal environmental groups and mounting public outrage over the issue.

7 CFCs, used in a wide range of manufacturing processes from refrigeration to solvents, are considered something of a wonder chemical since they are nontoxic, nonflammable and stable. But the chemicals also are the prime destroyer of the ozone layer that protects earth's surface from too much ultraviolet radiation.

8 "The door on CFCs is going to close, and they are going to be highly regulated if not outright prohibited sooner than later," said AT&T engineering vice-president Dave Chittick. "And the way we see it, if you don't know you have a problem you aren't looking for a solution."

9 He said AT&T's cutback will not be easy. He said his company used CFCs in hundreds of manufacturing processes. "Inventing our way out of this is going to be an enormous task," he said.

10 Gore, along with other politicians in both the House and Senate, has introduced legislation to reduce and eventually ban ozone-depleting chemicals. Legislatures in states including Vermont and Hawaii have similar legislation in place. And CFCs are to be reduced worldwide by 50 percent by the end of the century under an international agreement.

11 Several industry groups have recommended that their member industries stop releases of CFCs and encourage recycling.

Vocabulary

Head **ozone**   one of the natural gases in our atmosphere (O_3) (see ¶7)

¶2   **purge**   to clean out or get rid of (remove) something unwanted

¶4   **solvent**   chemical that dissolves another substance

¶5   **offset**   to balance

        cut back   to reduce

¶6   **eliminate**   to get rid of all of something

        prod   to poke or punch something (someone), especially in order to make it move forward

        pending   upcoming, waiting to be decided

        mounting   increasing

        outrage   shock or anger caused by an offensive/shocking act

¶7   **stable**   unchanging

¶8   **outright**   completely

        sooner than later   sooner (*not* later) [from the phrase: *sooner or later*]

¶10   **eventually**   at some time in the future

        ban   to forbid/stop/prohibit

        deplete   to decrease, to use completely

Questions

1. What are CFCs? Where did you find that information?

2. a. Who says it will *not* be easy to reduce emissions of CFCs?

   b. Who says it *will* be easy? Anyone?

3. What is Congress (House of Representatives and Senate) doing about CFCs?

4. Why is the ozone layer important?

5. Has any worldwide progress been made since this article was written (1989)? Discuss what you know about other countries' actions. Use some of these words: *emissions, potential, proceed, recycle, **cut back, deplete, eliminate***. (Do the last three expressions have the same meaning?)

6. *Extra-credit Project:* Find out whether Nissan Motors (or any car manufacturer) has been successful in replacing CFCs in its automobile air conditioners (¶3). Visit or call a car dealer or study advertisements for information.

MARCH 31, 1989

US declines to take control of effort to clean up spill

By John W. Mashek
Globe Staff

Barges and fishing boats struggle with an oil slick that now covers an estimated 575 square miles. Page 6.

1 WASHINGTON – The Bush administration concluded yesterday that there was no need for the government to assume control of cleaning up the huge oil spill in Alaska, although the chief US environmental official conceded that it was "a disaster of enormous potential, magnitude and impact."

2 Transportation Secretary Samuel Skinner and William Reilly, the Environmental Protection Agency administrator, both said that cleanup efforts were proceeding at full speed after a slow start. They spoke after a meeting with President Bush.

3 "At this point, there is not a need to federalize this effort — that will be held in abeyance — and in fact, such a decision might be counterproductive because of the coordination that is ongoing," Skinner said.

4 Reilly, who made his description of the spill as a "disaster" while appearing before reporters with Skinner, also said the oil had spread to more than 100 miles from the site of the accident.

5 Skinner said the Coast Guard had 300 people involved in the effort, augmenting more than 100 from other state and local agencies. Exxon, the company whose tanker caused the spill, had more than 300 employees on the scene. The Coast Guard and the company have dispatched numerous vessels and helicopters to help control the slick, he added.

6 By leaving Exxon in charge, the government is giving the company a vote of confidence in its cleanup efforts, a White House official said. If the government were to take control of the cleanup, it would incur all expenses, which it might be able to recover later from Exxon in court, the official said.

7 Despite assurances that an effective cleanup plan was in place, environmental groups are skeptical because of what they have called lax standards in the first place. For example, Gaylord Nelson, the counselor to the Wilderness Society and a former senator from Wisconsin, said Exxon and the government were "grossly negligent."

8 "Exxon was negligent for obvious reasons and the government needs tighter controls for ships up there. It's goofy to let a ship go out in a sea lane with icebergs," Nelson said.

9 Coast Guard Commandant Paul Yost, who made an inspection trip to Alaska with Skinner and Reilly earlier this week, said it was "almost unbelievable" that the tanker, the Exxon Valdez, struck a reef outside the 10-mile shipping lane.

10 "This was not a treacherous area, not treacherous in the area where they ran aground," he said. "It's 10 miles wide. Your children could drive a tanker through it."

11 The first priority, he said, was to protect fish hatcheries on the uninhabited islands near Valdez. He said it was inevitable that the spill would affect sea otters and sea lions.

12 Asked if the disaster had changed his mind about future oil drilling in the pristine Arctic National Wildlife Refuge, Reilly said the nation had energy choices that imposed some risks. "I think all things considered, it is inconceivable that any nation would walk away from the resources that may exist in the magnitude that is potentially there in Alaska," he said.

13 Could damage have been more limited if Exxon had acted faster? Skinner responded that more than 10 million gallons spilled into the water in the first five hours last Friday. But he said some of the spillage could have been contained if a response team had moved in faster.

14 "We're going to learn. If we don't learn from this experience, we are just not performing our job," Skinner said after fielding a number of questions on the effort.

15 Potential civil penalties against Exxon await an investigation by the Coast Guard, the officials said. The state of Alaska, meanwhile, is conducting a criminal investigation.

16 In a separate meeting with reporters, Attorney General Dick Thornburgh said the natural resources division of the Justice Department would assess the legal grounds for any civil or criminal action after the Coast Guard investigation is completed.

17 Recognizing the environmental impact of this largest spill in US history, Bush brought up the subject in a speech to the American Association of Community and Junior Colleges.

18 "We're doing all we can at the federal level to speed up this undertaking," Bush told the educators. "The cleanup will not be easy. It is in remote areas and it's very complicated."

Vocabulary

¶1　**assume**　[here] to take or take over
　　　concede　to admit as true (unwillingly)
　　　impact　effect; also, the force of one thing hitting another
¶3　**federalize**　to make *federal*/national
　　　in abeyance　not in use at this certain time [formal]
　　　counterproductive　having an opposite effect; contrary to being useful
¶5　**vessel**　ship or boat
　　　slick *[noun]*　covering of oil in water
¶6　**in charge**　as managers, having the responsibility
¶7　**skeptical**　doubting, unwilling to believe, distrustful
　　　lax　weak, lacking control, relaxed
　　　grossly　inexcusably (with no excuse)
　　　negligent　not caring (for/about something), not giving the necessary attention
¶8　**goofy**　silly [informal]
¶9　**reef**　sharp underwater rocks
¶10　**treacherous**　dangerous (in an unexpected way)
¶11　**inevitable**　not preventable, certain to happen
¶12　**pristine**　pure, unspoiled, like new
　　　refuge　shelter, safe place
　　　inconceivable　unthinkable, impossible
　　　resources　[here] the land, mineral wealth, natural energy sources, etc., that an
　　　　　　　　　area/country has
¶14　**field (questions)**　to get (answer) successfully [originally a sports term]
¶15　**civil penalties**　punishment for breaking civil law (law dealing with private
　　　　　　　　　rights of citizens, not with crimes)

Note: On March 24, 1989, the oil tanker Exxon Valdez hit a reef near the Alaskan port Valdez. Details of the accident are not reported in this article because it is assumed that readers are familiar with the week-old story.

Questions

1. Who is working on the cleanup?

2. Why isn't the federal government (President Bush's administration) taking active leadership in the cleanup?

3. Considering ¶1–5, how do you interpret Bush's words in ¶18?

4. From what you know now, long after the Valdez oil spill, do you think the President's decision was wise? Was it typically American?

5. What animals were affected by the oil spill?

Note: The following article describes the cleanup situation 4½ months later.

SAMPLE ARTICLE 7.5-3

8/16/89

Cleaning it up their way: Alaskans split from Exxon

by Dianne Dumanoski

1 ALASKANS, AIDED by volunteers from as far away as Europe, have started an independent cleanup effort in an area affected by the Exxon Valdez oil spill, contending that Exxon will not let its cleanup crews do a proper job.

2 Exxon crews are directed to wash only the tops of the tar-covered rocks, said Jim Heinzen, a commercial fisherman from Homer who organized the effort in the Kenai Peninsula. Using a special rock-washing device built by a local inventor, the volunteer crews are doing an overall cleaning, he said.

3 "The volunteers include people who worked for Exxon and who evolved their own techniques that Exxon wouldn't accept," he added.

4 Disputing these accusations, Exxon spokesman Fred Davis said the cleanup is proceeding on schedule and to the satisfaction of the Coast Guard, which is overseeing the effort.

5 According to state officials, volunteer crews have also been organized in Valdez and Kodiak Island.

6 The volunteer cleanup will continue after Exxon pulls out of Alaska in mid-September and, Heinzen said, "in the spring, we'll clean up the beaches the way Alaskans want them cleaned."

Reprinted courtesy of The Boston Globe.

Vocabulary

Head	**split**	to separate, go away from (each other)
¶1	**contend**	to claim, say with strength
	crew	team/group workers (especially on a ship)
¶2	**tar**	thick, sticky, black substance derived from a natural material
	device	a machine or instrument, especially one cleverly designed
¶4	**dispute**	to argue against, disagree with
¶6	**pull out**	[here] to leave (like a train from a station)

Questions

1. Who is helping Alaskans clean up *their* way?
[*Note:* The headline uses a special phrase to attract attention, the phrase "their way." The emphasis is on "their," as opposed to the way/method of anybody else. A song, "*I'll do it my way,*" sung by Frank Sinatra, made the phrase popular. It expresses an individualism that many Americans value, and it seems appropriate as a headline for this story.]

2. In the previous article, President Bush's administration expressed confidence in Exxon's cleanup efforts. In this later story, is any group satisfied with Exxon's work?

3. Have you ever been a volunteer for any environmental group? If so, tell the class about your experiences. Use some of the Essential Vocabulary, such as: *cleanup, proceed, effort, environment, pollute, toxic, potential, recycle.*

4. Have you ever lived in an area affected by an oil spill?

5. Are the Valdez oil spill and the cleanup effort still in the news?

4/16/89

Environmental Notebook

DIANNE DUMANOSKI

Ecologist bearish on ecotourism future

1   Ecotourism may be booming now, but a leading Canadian ecologist predicts that it will soon be bust because wild places are going fast.

2   David Suzuki, who is also a science broadcaster in Canada, made the dire forecast last week in a speech at an international tourism conference in Indonesia. "In 30 years," he warned, "there will be no wilderness left to visit except for a few little islands we set aside as preserves."

3   In his view, the developed world is ignoring evidence that the planet is being pushed to the limit by growing numbers of people consuming more goods and producing increasing amounts of waste. Rich countries, he said, should begin by setting a better example at home. "As long as we are consuming at the rate we are," he said, "we have no right to say anything."

4   Fish and other aquatic species in North America are losing ground even faster than land-dwelling creatures, say Nature Conservancy scientists. They find that 30 percent of the 700 native freshwater fish species are in jeopardy because of water pollution, stream impoundments, and habitat loss.

Reprinted courtesy of The Boston Globe.

Vocabulary

Head **ecologist**   scientist who studies the relationships of all living things with their environment

bearish [idiom from the stock market]   pessimistic

ecotourism [new word]   tourism of wilderness areas

¶1   **booming**   rapidly growing/increasing, successful (for a business)

bust [slang]   bankrupt, or a business failure

going   [here] disappearing, becoming lost

¶2   **broadcaster**   radio or TV speaker

dire   deeply pessimistic

¶3   **ignore**   pay no attention to

goods   things produced by business and industry to be sold

¶4   **aquatic**   living in (or near) water

species   [here] kinds of living beings (plants and animals)

lose ground [idiom]   to become weaker

land-dwelling   living on land

jeopardy   danger

impoundment   legally taking control of, by an authority [formal]

habitat   natural environment in which a creature lives

Questions

1. *Looking at Language:* "Bearish" is a word from stock-market talk.
   a. Find two other stock-market terms in the first paragraph.
   b. Why are these terms used in an article about the environment?

2. Why is the ecologist bearish?

3. Which are more in danger of dying out, fish or land animals?

4. Compare David Suzuki's message with that of Sting on p. 108.
   a. Do you think the two men have similar messages?
   b. Do they have similar backgrounds?

5. Is there any news about the loss or preservation of wilderness areas in your current newspaper?

6. Is environmental protection or preservation an issue in your country?

Essential Vocabulary

Many newspapers include a Science Section once a week. Articles in that section are usually long and give details and background information. The National News section can also contain general-interest stories about science and technology. Some vocabulary is common to many of these reports.

A. Read the following fictional news article about the real National Science Foundation. It contains all 11 essential words (some twice) in boldface. On the basis of the article, try to write your own definitions of these words (some are written for you). Read the whole article before you begin the definitions.

PRESIDENT PRAISES SCIENCE FOUNDATION

WASHINGTON, D.C. – Under this President's **administration**, the National Science **Foundation** has achieved a new **image**. The organization has received over $2.1 **billion** from the **federal** budget this year, a 10% increase over last year. In contrast, under the last **administration**, financial support had dropped about 2% per year.

The President called for a **massive** new effort to increase top-quality **research** in all the sciences.

"The President's attitude toward science is **crucial** to us," responded the spokesperson for NSF. "It generates interest in scientific and **technological** progress within the **federal** government. And then, when the public **perceives** the benefits of **research**, that gives science courses at all levels of education a more positive **image**."

The **foundation** dispenses the money to hundreds of scientists at universities and institutes across the United States. It receives in return detailed reports of the results of the **studies** that it supported.

---

administration _____

billion _____

crucial _____

federal _____

foundation <u>organization that gathers or holds money *(funds)* for a purpose</u>

image _____

massive _____

perceive _____

research _____

study–studies <u>(scientific) investigation(s) or learning</u>

technological <u>concerning (practical) sciences as used in industry</u>

B. Can you match each science below with the correct definition?

_____ 1. **aeronautics**

_____ 2. **astronomy**

_____ 3. **engineering**

_____ 4. **bioengineering**

_____ 5. **genetics**

a. the science of applying biology to industrial uses

b. the science of applying the use of power to industry, as in the construction of machines, bridges, etc.

c. the scientific study of the flight of airplanes, etc.

d. the science of the planets, stars, etc., in the universe

e. a branch of biology that studies heredity; the scientific study of genes, the chemical parts of a chromosome (in a cell) that carry inherited characteristics from parents to child

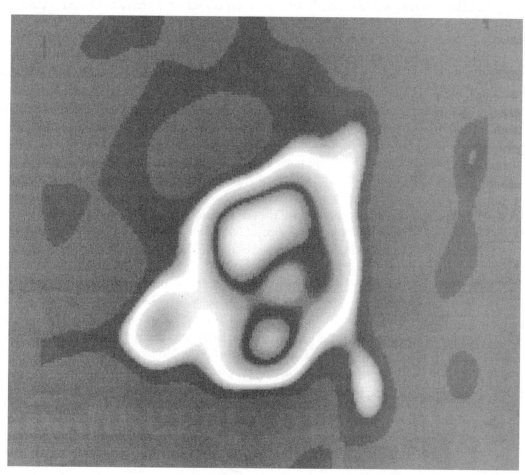

An astronomer's image of an exploded star. The star's remains are flying through the universe at a speed of 10,000 km per second.

Business News

Introduction: Business News and the News Business

Business news is generally contained in a separate section of the newspaper, following the national and international news and the editorial/Op-Ed pages. Articles about the growth or losses of companies, financial or industry trends, labor–management relations, and investments are of interest to business people. In addition, stock market tables are printed in the national papers, the *International Herald Tribune*, and large metropolitan journals.[1] (Those tables plus other statistical business news are a major source of income for wire services.)

Other articles are written to inform the general public about trends in the business world. Issues that can affect everybody, especially buyers of products, are called *consumer issues*. They can deal with health or safety problems of a product, with environmental effects of industrial production, with prices or mortgages (bank loans for buying a house), and so on. See Section 8.2 for examples.

In some cases consumers' concerns are contrary to the point of view of the business or industry involved. Companies that advertise a lot in newspapers try occasionally to influence the publishing of (bad) news about themselves or their products. For example, author Martin Mayer writes that a 1986 consumer service article about how used-car salesmen deal with customers was run by many papers. The story

> ... annoyed automobile dealers. One paper, ... Wichita [Kansas] *Eagle & Beacon*, responded to threats of the local auto dealers by publicly apologizing for the piece as "inadequately researched," which may indeed have saved some advertising revenues—at a very high cost.[2]

After all, a newspaper's survival depends on its income from advertising, which is generally about three-quarters of its total income; and automobile companies place a great number of advertisements. However, most editors, whose primary interest is *news*, and publishers resist such efforts successfully.

The content of the Business section of each newspaper reflects the concerns and financial status of its particular readers. This includes the advertisements as well as the articles. For example, the advertising manager of Bloomingdale's, an expensive department store, explained bluntly to the tabloid *New York Post* why Bloomingdale's did not place any advertisements in that paper but only in the *New York Times*: "Their [the *Times'*] readers are our customers; your readers are our shoplifters."[3] (A shoplifter is someone who takes something(s) from a store without paying.)

In metropolitan newspapers, many of the articles found in this section are local. A successful metropolitan paper helps business people to stay well informed about the business community of which they are a part. In many big city areas, small suburban papers cover local news thoroughly and create real competition for metropolitan dailies.

On the following pages are examples from both national and metropolitan newspapers.

Essential Vocabulary and Sample Articles

8.1 WORKPLACE ISSUES: LABOR AND MANAGEMENT

Essential Vocabulary

A. The following 14 words are essential for the understanding of newspaper articles on labor-and-management issues, such as strikes and contract negotiations. (If you have already completed several of the other sections in this book, you will recognize some of the vocabulary.) Match each word on the left with the correct definition on the right. How many can you match without using a dictionary? _____

_____ 1. **allegation/alleged**

_____ 2. **bargaining**

_____ 3. **contract**

_____ 4. **employee**

_____ 5. **file** *[verb]*

_____ 6. **fire** *[verb]*

_____ 7. **issue** *[noun]*

_____ 8. **labor**

_____ 9. **negotiate**

_____ 10. **suspend**

_____ 11. **strike** *[noun]*

_____ 12. **union**

_____ 13. **uphold**

_____ 14. **work force/workforce**

a. a paid worker

b. workers/employees in general, as a group

c. workers, as a group, especially those who use their hands at work

d. club or society; [here] organized group of workers in similar jobs

e. discussing the content of a contract, etc.

f. an important topic not easily solved

g. a formal, lawful agreement

h. refusal to work (work stoppage) because of a disagreement [also a verb]

i. to delay or stop for a period of time

j. to talk together and try to come to an agreement on

k. to record or send in officially

l. to confirm, declare to be right

m. to end the employment of a person because of something bad/wrong that he or she did

n. charge/accusation not yet proven; charged as, or declared to be, something without proof [Journals use it for legal reasons.]

B. Fill in the blanks with nine words from the Essential Vocabulary list.

WASHINGTON – The Supreme Court decided yesterday that airline and

railway companies can require drug tests for their _____.
                                                          1

_____ leaders had opposed the measure, saying that it is
        2

not part of their _____ _d_ contract.
                          3

Important in this case was the fact that routine urinalysis is already

provided for in the unions' _____s_. Adding a drug test did not
                                    4

require new collective _____, the high court ruled.
                                5

Another recent Supreme Court decision _____ the
                                               6

government's mandatory drug testing order for _____s_ who
                                                       7

operate dangerous equipment, carry guns, or work in drug law

enforcement.

Union leaders have been actively involved in this _____
                                                          8

but had not threatened to go on _____ over it.
                                        9

Extra Vocabulary

mandatory: compulsory/forced/obligatory
urinalysis: chemical analysis of urine (yellow fluid waste passed from the
         body)

SEPTEMBER 14, 1988

Strike enters 4th day at Wire Belt Co.

1   About 45 Hispanic employees of a Winchester conveyor-belt company yesterday entered the fourth day of a strike to protest the alleged discriminatory firing of a Puerto Rican worker.

2   The non-union workers of the 115-employee Wire Belt Co. of America stayed outside the River Street firm in a workday vigil they have kept since Miguel Ramos was fired for fighting last Thursday with white co-worker Robert Hall.

3   They say Ramos' dismissal was racially motivated, and are refusing to work until both men are either fired, suspended or Ramos is rehired, said Willie Candelario, an employee spokesman.

Reprinted with permission of the Boston Herald.

Vocabulary

¶1   **Hispanic**   person in the U.S.A. who comes from a Spanish-speaking culture or country

  discriminatory   for biased reasons, based on unfairly treating people differently (because of sex, race, religion, background, etc.)

¶2   **vigil**   act of remaining watchful (especially at night)

¶3   **dismissal**   sending an employee away and ending his/her employment (fault is not implied in this verb)

  racially motivated   done because of (a person's) race (or background)

Reading for Information

Write out the answers to the Five W's and the H question.
(You can use the example on p. 63 as a model.)

What: _____

Who: _____

Where: _____

When: _____

How: _____

Why: _____

Questions for Discussion

1. Are strikes common in your country? Use some of the Essential Vocabulary in your answer, such as: *issue, employee, labor, union, workforce, negotiate, bargaining, contract, strike.*

2. Are there any articles about strikes in your current paper?

3. Do you think there are racial problems where you live?

4. Are there any articles about alleged racial discrimination in current American newspapers?

3/10/89

Eastern seeks protection under bankruptcy laws

Unions pledge fight over plan

SAMPLE ARTICLE 8.1-2

3/10/89

'Continental-type deal'?

1   Union officials see Eastern Airlines' bankruptcy filing yesterday as an attempt by Texas Air Chairman Frank Lorenzo to repeat the success he had when he put Continental Airlines into bankruptcy in September 1983.

2   Continental, then the nation's eighth-largest carrier, was closed for three days.

3   It reopened as a discount carrier, offering tickets for domestic flights for only $49.

4   More important, Lorenzo was able to scrap union agreements, sack two-thirds of his employees and cut salaries by up to 50 percent.

5   Experts said a similar scenario is unlikely in the Eastern case. In response to the Continental action, Congress amended the bankruptcy laws in 1984.

6   Bankrupt firms must now negotiate with unions and prove economic need before they break labor agreements. A bankruptcy judge will allow Eastern to break labor agreements only if it shows it cannot survive otherwise.

— JEFFREY KRASNER

Reprinted with permission of the Boston Herald.

Vocabulary

1st Head   **bankruptcy**   the state of not being able to pay company debts
2nd Head   **deal**   business arrangement or agreement
¶2   **carrier**   [here] airline
¶3   **domestic**   [here] of/within one country, not international
¶4   **scrap**   to throw away, discard, or do away with
        sack   to fire employee(s) [informal]
        salary   regular monthly or biweekly pay for work
¶5   **amend**   to change the words of (a rule or law)

Questions

1. Which bankruptcy happened first: Continental or Eastern Airlines?

2. How many years are between the two bankruptcies?

3. Why do you think the unions will fight Lorenzo's plan to declare bankruptcy?

4. Can Frank Lorenzo "scrap union agreements" with Eastern, now that it is bankrupt?

SEPTEMBER 1, 1989

Unions Bet Bargaining Chips on Family Benefits

By Bob Dart
Journal-Constitution Washington Bureau

1 WASHINGTON – Labor Day may take on a new meaning in the 1990s as unions shift their demands from bigger paychecks to better family benefits in an increasingly female work force.

2 Benefits that help workers balance job and family commitments — such as time off for pregnancy, delivery and baby bonding — likely will replace financial demands as the dominant issues for the American labor movement in the next decade, according to a report issued Thursday by the Bureau of National Affairs (BNA).

3 Rather than bargaining over whether members will get a 50-cent or 55-cent-an-hour raise, union negotiators will be asking for parental leave, flexible work schedules and more employer help in caring for children and aged parents, the private business research organization predicted.

4 BNA is a leading publisher of print and electronic news and information services, reporting on developments in labor relations, business economics, law, taxation, environmental protection and other public policy issues.

5 "It's not just how much money we can squeeze out of [management] anymore. . . . A lot of our members are interested in the more intangible benefits," Howard Evans, president of the American Postal Workers Union's Syracuse, N.Y., local, said in the report.

6 However, unions may find bosses as hard to budge on family-aid benefits as on traditional issues of wages and working conditions.

Rather than bargaining over whether members will get a 50-cent or 55-cent-an-hour raise, union negotiators will be asking for parental leave, flexible work schedules and more employer help in caring for children and aged parents.

7 With medical costs rising, the basic family benefit of health and hospitalization insurance is becoming an increasingly touchy issue between employers and employees. Thousands of telephone workers went on strike in August at least partly because some Bell operating companies proposed changes in health-care coverage.

8 Union demands for new — and costly — family benefits such as assistance in child care or elder care probably will meet resistance from employers. BNA surveyed 250 firms and found only 19 — 8 percent — provide any type of child-care assistance under their union contracts. Another 8 percent planned to negotiate such a benefit in 1990, the survey found.

9 While 75 percent of the firms provide for maternity leave in union contracts, only 12 percent have provisions for paternity leave. In dual-income families, fathers increasingly are demanding time off for child-rearing duty.

10 Historically male-oriented unions are having to shift their stances at the bargaining tables to take into account changing demographics of the work force. More than 70 percent of the nation's women ages 25 to 34 were employed outside the home in 1988 — double the percentage of 1950, according to the Department of Labor. In the final 15 years of the 20th century, 60 percent of the new entrants into the labor force will be women.

11 Likewise, working couples will be more concerned with care for their elderly parents as life spans continue to grow and the baby boomers enter retirement.

12 Union members now feel that bargaining for child-care assistance and other family-type benefits is an obligation of organized labor, the report said. Indeed, the report said, "signs of organized labor's increasing interest in work and family issues are everywhere."

13 ■ In May, the Communications Workers of America reached an agreement with American Telephone and Telegraph Co. that provides child-care benefits, more leave for family problems, reimbursement for adoption expenses and other family benefits.

14 ■ The Coalition of Labor Union Women, the AFL-CIO and the Labor Department sponsored seven regional conferences last spring on "Bargaining for Our Families" in which union representatives discussed ways to bargain and lobby for work and family benefits.

15 ■ The AFL-CIO recently held a "Children's Day on the Hill" in which thousands of working parents lobbied Congress for legislation dealing with work and family issues.

Vocabulary

Head   **bet . . . chips on . . .** *[idiom from gambling]*   to be willing to take a risk in the
            hope of gaining . . . (something valuable)

    benefits   [here] money or other advantages given to employees by the employer

¶1   **Labor Day**   the first Monday in September, an annual legal holiday in the
            U.S.A. in honor of workers

    take on   [here] to begin to have

    shift   to move from one position to another

¶2   **commitments**   responsibilities

    delivery   [here] having/bearing a baby

    baby bonding   forming a loving attachment/relationship with a baby

    issued   given out, provided [*verb:* to issue]

    Bureau   office, especially one that collects facts

¶3   **leave**   period of permitted absence from work (a week or more)

¶5   **intangible**   not material

    local *[noun]*   local union; [here] the union of Syracuse, New York

¶6   **budge**   [here] to cause to move or change positions a little, to push

    aid   help

¶7   **touchy**   sensitive (emotional)

    propose   to suggest

    coverage   [here] insurance

¶8   **survey** *[verb]*   to poll, to question in an organized way

¶9   **child-rearing**   bringing up, taking care of, a child or children

¶10   **male-oriented**   directed toward or concerned with the interests of men (*males*)

    stance   [here] position or way of thinking about an issue

    demographics   population statistics

¶11   **likewise**   also; similarly

    lifespan   length of a human life

    baby boomers   generation of people born after World War II, from 1946 to
            1963 in North America

¶13   **reimbursement**   paying back, payment to an employee from a company for
            money already spent by the employee

¶14   **lobby for**   to be active in efforts to achieve positive changes in

¶15   **dealing with**   [here] about, concerned with

Reading for Information

1. Scan (look quickly through) the article for the following abbreviations. Are they defined?
   If so, in which paragraph? If not, why not? Can you define them yourself?
   a. BNA
   b. N.Y.
   c. Co.
   d. AFL-CIO

2. a. What were traditional bargaining issues between labor and management in the past?

   b. What kind of issue is important in the '90s, according to the article?

3. List the specific employee benefits that are mentioned in the article. (Some are mentioned
   more than once.)

Questions for Discussion

1. a. What event is the basis for Sample Article 8.1-3? In which paragraph is it reported?

    b. Is this a hard news story, a feature story, or a blend of both? Give reasons for your answer.

2. Does your family's employer provide any of the benefits that you listed in item 3 (previous page)? Do you have additional benefits? (*Option*: Read Sample Article 7.4-2, on universal health care (p. 144), to get some ideas of other benefits.)

3. If you know about typical benefits provided by companies in another country, compare them with those mentioned in the article or with those that you have discussed in class.

4. Look through a current newspaper for stories on labor/management relations. (In which sections of the paper will you look?) What issues are reported? Use some of the Essential Vocabulary in your answer if possible, such as: *union, workforce, labor, employee, negotiate, bargain, uphold, contract, issue.*

5. *Concluding Discussion*:

    a. How many of the four articles in Section 8.1 (including the article in Essential Vocabulary) are about unions or union workers?

    b. On the basis of your own experience and reading, compare union issues in the United States and your native country.

Consumers (people who buy and use things, that is, just about everybody at some time!) are concerned about *safety, quality,* and *prices* of the things they buy. This section offers some examples of consumer news.

Essential Vocabulary

The crossword puzzle below includes the 10 words that are important for understanding articles about consumer issues. Clues for these essential words are marked with an asterisk (*). The other words often appear in the Business Section, too. *Challenge:* Cover the bottom right corner of this page and try to solve the puzzle first without looking at the list.

ACROSS

*2. buy

5. get money for work

6. rise fast and far

7. short (tabloid) word for *executive, manager

*8. smaller/secondary company under a main one

*11. understand, see, feel

*14. guarantee *[noun]*

DOWN

*1. public attention

*2. before(hand)

*3. buys and uses (also, eats)

*4. frighten

*9. low price for a good item, favorable deal

10. room (abbreviation used in the Classified Ads)

12. Individual Retirement Account (abbreviation)

13. begin a first job = _____ the workforce

Essential Vocabulary

bargain
consume
executive
perceive
previous
publicity
purchase
scare
subsidiary
warranty

JULY 21, 1989

New milk-production drug runs into strong opposition

By John Larrabee
USA TODAY

1 WHITINGHAM, Vt. – Leon Corse starts work at 4 a.m. and quits at sunset. Each morning he milks 50 Holsteins. Then there's hay to mow and wood to cut. In the summer, he'll go six weeks without a day off.

2 Like most New England dairy farmers, Corse, 36, would welcome any innovation that promises to ease his workload.

3 So why is Corse reluctant to inject his cows with BST, a new drug designed to boost each cow's output by a gallon a day?

4 "If you push the cows too hard, they tend to have health problems," says Corse. "They would be under more stress, just like an executive with too many responsibilities."

5 BST — bovine somatotropin — is a genetically-engineered hormone that can increase a milk cow's output 10 to 25 percent. To the pharmaceutical companies that hope to market the drug it's a revolutionary advance — one of the first uses of biotechnology in agriculture.

6 But in New England's top dairy state, many farmers can't understand why the drug was invented in the first place. They fear it will harm livestock, scare consumers, and drop the price of milk.

7 The four companies developing BST — Monsanto, American Cyanamid, Elanco and Upjohn — hope to see it go on the market next year. The FDA [Food and Drug Administration] decided BST poses no threat to humans, but has not licensed its commercial use.

8 Some dairy operators "don't fully perceive the economic benefits," says Monsanto spokesman Larry O'Neill. "Like every other dairy production tool, BST should be allowed to succeed or fail."

9 The Foundation on Economic Trends — a Washington, D.C., bioengineering opponent — starts an international anti-BST campaign next month.

10 Jeremy Rifkin, director of the group, vows "a massive consumer campaign in any country that attempts to put this on the market."

11 In a 30-second TV spot he produced, a syringe lies next to a glass of milk while a voice asks: "What are they doing to our milk?" It has yet to air.

12 Manufacturers are outraged by the TV spot. "It's reckless, irresponsible, and wrongly alarming," says O'Neill. "It's not consumer education."

13 Food industry executives are caught in the middle. Many processors and supermarkets quietly refuse to handle milk from BST-treated herds.

14 One of their biggest fears: Publicity about the drug will cause consumer backlash. Many were upset when the Massachusetts Commissioner of Agriculture called BST "crack for cows."

15 Says Doug Dimento, a spokesman for New England's Agri-Mark co-op: "We don't want to damage milk's image as pure and nutritious."

Vocabulary

¶2   **innovation**   the introduction of a new invention/thing or idea

¶3   **reluctant**   not eager, unwilling and hesitant

      boost   to increase or raise

¶5   **hormone**   a biological substance (usually) produced in the body to influence growth and development

¶6   **dairy** *[adj.]*   concerning milk products; or *[noun]* place where milk products are prepared

¶11   **TV spot**   advertisement on television

      syringe   hypodermic needle used to inject drugs into the body

      air   to be broadcast on TV or radio

¶14   **backlash**   strong (public) feeling against a policy or movement

      crack   popular and inexpensive form of the addictive drug cocaine, used for pleasure

¶15   **nutritious**   healthy and good for the body, said of food

Questions

1. Why doesn't Mr. Corse want BST to become available?

2. Are Jeremy Rifkin's objections the same as Leon Corse's?

3. What is the counterargument of the companies that are developing BST?

4. What is New England's "top dairy state" (¶6)?

5. Do you know of any stores or markets in your area where you can buy organically produced foods? "Organic" usually means it is produced without pesticides or certain chemical fertilizers or additives.

6. As consumers become more interested in how foods are produced and treated, the issue becomes more newsworthy. Are there any articles about this topic in your current paper?

7. Are consumers in your country worried about the safety and quality of foods? Give some examples and try to use some of these words: *consumer, perceive, publicity, scare, bargain.*

AUGUST 14, 1989

US drivers give Asian cars highest satisfaction rating

Reuters

1   AGOURA HILLS, Calif. – Cars produced by Asian manufacturers continued to win the highest customer satisfaction from American car owners, according to a survey released last week.

2   The Asian cars, however, held a narrower point lead over US-made rivals than previously, J. D. Power and Associates, an automotive research firm, reported in its annual Customer Satisfaction Index.

3   Acura, the luxury car division of Japan's Honda Motor Co., received the highest customer satisfaction rating, with 147 points, for the third consecutive year. Mercedes-Benz had the second-highest rating of 138 points, followed by Honda with 137 points.

4   Of the 16 carmakers that matched or exceeded the industry average customer satisfaction score of 118 points, seven were Asian, five were European and four were American. The survey releases only the names of autos that do better than the industry average, not those that do worse.

5   The index is based on the opinions of about 24,000 owners of 1988 model-year cars 12 months after purchase. The survey measures 23 components of ownership and service experiences.

Customer satisfaction

Ranking of 1988 model year cars according to customer satisfaction

Rank	Model	Rating
1.	Acura	147
2.	Mercedes-Benz	138
3.	Honda	137
4.	Toyota	134
5.	Cadillac	131
6.	Nissan	128
7.	Subaru	126
8.	Mazda (tie)	125
9.	BMW (tie)	125
10.	Buick	123
11.	Plymouth	122
12.	Audi (tie)	121
13.	Volvo (tie)	121
14.	Hyundai	119
15.	Porsche (tie)	118
16.	Mercury (tie)	118

Source: J.D. Power and Associates

Globe staff chart / Neil C. Pinchin

Reprinted by permission of Reuters. Chart reprinted courtesy of The Boston Globe.

Vocabulary

Head **rating**   placement in a list of things
¶1   **survey**   poll, organized questioning of many people
     release   to publish, make available to the public
¶2   **point lead**   percent lead, percent by which they are in front
     rival   competitor
     annual   yearly, every year
¶3   **consecutive**   following regularly; [here] three years in a row
¶4   **match**   [here] to be equal to, or to make an equal offer
     exceed   to be greater than
¶5   **components**   aspects, or parts

Questions

1. *True or false?* Write T or F in the blanks on the left.

   _____ a. Acura had the highest rating for 1987 as well as 1988 models.

   _____ b. Mercury was below the industry average.

   _____ c. The best-rated American-made car was the Cadillac.

   _____ d. All the cars that are not on the list rated below the average satisfaction level.

2. Can you identify the cars that were made in these countries? (*Hint:* See ¶4.)

   a. Japan: _____

   b. Germany: _____

   c. the U.S.A.: _____

   d. Sweden: _____

   e. Korea: _____

3. If you, or your family, own a car, what kind is it? Are you satisfied with it?

4. What kind of car is most popular in your country?

APRIL 4, 1989

Chrysler offers no-interest, 2-year loans to buyers

By Frederic M. Biddle
Globe Staff

Auto financing

AUTOMAKER	CUT-RATE FINANCING OFFERED
Ford Motor Co.	2.9%
Chrysler Corp.	0%
General Motors Corp.	2.9%

1   In a virtual replay of Detroit automakers' interest-rate wars of 1986, Chrysler Corp. yesterday offered interest-free loans on most of its cars and trucks.

2   The loans are being offered indefinitely by Chrysler's credit subsidiary on most 1988 and 1989 Chryslers, Dodges, Plymouths and Eagles, on purchases to be paid for in 24 months or less. The offer undercuts the 2.9 percent loans offered last week by GM and Ford.

3   The zero-percent lure is an attempt by Chrysler to sell the too-many cars lying unsold on its dealers' lots during the big spring car-buying season. So far, Big Three automakers' 1989 sales are trailing last year's by 8 percent, and about 20,000 fewer cars were built than had been planned at the beginning of the year.

4   And as increasing interest rates begin to scare off consumers, Chrysler and other automakers are abandoning the so-called new car "warranty wars" of the past two years, to return to familiar territory.

5   "Interest rates are the new battlefield," said Detroit auto analyst Arvid F. Jouppi. And Chrysler executives are leaving no doubt as to whom they expect to snap at the new loans —

namely, buyers who normally pay cash for their new cars.

6   "This attracts the more affluent buyer, the more stable buyer, who perceives having, say, $12,000 to use for two years at no interest to be a once-in-a-lifetime deal," said Jeremiah Farrell, president of Chrysler Credit Corp. The deal doesn't include the Dodge Caravan/Plymouth Voyager minivan, the automaker's biggest seller.

7   Chrysler's sales are off 20.7 percent for the first three months of this year compared with last year, Farrell said, and the company is expected to build nearly 16 percent fewer cars during the second quarter of this year than during the same period last year.

8   "I think this opens Chrysler up for some additional loans losses," said Paul Kleinaitis, a Duff and Phelps Inc. analyst. "It brings in more marginal customers" who otherwise might not be willing to get themselves in over their heads by buying a car they cannot afford.

Vocabulary

Head **interest**   money paid, for example to a bank, for the use of their money

       loan   money that is borrowed and must be repaid

¶1 **virtual**   in fact (even if it is not said)

       rate   value, amount

¶2 **undercut**   to go below, reduce by more than (someone else)

¶3 **lure**   something used to attract

       trailing   falling behind, losing in a race or competition

¶4 **abandon**   to give up, stop; or to leave

¶6 **affluent**   wealthy, rich

¶7 **off**   lower/less [Note word placement: ". . . are *off* 20.7%" but ". . . are 20.7% *lower*"]

Questions

1. What happened to interest rates on car loans in 1986?

2. What is happening to interest rates at the time of the article?

3. Who benefits from low interest rates?

4. What kind of buyer does Chrysler hope to lure with 0% interest?

5. Why did Chrysler decide to offer zero-interest loans?

6. Is Chrysler experiencing a growth or decline in business?

7. Is it more common for Americans to buy cars with a loan or to pay cash? How is it in your country?

8. What are the interest rates on car loans in your city?

Foreigners are spending plenty but prices are bargains to them

By Carolyn White
USA TODAY

1 Martin Barrier, owner of Martin's Discount Golf and Tennis in Myrtle Beach, S.C., still is on cloud nine.

2 A group of 25 Swedes, in the U.S.A. for a golf holiday several weeks ago, left Martin's with 11 full sets of golf clubs and nearly $7,000 in merchandise after a two-hour shopping spree.

3 "One Swedish golfer told me that in his country, a set of Ping 8 irons costs $1,000. He bought them here for $445.

4 "In some instances, they're saving up to 200 percent," added Barrier. "They came to the USA with little or no equipment at all. They plan to purchase a new set here, sell their old sets for nearly enough to pay for their trip.

5 "We had more foreign business the last 12 months, than during the previous 18 years."

6 Six weeks ago, six Japanese golfers spent $4,000 in a single afternoon. "They saved almost half of what they'd pay in their country," Barrier said. "They plan to come back next year and bring about 300 guys. I can't wait for that."

7 What's behind the hot sales? The decline of the dollar, the lack of golf facilities in other parts of the world (Myrtle Beach has 58 clubs compared with 25 in West Germany) and the sport's growing popularity.

8 Other groups, from Canada, West Germany, France and Australia, have purchased a large amount of equipment from Martin's four Myrtle Beach outlets.

9 But nobody tops the Japanese, according to Buzz Gill, who oversees pro shop operations for Landmark Land Co., which owns eight country clubs and 19 18-hole courses.

10 "None of the other foreigners buy like the Japanese. It's not even a contest," said Gill. "The golf boom and craze has hit Japan but there are few places to play there. They watch the Bob Hope Classic and the PGA West on TV. When they get over here, they want to buy the equipment with those logos on it.

11 "They always look for the logo 'Made in the U.S.A.' Money seems to be no object for them. But quality certainly is. They're buying good and expensive equipment. And they're buying it retail."

12 Gill says the Japanese pay 250 percent more for soft goods and double the price for hard goods in Japan. "A day of golf in Japan, including greens fees, costs $250," Gill said.

13 A golf shirt, purchased for $40 in the USA, would cost nearly $100 in Japan. "Joining a country club in Japan costs between $250,000 and $1 million," Barrier said.

14 "But they can fly here for $2,000 then eat, sleep and play golf for nearly $100 a day."

15 Other sales: A Japanese group plans to buy Riviera Country Club in Los Angeles for $100 million. In 1986, Japanese businessmen purchased La Costa Golf Course in Carlsbad, Calif.

Vocabulary

¶1 **discount**   reduced prices

on cloud nine *[idiom]*   very happy, like in a dream

¶2 **merchandise**   things to buy, goods for sale

shopping spree   fun shopping trip for many purchases

¶6 **guys**   people, especially men/boys [informal]

¶7 **hot**   popular, growing increasingly attractive [informal]

¶8 **outlet**   store that sells at reduced prices

¶9 **top** *[verb]*   to be greater than, at the *top* of the list, surpass

¶10 **boom**   a rapid growth or increase

craze   very popular thing for a short time, a fad

PGA West   major golf tournament/contest

logo   symbol, picture, or word that represents one brand

¶11 **retail**   [here] at a regular store price

Questions

1. How many golf courses are in each of the following four places? (Is it reported?)
   a. Japan
   b. Germany
   c. the U.S.A.
   d. Myrtle Beach, U.S.A.

2. Compare the price of playing golf plus buying equipment in Japan, Sweden, the U.S.A., and your country.

Essential Vocabulary

A. The following 14 words are essential for the understanding of articles about personal finances, investments, and money in the Business or Financial section of the newspaper. Match each word on the left with the correct definition on the right. How many can you match without using a dictionary? _____

_____ 1. **bullish**

_____ 2. **consumer**

_____ 3. **dampen**

_____ 4. **Dow Jones average**

_____ 5. **forecast**

_____ 6. **gain**

_____ 7. **inflation**

_____ 8. **interest rate**

_____ 9. **pace**

_____ 10. **plunge**

_____ 11. **soar**

_____ 12. **stocks**

_____ 13. **up**

_____ 14. **wages**

a. prediction of future events or trends
b. expecting a rather high stock market; optimistic
c. general rise in prices (indicating that money is losing value)
d. the cost of using borrowed money, figured as a percentage of it
e. units of ownership in a corporation
f. person who buys and uses (*consumes*) things
g. rate or speed
h. to increase; an increase
i. to rise far and fast
j. higher than before
k. payment for work (especially if received daily or weekly)
l. to make less strong, to decrease
m. to fall (suddenly) downward
n. most widely used stock market average, based on 30 industrial stocks, 20 transportation stocks, and 15 public utilities (gas, water, electricity)

B. Answer the following questions about the Essential Vocabulary.

1. Which words refer to an *increase* in something?

_____

2. Which words refer to a *decrease* in something?

_____

APPENDIX 1

Notes and References

Chapter 1

1. Mark S. Hoffman, ed., *The World Almanac and Book of Facts 1991* (New York: Pharos Books, 1990), p. 314. This reference book and others similar to it are available in most public libraries in North America.

2. David Petersen, *Newspapers* (Chicago: Regensteiner Publishing Enterprises–Children's Press, 1983), p. 6. [Very easy to read: written for elementary school children.]

3. A history and description of the *Wall Street Journal* is included in Martin Mayer, *Making the News* (New York: Doubleday & Company, 1987), pp. 225–233. [Advanced-level reading.]

4. Betty Lou English, *Behind the Headlines at a Big City Paper* (New York: Lee & Shepard Books, 1985), p. 117. The author writes about the organization and the people of the *New York Times* [Easy to read.]

5. Peter Prichard, an editor of *USA Today*, tells how the number of readers for *USA Today* and the *New York Times* was computed in his book, *The Making of McPaper. The Inside Story of USA Today* (Kansas City/New York: Andrews, McMeel & Parker, 1987), p. 316. But Mayer, in his book, *Making the News*, pp. 234–236, writes that *USA Today*'s figures are inflated because of special arrangements for bulk shipments to hotels and airlines, which give the paper away free to customers. Many of these free copies, he argues, are never read at all. Mayer, a professional nonfiction author, also gives a short history of the development of the paper.

   In 1990 the circulation of *USA Today* was listed as just over 1,300,000. Hoffman, ed., *The World Almanac and Book of Facts 1991*, p. 314.

6. The number of countries was stated by the founder of *USA Today*, Al Neuharth, and quoted in: "Thank You, Mr. Dictator," *Newsweek*, June 13, 1988, p. 65.

7. Hoffman, ed., *The World Almanac and Book of Facts 1991*, p. 314.

8. Carlin Romano, "The Grisly Truth About Bare Facts," in *Reading the News*, ed. Robert Karl Manoff and Michael Schudson (New York: Pantheon Books, 1987), p. 75. [Difficult reading.]

9. Howard E. Smith, Jr., and Louanne Norris, *Newsmakers. The Press and the Presidents* (Reading, Mass.: Addison-Wesley, 1974), pp. 90–96. The authors include a discussion about presidents who have tried to control newsmaking, sometimes successfully, during war times (through the early 1970s). [Intermediate-level reading.]

Chapter 2

1. Louis Solomon, *America Goes to Press* (London/New York/Toronto: Crowell-Collier Press, 1970), p. 147. [Advanced-level reading.]

2. *Newspaper in the Classroom* (Boston: *The Boston Globe*, 1984), p. 15. [Published for teachers.]

3. Peter Prichard, *The Making of McPaper. The Inside Story of USA Today* (Kansas City/New York: Andrews, McMeel & Parker, 1987), pp. 6 and 178d. [Advanced-level reading.]

4. Prichard (see note 3), pp. 178d and 302–303.

5. The study was done by this author June 6–10 (Monday–Friday), 1988, except for the *Monitor*, which changed its policy in late 1988 and was studied in June 1991. The headlines of the five dailies were noted and analyzed.

   A second, control study by this author of 14 randomly selected *New York Times* front pages from 1/1/88 through 4/11/88 shows a distribution only slightly different from the June results for that paper—namely, foreign news 37%, national news 44%, state news 3%, and local news 15%.

   Daniel C. Hallin reports statistics for the *Los Angeles Times* July 28 through August 3, 1985, as follows: international [foreign] news 33%, national news 53%, state news 5%, and local news 15%. Daniel C. Hallin, "Cartography, Community, and the Cold War" in *Reading the News*, ed. Robert Karl Manoff and Michael Schudson (New York: Pantheon Books, 1987), p. 119. [Difficult to read.]

6. A random sampling of six front pages of the *International Herald Tribune* in July and August, 1988, showed the following results: foreign news (non-American) 74%, national (U.S.) news 26%, state and local news (within the U.S.A.) 0%.

Chapter 3

1. Most of the headlines without page number references are fictional.

2. Statistics from the June 1988 study show that the *Monitor* has 36% noun phrases, 61% sentences in the active voice, 3% sentences in the passive voice in its headlines. The *Globe*: 19% noun phrases, 57% active sentences, 24% passive sentences. The *Herald*: 16% noun phrases, 81% active sentences, 3% passive sentences. *USA Today*: 14% noun phrases, 86% active sentences, 0% passive sentences. The *Times*: 7% noun phrases, 67% active sentences, 26% passive sentences.

3. Data for the front pages June 6–10, 1988. Names were included in headlines in (1) the *Times* for 18 persons, 18 countries, and 6 mostly local places out of 36 headlines; in (2) the *Globe* for 12 persons, 6 foreign countries, and 11 mostly local places out of 40 headlines; in (3) the *Monitor* for 8 persons, 10 foreign countries or regions, and 1 American state out of 23 headlines; in (4) the *Herald* for 13 persons, 8 sports teams, 1 foreign country, and 2 local places out of 29 headlines; and in (5) *USA Today* for 7 persons, 2 countries, and one state out of 29 total headlines.

4. James W. Carey, "The Dark Continent of American Journalism," in *Reading the News*, ed. Robert Karl Manoff and Michael Schudson (New York: Pantheon Books, 1987), p. 180. [Advanced-level reading.]

5. You might want to buy a dictionary of American idioms. Then you could look up any idiom that you read in the newspapers.

Chapter 4

1. The five newspapers are the *Globe*, the *Herald*, the *Times*, the *Tribune*, and *USA Today*. Analyzed were the first ten datelined articles in each paper, except for *USA Today*, where, because of its different organization, articles from the front page and the "Second Front Page" were chosen.

2. Examples in this chapter are taken from newspapers appearing Wednesday, July 20, 1988, unless otherwise stated. Underlinings were added by this author.

Chapter 5

1. For detailed discussions of the difficulties of answering these questions, see: James W. Carey, "The Dark Continent of American Journalism" in *Reading the News*, ed. Robert Karl Manoff and Michael Schudson (New York: Pantheon Books, 1987), pp. 146–196.

2. Carey (see note 1), pp. 150–151.

3. Peter Prichard, *The Making of McPaper. The Inside Story of USA Today* (Kansas City/New York: Andrews, McMeel & Parker, 1987), p. 293.

4. Prichard (see note 3), pp. 294ff.

5. Daniel C. Hallin, "Cartography, Community, and the Cold War" in *Reading the News*, ed. Manoff and Schudson (New York: Pantheon Books, 1987), pp. 121–122.

6. Charles Kuralt, "Foreword" in Prichard (see note 3), p. xi.

7. Hallin (see note 5), pp. 130–131.

Chapter 6

1. Daniel C. Hallin, "Cartography, Community, and the Cold War" in *Reading the News*, ed. Robert Karl Manoff and Michael Schudson (New York: Pantheon Books, 1987), pp. 139–141.

2. Dan Rather, "The Threat to Foreign News," "My Turn" Series, *Newsweek*, July 17, 1989, p. 9.

3. Rather (see note 2).

4. Hallin (see note 1), pp. 134–143. Adapted courtesy of Daniel C. Hallin.

5. Hallin (see note 1), pp. 143–144.

1. For clear, detailed explanations of stock market and financial vocabulary, see: Gerald Warfield, *How to Read and Understand the Financial News* (New York: Harper & Row Perennial Library, 1986). [Written for Americans, advanced-level reading.]

2. Martin Mayer, *Making the News* (New York: Doubleday & Company, 1987), p. 223. Mayer gives a few additional examples of consumer and political news stories that aroused local businessmen on pages 223–224 and 243.

3. Mayer (see note 2), p. 204.

Newspaper Literacy List: Commonly Occurring General Vocabulary

abandon   to leave completely, desert; or to give up, stop

aim at   to have as a goal, to direct toward (also, *to take aim at*)

alleged(ly)   supposed or stated but not proven [formal]

arrested   taken by police and charged with a crime

attorney   lawyer [American]

ban   to forbid/stop/prohibit

bargain *[noun]*   discount or reduced price; or something that is sold for a reduced price

boom   to increase quickly; or a sudden increase

boost   to increase/raise

concede   to admit (unwillingly) as true, or to yield

confrontation   face-to-face opposition or challenge, usually emotional

consumer   person who buys or uses things

crucial   all-important

custody   care, or the legal right of caring for someone

dealer   person in a specified business (examples: *drug dealer, automobile dealer*)

despite   in spite of

donor   person/country that gives/donates something

drugs   medicines, either used legally/correctly, or used improperly/illegally and habitually for pleasurable effects

ease   to do something gently/carefully

estimate   to guess, or to calculate approximately

environment   the (natural) surroundings

eventually   at some time in the future

federal   national, or relating to the central government

file (for)   to record or send in officially

fire *[verb]*   to dismiss or discharge an employee from a job for some fault of the employee; or to fuel/strengthen or arouse

Hispanic   person in the U.S.A. who comes from a Spanish-speaking culture/country

hot   popular [informal]; or controversial

interest rate   the cost of using borrowed money (figured as a percentage of that money)

issue   important topic or subject (that is not easy to solve)

joint   together

likely   probably or probable

massive   very big (and powerful)

negotiate   to try to reach an agreement through discussions/talks

off   away from (example: *off the coast*); or low(er)/less (example: *business was off*)

official   high-level employee of, or person who holds an office in, the government or a large organization

perceive   to understand, see, feel

plant   factory, especially one that produces energy

poll   (results of) questioning many people in an organized way

potential(ly)   possible/possibly in the future

resident   person living in a specified city/place

retail *[noun]*   store that sells goods to the public; or *[adjective]* at regular store prices (not wholesale)

search *[verb]*   to look for or examine carefully in order to find something; or *[noun]* examining, investigation

seek   to try to get, to ask for, to look for

serve a term   to spend time in (for example, in a position/office, or in prison as punishment for crimes)

soar   to rise fast (and far)

target *[verb]*   to aim at, to make into a target *[noun]* or goal to achieve

tough   hard, difficult

toxic   poisonous

trade *[noun]*   buying and selling, commerce

TV spot   advertisement on television

victim   person/thing that is harmed or suffers through another's fault

virtually   almost, very nearly

Page numbers in **boldface** refer to photographs.

APPENDIX 4

Answer Key to Part Two

6.1 Disasters

ESSENTIAL VOCABULARY
p. 78

1. the number of deaths, or the cost in lives   **2.** the crash is said to be caused by mechanical failure, or mechanical failure is said to be responsible for the crash   **3.** high-level employees (manager/executive) of the airline, or high-level persons who represent the airline   **4.** several miles away from the coastline/land (still over water)   **5.** hit the ground   **6.** passengers had been taken out quickly, or passengers had been helped to escape/flee/leave quickly   **7.** Fire was a danger for rescue workers   **8.** the fire   **9.** completely destroyed/wrecked the church   **10.** behind it, in the path it had taken   **11.** at the beginning of the 1900s, or around 1900; *century* = 100 years

SAMPLE ARTICLE 6.1-1
(Blasts rock oil tanker . . .)
p. 80

Reading for Information   **1.** (the) Haven, ¶2.   **2**   Troodos Shipping owned it (and chartered it to the national Iranian Tanker Co.), ¶11.   **3.** at least three, perhaps as many as six, ¶10.   **4.** fishing areas near Arenzano (or the Bay of Genoa), where the ship is now, ¶5–6.   **5.** the Mediterranean Sea (along the Italian Riviera), ¶6.   **6.** March 1978, ¶13.

Questions for Discussion   **1.** A fire; the cause of the fire is not mentioned, ¶10.   **4.1.** (the) Exxon Valdez, ¶9.   **4.2.** Exxon, ¶5.   **4.3.** No death toll is given.   **4.4.** more than 100 miles of water off Alaska, ¶1, ¶4.   **4.5.** Fish hatcheries (breeding areas) on the islands near the tanker, and the living areas of sea otters and sea lions, ¶11.   **4.6.** The U.S.A.'s worst oil spill is this one (¶17), which happened "last Friday" (¶13) in March 1989 (date of article). Discussion should include: the Valdez spill was much larger but caused no human deaths; the Valdez spill is not blamed on a fire as the Haven's is but rather seems to have been caused by human negligence; the Italian government is organizing national forces, such as the navy, whereas the U.S. government is not organizing the clean-up in Alaska, which instead is being done by the Coast Guard and the oil company Exxon.

SAMPLE ARTICLE 6.1-2
(Killer 'cane!)
p. 82

1. The word *'cane* is short for *hurricane*; it is used because it is short and makes alliteration with *killer*. It refers to the hurricane named Gilbert, which is the worst storm of the 20th century (up to that date). Thousands of people are running away or evacuating areas in its path. The headline and subheadline are dramatic, using colorful words to create interest. **2.a.** Galveston, Texas, U.S.A. (see dateline). **b.** Mexico (¶1, 2, 6); U.S.A. (¶1, 3, 4, 5); Jamaica and the Dominican Republic (¶7). **3.a.** most powerful (adj.) storm; dead (adj.) aim; deserted (adj.) streets; (monster (noun used as an adj.) storm); direct (adj) hit; catastrophic (adj.) damage; horrible (adj.) sound of the wind. **b.** They help the reader experience the story, bring it to life. **c.** flee, take dead aim, flattened, forced, (flee), roamed, (clocked), churning, smash, evacuated. **d.** Usually it is not considered good journalism, because readers should get an objective report and form their own judgments. Since "color" words reflect the reporter's views, the article becomes like a feature article and loses objectivity. However, in extreme situations, adjectives are helpful in describing the situation vividly. Some newspapers, like the *Boston Herald,* allow more than other papers do. **5.** In the U.S.A. hurricanes are fairly common along the southeastern coastlines; few go as far north as New York. (Tornados are fairly common in the Midwest and South in late summer.)

SAMPLE ARTICLE 6.1-3
(Jamaica seeks aid. . .)
p. 84

1. Kingston (the capital), Jamaica. **2.a.** Four days. **b.** Yes; both report about 500,000 homeless people. The *Herald* says "at least 20 deaths," while the *Monitor* later can be more exact: "36 people dead." **3.** no

SAMPLE ARTICLE 6.1-4
(Peru's cholera toll. . .)
p. 85

1. January 1991 **2.** 89,000 **3.** 535 **4.** all of Latin America, including, for example, Argentina

6.2 Unrest

A. 1.h **2.**k **3.**j **4.**g **5.**i **6.**d **7.**b **8.**l **9.**c **10.**n **11.**e **12.**a **13.**f **14.**m
B. *Nouns:* arrest, arms, civilian, clash, confrontation, fire, protest, rally, troops. *Verbs:* arrest, clash, disperse, fire, protest (armed, wounded = past participles), ["rally" can also be a verb]. *Adjectives:* armed, civilian, defiant, massive, wounded. *Prefix:* anti-.   **C. 1.** clashed   **2.** civilian (or defiant, armed)   **3.** protest   **4.** troops   **5.** disperse   **6.** defiant   **7.** armed   **8.** fired   **9.** confrontation (or clash)   **10.** wounded (or arrested)

1.a. unarmed civilians (¶1), peaceful crowds (¶11) [Note: 'peaceful protest' (¶1) does not describe the *people*].   **b.** intensive fire (¶4), intense fusillade (¶8).   **c.** massacre (¶1), crushed (¶9), (also, cutting (¶1)).   **2.** This author's opinion: His style of writing, the inclusion of color, helps to bring scenes closer to his reader. Considering the seriousness of the events, his choice of words seems appropriate; he writes descriptively but without overreliance on colorful imagery.   **3.** Yes; he says, "This reporter saw. . ." (¶8), and the dateline is Beijing.   **4.** Yes, at the end of the article, ¶10–11.   **5.** Only one country, the People's Republic of China, was involved, but the events certainly dismayed people all over the world. Leaders of most countries commented on it.   **6.b.** President Bush's first reaction was to express deep "concern" about the crackdown. Then he ordered a freeze on shipments of weapons to China. Very few countries did not express sadness or condemnation, notably Vietnam and Cuba. Many countries told their citizens to leave China or Beijing.

1. The West Bank is on the western bank of the Jordan River between Israel and Jordan. Gaza is a city and a small strip of land bordering the southern tip of Israel's Mediterranean coast. See World Map on p. 77, or consult an atlas.   **2.** *Peace* (two or three) prayer service (¶3), shelter (¶9), (nap, ¶9). *Conflict* (nineteen to twenty-three): uprising, clash, (curfew), strike (¶1); confrontations, intifadah (¶2); gunfire, demonstrations, (occupation) (¶3); roadblocks, strife (¶4); battles (army of occupation, curfew), violence, disturbance (¶5); demonstrations (¶6); strike, intifadah (¶7); protesters, roadblock, fight (¶8); intifadah (¶9)
3. ¶8 states: "Protesters. . .welcomed two American reporters. . . ." Since he then writes further, giving exact details, readers will assume that he was one of the two reporters. (However, it is also possible that another reporter told him the story.)

1. West Germany, the Netherlands (Holland), Switzerland, England (Great Britain).   **2.** They concerned nuclear power/energy; the demonstrators opposed its use on the anniversary of the Chernobyl disaster.   **3.** See ¶2: "Protests turned *violent* in Switzerland. . .and in the Netherlands. . ." but not in W. Germany (¶10: "a peaceful demonstration") and England (¶13: "peaceful march"). More vocabulary of violence: Switzerland (¶4): "hurt," "police fired tear gas and rubber bullets," "smashed," "damaged"; Holland (¶8): "clubs," "blockade," "injured."   **4.a.** *Protesters*: Switzerland: 10,000 at the rally, at least "thousands" broke away; Holland: 200; W. Germany: more than 11,000; England: 48,000–100,000. *Arrests*: Switzerland: no number reported; Holland: none; W. Germany: none; England: three. *Injuries*: Switzerland: 18 (unconfirmed), compared to 2 in Holland and none anywhere else. Probably the most damage was done in Bern, too, so that seems to have been the most *violent*.   **b.** Police gave the number of protesters; only in England did the rally organizers offer a different statistic. The difference between the numbers given for London show how important it is to know the source of information. Since the reporter was not present to verify either number, the reader must decide where the truth lies. The number of injured protesters in Bern was given by an organizer; the police refused to support or deny the number.

1. *verbs*: beat, crush, defy, clash, would be, grow. The first headline is a *noun phrase*: "clashes" is a noun there. The verbs are all in the active voice, emphasizing the news-making action.   **2.** Added words are in italics: **a.** *There are* ethnic clashes in Soviet Azerbaijan. OR Ethnic clashes *are taking place (happening/appearing)* in . . . .   **b.** Prague police beat protesters *and* crush *a* rally.   **c.** no change.   **d.** Zulus *and their* political rivals clash over Natal Province.   **e.** Baker *says/said an* attack on Iraq would be fast *and* massive.   **f.** no change. [Review Chapter 3 if this exercise was difficult.]   **3.** *Who, what,* and *where* are answered most often. Readers must read the lead or farther to find answers to the other information questions. These findings are quite typical of headlines in general (see Chapter 5).   **4.a.** Azerbaijan, formerly part of the Soviet Union, is located just north of Iran and west of the Caspian Sea. **b.** Prague was at that time the capital of the former Czechoslovakia, an Eastern European country bordering on Poland (north), Ukraine (east), Hungary and Austria (south), and Germany (west).   **c.** China covers most of eastern Asia. It borders on the Pacific Ocean and North Korea to the east, Russia and Mongolia to the north, and several countries to the south and west.   **d.** Natal Province is part of South Africa, lying on the east coast just south of Mozambique.   **e.** Iraq is in the Middle East, west of Iran, north of Saudi Arabia and Kuwait, east of Jordan and Syria, and south of eastern Turkey.

6.3 Summits and Talks

1. agreement   **2.** list/schedule of topics to be discussed at a meeting   **3.** a positive decision/event/discovery that leads to further action (toward agreement)   **4.** something given up without adequate return payment   **5.** topic or problem (that is not easy to solve)   **6.** shared   **7.** reach an agreement through talks   **8.** treaty/agreement   **9.** tried, or searched for   **10.** decision/agreement   **11.** representative whose job is to present a person's or company's views to the media (and public)   **12.** meeting of very high government officials, such as heads of state (also, top of a mountain)   **13.** relations   **14.** an agreement to stop fighting

**SAMPLE ARTICLE 6.3-1
(Breakthrough not likely . . .)
p. 96**

1.a. Mikhail Gorbachev (Soviet Union), George Bush (United States), and the other, unnamed leaders of the Group of Seven: Japan, Great Britain, Canada, Germany, France, Italy.   **b.** No.   **2.** Emigration (¶7) and free trade (¶12); these are issues among the Group of Seven.   **3.** *In favor*: Germany, France, and Italy; they do not want the USSR to become so poor and weak that its citizens emigrate into their lands (¶7). *Against*: the U.S.A., Japan, Britain, and Canada; they want the USSR to start some reforms first, before such aid is given.   **4.** A free-trade pact: Japan rejected (did not accept) it (¶12).   *Follow-up Notes*: During Bush's and Gorbachev's meeting, the two leaders were able to reach agreement on START. On January 1, 1992, the Soviet Union ceased to exist.

**SAMPLE ARTICLE 6.3-2
(Prime Ministers . . .)
p. 98**

1. Preliminary talks (¶6) between high officials (¶14) have taken place; their goal has been to arrange a summit of their highest leaders, which has not yet taken place, and some skeptics think it still might not (¶3–4).   **2.** Changing world conditions, the reunification of Germany, and the South Korean/Soviet summit in San Francisco (¶7).   **3.** A summit and the weather (¶5).   **4.** Military issues (and perhaps more) (¶8–9).   **5.** Possible topics are given in ¶11—for example, reunification of families.

**SAMPLE ARTICLE 6.3-3
(Spain Cites Progress . . .)
p. 100**

1. A group of Basque fighters who want to separate from Spain (¶1, 4) (the name comes from "Basque Homeland and Liberty" in the Basque language).   **2.** No, they are in progress at the time of this article.   **3.** A truce with ETA and an end to violence, especially before the Olympics in 1992 (¶1–2, 4).   **4.** Separation from Spain; to have their own country; this answer is implied by the use of the adjective "separatist" in ¶1–2, 4, and in the group's name (¶4).   **5.** b (¶8)

6.4 International Trade

1.d **2.**c **3.**a **4.**i **5.**b **6.**g **7.**l **8.**k **9.**e **10.**h **11.**j **12.**f

1.a. (¶6) Singapore's Prime Minister.   **b.**(¶8) South Korea's foreign minister.   **c.**(¶9) Deputy (representative/substitute) for Mr. Kwang.   **d.** Yes.   **2.a.** (¶3) General Agreement on Tariffs and Trade.   **b.** (¶7) The Association of South East Asian Nations.   **c.** (¶11 and 14) European Community.   **d.** No, not EC.   **3.** Asians see some U.S. and EC policies as protectionist and exclusive (¶1, 4, 13), but Asian countries rely on both those markets to stay strong and grow (¶8, 11, 14). The problem is thus how to continue to expand in spite of a more restrictive western market. Their answer may be to increase trade relations and political cooperation among themselves (¶1, 6, 9).   **4.a.** "Tokyo" and "Canberra" are the capitals of their countries (Japan and Australia) and thus stand for them here. The study is the one described in ¶4 (first sentence) and ¶5 (last sentence).

1. The headline means: The difference between imports and exports (trade gap) was 21% greater in November (1988) than in October (1988). **2.a.** monthly (¶2).   **b.** February.   **3.** bad: sticky, not coming off, disturbing, the opposite of what . . . the Fed wants, doesn't bode well. **4.** *Upward/bigger:* surge, balloon, widen, grow, rise, raise, jump; *Downward/smaller:* shrink, drop, weaken, slip

Reading for Information   **1.** The headline means: The United States is imposing trade sanctions, a kind of economic punishment, on the European community. EC = European Community.   **2.**b   **3.a.** yes: $100 million.   **b.** no.   **4.** because West Germany and Italy strongly supported the EC's ban on meats (¶8)
Questions for Discussion   **1.a.–b.** Answers will vary.   **c.** because tomatoes are a major ingredient in pizzas

1.a. Sting says that the rain forest must be preserved because it produces air.   **b.** The Brazilian government says that it must develop the rain forests in order to pay its foreign debt (by generating a healthy economy). **2.** Answers will vary.   **3.a.** the international or the business/financial section.   **b.** the international or the travel section or with other environmental issues.   **c.** the travel or international section.   **d.** the arts/entertainment section, a gossip column, or a "People" feature or column.

7.1 Elections

A. 1.f **2.**l **3.**e **4.**a **5.**i **6.**c **7.**b **8.**o **9.**j **10.**g **11.**d **12.**k **13.**m **14.**n **15.**h **B. 1.** poll **2.** lead **3.** primary **4.** base **5.** runn(ing) **6.** spots **7.** campaign **8.** candidate **9.** nomination **10.** lean **11.** incumbent

SAMPLE ARTICLE 7.1-1 (Campaign sniping ends. . .) p. 118

1. a **2.** Edward R. Vrdolyak, Republican (¶3); Timothy C. Evans, independent (¶4); Richard M. Daley (Democrat) (¶5); Eugene Sawyer (Democrat) (¶6); Dr. Herbert Sohn, Republican (¶10). **3.** He is an independent candidate (i.e., he does not belong to either one of the two major parties). There are very few independent candidates running for elected office, especially above the local level, because they lack a party base. **4.a.** Yes: "Richard M. Daley is expected to win" if the turnout is as expected (¶5). **b.** Yes: the Democratic primary winner (likely Daley) traditionally is also elected Mayor (¶2) (i.e., there is not enough support for a Republican mayor, no matter who wins the GOP primary). **5.** Yes: Daley is white. [This is not stated expressly in the article but can be inferred from the contrasting statement in ¶6: "*But* an outpouring of black votes . . . could upset Daley's equations."] Eugene Sawyer is black. (Jewish voters as a group are also mentioned (¶7), but they constitute an ethnic/religious group rather than a racial one.) **6.** Yes: Details are given in ¶8 and 9.

SAMPLE ARTICLE 7.1-2 (Keys to the election) p. 120

1. The Republican heartland, from Orange county to San Diego—GOP; the central valley—GOP; northern California/San Francisco Bay area—Democratic; and Los Angeles—Democratic. **2.** California has the largest number of votes in the Electoral College (¶2) because of its high population; the Electoral College ultimately chooses the President (see the Introduction). **3.** The journalist does not answer this question—see ¶14 and 15. **4.** have the best shot at (¶5), attacking (¶6), targeting (¶11), capture (¶12)

SAMPLE ARTICLE 7.1-3 (Florida race . . .) p. 122

1. c: The title of the office is given in ¶1, "the late *Rep*. Claude Pepper." In ¶4 the "18th congressional district" is mentioned; only Representatives have districts, whereas Senators represent and are elected by an entire state. **2.a.** He used to be a Representative; he was a Representative until he died (¶1: "the *late* Rep. Claude Pepper"). **b.** She will probably become the Republican nominee to run against a Democrat for the Congressional seat (¶10, 13) **c.** Castro became head of the government (dictator) in Cuba. **d.** There will be a special election for the vacant seat in Congress. (As a rule, elections above the local level take place on Election Day in November.) **3.a.** No: Jack Gordon decided not to run; and Claude Pepper died—it is his seat that has become vacant. **b.** Ileana Ros-Lehtinen, Republican (¶10), Carlos Perez and David Fleischer, also Republican (¶13), and Democrats JoAnn Pepper and Marvin Dunn (¶15). **4.** It is not suggested explicitly, but ¶11 concludes that "the next member of Congress from the 18th district will likely be a Cuban American." Of the two Hispanic candidates, Ros-Lehtinen is shown as leading. Therefore, the reader can get the impression that she is the probable winner. **5.** Race may play a role in the Democratic primary, in which the contest includes a black candidate. (Readers will assume that JoAnn Pepper is white—and that is a correct assumption.) Jack Gordon mentioned racial and ethnic groups in his complaint about the primaries (¶1). But ethnic groups are more important in this race.   **6.** fuel high emotions (¶2); inflammatory (¶3); fiery nature of politics (¶4); fire Latin pride (¶11).   *Extra Credit*: undercurrent (¶7); the image is of running water.

7.2 The Economy

<table>
<tr>
<td>

ESSENTIAL VOCABULARY
p. 125

</td>
<td>

A. 1.m **2.**a. **3.**j **4.**b **5.**i **6.**d **7.**c **8.**l **9.**g **10.**k **11.**h **12.**f **13.**e.
B. cut, deficit, recession

</td>
</tr>
<tr>
<td>

SAMPLE ARTICLE 7.2-1
(Washington
prediction . . .)
p. 126

</td>
<td>

Reading for Information   **1.**b. (¶1, 12)   **2.**a (¶2)   **3.**a (¶1, 11)
4.b (¶3)   **5.**c (¶8)
Questions for Discussion   Both parties' views on the prediction are given. The Republicans, Brady and others, are optimistic about the forecast of a healthy economy; the Democrats praised their forecast. On the economy itself, only the administration's view is reported; the Democrat's own projections or forecast of the economy are not given. Note that this article is based exclusively on information from sources within the government; no independent experts are quoted.

</td>
</tr>
<tr>
<td>

SAMPLE ARTICLE 7.2-2
(Brady upbeat . . .)
p. 128

</td>
<td>

1. He is optimistic because the outlook/forecast for the economy is good; however, the recession is not over (¶2–3).   **2.** First, interest rates should be lowered; the Federal Reserve Board does that (¶1). Second, a cut in federal income taxes on capital assets should be adopted (made) (¶8). The article does not say who should do this, but that is the task of Congress, which makes all laws, including tax reforms.   **3.** no   **4.** Answers should include: In both articles the administration is optimistic about the economy; but in 1989 their experts did not foresee the recession, which developed during late 1990 and was obvious in 1991. In 1989 Darman thought the deficit was being reduced (¶4); but in 1991, when the deficit was still very high, Brady again thinks it is on a "downward course" (being slowly reduced) (¶6). Note: It is important for a president to show that the economy is not so bad; a bad economic situation often helps defeat the party of the president in elections. For both articles, the journalists did not do investigative reporting (see p. 10) but simply reported what government officials said.

</td>
</tr>
<tr>
<td>

SAMPLE ARTICLE 7.2-3
(Income, spending
up . . .)
p. 130

</td>
<td>

1. Income and spending (have) increased sharply (a lot).   **2.** *b, c, d*; there is no information about *e* in the article.   **3.** October (¶7)

</td>
</tr>
</table>

7.3 Guns, Drugs, and Crime

ESSENTIAL VOCABULARY
P. 131

1.o 2.j 3.a 4.e 5.p 6.l 7.b 8.d 9.k 10.c 11.h 12.n 13.r 14.m 15.q 16.g 17.i 18.f

SAMPLE ARTICLE 7.3-1
(Rifle cheap . . .)
p. 132

1. The children were certainly defenseless, but a *massacre* generally means many, many people, not five; so the word is an exaggeration here.
2. assault rifle and hunting rifle; automatic rifle and machine gun.
3. $150; your own opinion.

SAMPLE ARTICLE 7.3-2
(Inner-City Teen Talks . . .)
p. 134

1. It is a news article; the immediate news is that Detra J. reported to the hearing.   **2.** strengthen families and end drug traffic; provide more positive role models; provide attractive activities in inner cities; more programs for disadvantaged youths, more communication between parents and children, and more jobs for more pay (¶13–16).   **3.** Answers will vary.   **4.** Yes: to gain money, respect from their peers (other youths), and popularity with girls (¶4); and to get a gun for protection and prestige (¶6).   **5.** no   **6.** He says taking drugs "was fun."

SAMPLE ARTICLE 7.3-3
(Junkie . . .)
p. 136

1.a. Carlos Colon.   **b.** in jail, until someone pays the $20,000 bail (¶7).
2. robbery (a car was broken into), assault (on Dan Rowan), weapons possession, and drug-implement (needle) possession (¶7–8).   **3.** No reason is given. Possible reasons: He is innocent; or he and his lawyer want to delay sentencing by insisting on a trial and an appeal afterward (he has a right to these); or he may hope his trial will become invalid for some reason—for example, a technicality of procedure.   **4.** If Colon has AIDS, his needle probably would have infected Dan Rowan, who would then be an HIV-infected person who could pass on the virus to others. Some people with AIDS have been charged with murder for such an assault as Colon's, since infecting someone with the AIDS virus is like imposing a death sentence.   **5.** The reporter uses informal, conversational language in the headline, and he uses names, quoting people as they talk about their emotions. (The original article was also accompanied by a photo of Dan Rowan and his wife.)

SAMPLE ARTICLE 7.3-4
(Boston homicide . . .)
p. 138

1. No, only 60 suspects could be arrested (¶10) and trials cannot be held without the suspect present. In some cases the criminals may still be unknown, since only 66 arrest warrants were issued.   **2.a.** black males, more than 60% (¶3).   **b.** no   **c.** gun (¶12).   **d.** drugs: 34 of 102 cases (chart), or one-third of the cases (¶1)

VERDICTS AND SENTENCES IN THE HEADLINES
p. 140

1. *active:* a, h; *passive:* b–f; *noun phrase:* g.   **2.a.** b, d, e, f, h.   **b.** f.
3.a. French – La Rouche; Irish – McDermott; Japanese – Otsuki; Polish – Barnoski; English – North.   **b.** Barnoski is the convicted felon; McDermott must have been the victim.   **4.** Both headlines tell the number of years in prison to which the criminal (thief, killer) was sentenced.

7.4 Health Crises and Policies

ESSENTIAL VOCABULARY
p. 141

ACROSS **1.** physician **3.** ethical **5.** HIV **8.** intravenous **10.** sp **11.** fund **12.** age **14.** treat **16.** sum **17.** disease **18.** RN
DOWN **1.** prevent **2.** ill **4.** coverage **6.** virus **7.** mandate **8.** infected **9.** spokesman **13.** AIDS **15.** test

SAMPLE ARTICLE 7.4-1
(Liver boy. . .)
p. 142

1. not famous, but unusual because of his rare disease **2.** yes, so far **3.** the parents of a brain-dead baby (¶14–15) **4.** no (¶19) **5.a.** No, the insurance pays (¶20). **b.** It seems the parents have to pay; the insurance doesn't (¶21–23). **c.** For some people it is typical; others have medical insurance that covers all costs from a hospital stay; still others (a sizable minority) have no health insurance at all.

SAMPLE ARTICLE 7.4-2
(Hatch opposes . . . health bill)
p. 144

1.a. Republican **b.** Democrats **2.** Against: He thinks it will be too expensive for some businesses, so they will cut their payrolls and employees will lose their jobs (¶4–6). **3.** Senator Edward Kennedy and Elliot Richardson support it, saying that it is not really different from other programs (¶10) and the current system (¶9).

SAMPLE ARTICLE 7.4-3
(Doc watches . . .)
p. 146

1.a. Dr. Kevorkian: As a pathologist, he had the knowledge and ability to make it and he believes strongly in the right to suicide with a doctor's help (¶13). **b.** Janet Adkins: She had Alzheimer's disease and did not want to finish her life in a vegetative state (¶1, 18). **2.** Susan Wolf opposes assisted suicide (¶7–8); Gerald Poisson thinks it depends on the facts of a case (¶10).

SAMPLE ARTICLE 7.4-4
(AIDS . . . Education)
p. 148

1.a. 33 of the 50 states mandate AIDS education in schools (¶2). **b.** Fewer states mandate sex education, but some do—the number is not given (¶3). **2.a.** F (¶6) **b.** F (it is mandatory for schools, but students do not have to take the class if their parents do not want them to – ¶9) **c.** T (¶6) **d.** T (¶8) **e.** T (¶2) **f.** F (at least in Oklahoma – ¶10) **g.** F (that number has HIV-infection, but not all have AIDS yet – ¶5) **h.** F (¶4)

SAMPLE ARTICLE 7.4-5
(. . . new AIDS drug . . .)
p. 150

1. FDA is explained in the lead: Food and Drug Administration. AIDS is not defined exactly; in ¶1 it is called "the deadly virus." The reporter probably assumes that readers know enough about AIDS that it does not need to be defined. **2.** It kills only infected T-cells and macrophage cells (not all cells); whereas AZT only prevents the duplication or spread of the virus and does not kill existing ones (¶2, 7–8). **3.** Both: two universities and Genelabs, a company (¶5). **4.** This information is not stated in the article but can be inferred (guessed): People could not buy it then because it had only been tested in the laboratory. The FDA requires a drug to be successfully tested on humans before it can be sold.

7.5 The Environment

ESSENTIAL VOCABULARY
p. 151

1.l **2.**i **3.**g **4.**f **5.**e **6.**a **7.**d **8.**h **9.**m **10.**b **11.**c **12.**j **13.**k
B. 1. cleanup **2.** proceed(ing) **3.** effort **4.** pollute(d) **5.** toxic
6. environment **7.** consumer(s) **8.** recycle(s) **9.** invent(ed)
10. potential **11.** emission(s) **12.** waste(s). *Preserve* is not used.

SAMPLE ARTICLE 7.5-1
(. . . ozone layer)
p. 152

1. chemicals, chlorofluorocarbons (¶1–2), that are used in coolants
(refrigeration) and as solvents, etc. (¶3, 4, 7); they are nontoxic,
nonflammable (do not burn easily), stable chemicals that destroy the
ozone layer (¶3, 7). **2.a.** AT&T (¶9) **b.** no one **3.** Lawmakers are
discussing laws that will reduce and ultimately ban chemicals like CFCs
(¶10). **4.** It protects the earth from the sun's ultraviolet rays (¶7), which
can cause sunburn and skin cancer in humans. **5.** The last three
expressions do not have the same meaning. *cut back* = reduce, use less;
deplete goes farther, meaning reduce to nothing/zero; *eliminate* = stop or
get rid of completely. **6.** A Nissan dealer in Toronto said Nissan had
indeed eliminated CFCs (1993).

SAMPLE ARTICLE 7.5-2
(US declines to . . .
clean up spill)
p. 154

1. the Coast Guard, state and local agencies, Exxon (¶5); *not* the federal
government **2.** It is already being done "at full speed" (¶2); it might be
"counterproductive" (¶3); the government trusts Exxon and doesn't want to
pay expenses (¶6). **3.** This author's opinion: His words sound
hollow/hypocritical, since he insists that the federal government should
stay out of the process. **4.** Answers will vary. This author's opinion: It
is a typically Republican decision, because Republicans generally are not in
favor of a big, active federal government. (President Bush is a Republican.)
5. fish, sea otters, sea lions (¶11)

SAMPLE ARTICLE 7.5-3
(Cleaning . . . Alaskans . . .)
p. 156

1. volunteers, including Europeans (¶1) **2.** The Coast Guard reportedly
is satisfied, according to an Exxon spokesman, who has an interest in
stating that; the Alaskans are not satisfied.

SAMPLE ARTICLE 7.5-4
(Ecologist . . . ecotourism)
p. 157

1.a. booming, bust **b.** In this article the environment is seen as part of a
business, the tourism business, so business and stock-market terms are
appropriate. **2.** He thinks there will be little wilderness left in 30 years
(¶2) because of people's consumption (consuming) and wastes (¶3).
3. fish (¶4) **4.a.** Yes, they are both worried about loss of natural
environments. **b.** No, Suzuki is a professional ecologist, a scientist
studying the environment; Sting is a singer with no professional
background relative to the environment.

7.6 Science

ESSENTIAL VOCABULARY
p. 158

A. *administration:* government (or officials) under a certain President
billion: a thousand million (1,000,000,000) *crucial:* all-important, very
important *federal:* national *image:* reputation or way of being seen
[sometimes also: picture] *massive:* very big and powerful *perceive:* to
understand, see *research:* advanced or controlled studies, investigations,
experiments ***B. 1.**c **2.**d **3.**b **4.**a **5.**e

198 APPENDIX 4 ANSWER KEY TO PART TWO

8.1 Workplace Issues: Labor and Management

ESSENTIAL VOCABULARY
p. 162

A. **1.**n **2.**e **3.**g **4.**a **5.**k **6.**m **7.**f **8.**c **9.**j **10.**i **11.**h **12.**d **13.**l **14.**b
B. **1.** workforce (or employees) **2.** Union **3.** negotiate(d) **4.** contract(s)
5. bargaining **6.** upheld **7.** employee(s) **8.** issue **9.** strike

SAMPLE ARTICLE 8.1-1
(Strike enters 4th day . . .)
p. 164

Reading for Information   *What:* a strike (continues for the fourth day).   *Who:* 45 Hispanic employees (are striking).   *Where:* at a conveyor-belt company in Winchester (Massachusetts).   *When:* yesterday was their fourth day (they started "last Thursday").   *How:* they are staying outside the company building.   *Why:* they say that Miguel Ramos was fired for racial reasons, which is discrimination.

SAMPLE ARTICLE 8.1-2
(Eastern/Continental)
p. 165

1. Continental (in 1983)   **2.** 5½ (6)   **3.** When Continental was declared bankrupt, the chairman, Lorenzo, dismissed two-thirds of his employees and reduced salaries, sometimes by 50%. The union's task is to save jobs, keep salaries up, etc., so of course they do not want to see the same things happen with Eastern employees.   **4.** The bankruptcy laws have been changed since 1983; now a company cannot break union/labor contracts unless it cannot survive without doing so.

SAMPLE ARTICLE 8.1-3
(Unions . . . Family Benefits)
p. 166

Reading for Information   **1.a.** BNA is defined as Bureau of National Affairs, a private research organization and publisher (¶2–3).   **b.** N.Y. is used in ¶5 but not defined; it means "New York state" and is a very common abbreviation that Americans read and write often.   **c.** Co. is used in ¶13 but not defined; it means "Company" and is a very common abbreviation, more prevalent (common) than the long form of the word.   **d.** AFL-CIO is used in ¶14–15 but not defined; it means "American Federation of Labor and Congress of Industrial Organization," the largest organization of unions in the U.S.A.; most Americans know the meaning of the abbreviation, although some may not be able to state exactly what the individual letters stand for.   **2.a.** money/wages (¶1–3, 5–6) and working conditions (¶6) **b.** family benefits   **3.** pregnancy and parental leave (¶2–3, 9); flexible work schedules (¶3); family aid programs (¶3, 8), including health and hospital insurance (¶7); leave for family problems (¶13); reimbursement for adoption expenses (¶13)

Questions for Discussion   **1.a.** the issuing of the report (¶2) **b.** The paragraphs on the BNA report are hard news, new information; paragraphs 10 and 13–15 are background information, making the article a blend of news and feature.   **2–4.** Answers will vary, depending on experiences.
5.a. three **b.** (Not all employees are organized in unions in the United States. There is general agreement that unions have lost power in the last 25 years or so.)

8.2 Consumer Issues

ESSENTIAL VOCABULARY P. 169

1. publicity **2. *ACROSS:*** purchase; ***DOWN:*** previous **3.** consumes
4. scare **5.** earn **6.** soar **7.** exec **8.** subsidiary **9.** bargain **10.** rm
11. perceive **12.** IRA **13.** enter **14.** warranty

SAMPLE ARTICLE 8.2-1 (New milk . . . drug) p. 170

1. Stress makes cows unhealthy (¶4).   **2.** While Rifkin is more concerned about consumers, Corse is worried about his cows' health; and Rifkin's group is against bioengineering (the science of combining biological and industrial research) in general (¶9).   **3.** It has economic benefits (¶8) and is a scientific advancement (¶5).   **4.** Vermont (see dateline: first line of ¶1)

SAMPLE ARTICLE 8.2-2 (US drivers . . .) p. 172

1.a. T **b.** F **c.** T **d.** T   **2.a.** six: Acura, Honda, Toyota, Nissan, Subaru, Mazda **b.** four: Mercedes-Benz, BMW, Audi, Porsche **c.** four: Cadillac, Buick, Plymouth, Mercury **d.** one: Volvo **e.** one: Hyundai

SAMPLE ARTICLE 8.2-3 (Chrysler offers . . . loans) p. 174

1. The U.S. automakers competed against each other in offering the lowest interest rates ("interest-rate wars" – ¶1).   **2.** The interest-rate wars have started again ("replay" – ¶1).   **3.** all car buyers   **4.** Buyers who normally would not buy on credit but with cash—they can keep some of that cash while slowly paying off the loan with no interest (¶6–7). But some market/business analysts say they will actually attract people who don't have much money instead (¶8).   **5.** They have not sold enough cars this year, so they need to attract customers with a better deal than the competitors have.   **6.** decline, compared to last year (¶7)   **7.** It is common to buy with a loan, on credit; but some people pay cash.

SAMPLE ARTICLE 8.2-4 (Foreigners are spending . . .) p. 176

1.a. "few" (¶10), no exact number is given **b.** 25 (¶7) **c.** no number given **d.** 58   **2.** *Japan:* 200–250% more expensive than in the U.S.A.; for example, a day of golfing costs $250 there, and $100 in Myrtle Beach (¶12–14). *Sweden:* equipment is about twice as expensive as in the U.S.A. (¶3–4). *U.S.A.:* the cheapest of the three countries.

8.3 Money

ESSENTIAL VOCABULARY p. 177

A. 1.b 2.f 3.l 4.n 5.a 6.h 7.c 8.d 9.g 10.m 11.i 12.e 13.j 14.k
B. 1. bullish, gain, inflation, soar, up 2. dampen, plunge (inflation: the value of money is decreasing)